STALKER, HACKER, VOYEUR, SPY

Confederation of Independent Psychoanalytic Societies
Boundaries of Psychoanalysis Series
Series editor: Fredric Perlman

When Theories Touch: A Historical and Theoretical Integration of Psychoanalytic Thought
Steven J. Ellman

Another Kind of Evidence: Studies on Internalization, Annihilation Anxiety, and Progressive Symbolization in the Psychoanalytic Process
Norbert Freedman, Marvin Hurich, Rhonda Ward, Jesse D. Geller, and Joan Hoffenberg

A New Freudian Synthesis: Clinical Process in the Next Generation
Edited by Andrew B. Druck, Carolyn S. Ellman, Norbert Freedman, and Aaron Thaler

The Second Century of Psychoanalysis: Evolving Perspectives on Therapeutic Action
Edited by Michael J. Diamond and Christopher Christian

Absolute Truth and Unbearable Psychic Pain: Psychoanalytic Perspectives on Concrete Experience
Edited by Allan Frosch

Battling the Life and Death Forces of Sadomasochism: Clinical Perspectives
Edited by Harriet I. Basseches, Paula L. Ellman, and Nancy R. Goodman

From Soma to Symbol: Psychosomatic Conditions and Transformative Experience
Edited by Phyllis L. Sloate

Critical Flicker Fusion: Psychoanalysis at the Movies
William Fried

STALKER, HACKER, VOYEUR, SPY

A Psychoanalytic Study of Erotomania, Voyeurism, Surveillance, and Invasions of Privacy

Helen K. Gediman

KARNAC

First published in 2017 by
Karnac Books Ltd
118 Finchley Road, London NW3 5HT

British Library Cataloguing in Publication Data

A C.I.P. for this book is available from the British Library

ISBN 978 1 78220 351 3

Edited, designed and produced by The Studio Publishing Services Ltd
www.publishingservicesuk.co.uk
e-mail: studio@publishingservicesuk.co.uk

Printed and bound in Great Britain by TJ International Ltd.

www.karnacbooks.com

CONTENTS

ACKNOWLEDGMENTS

I thank the Program Committee of Section I of Division 39 (Psychoanalysis) of the American Psychological Association for inviting me to participate in their 2006 panel, "Stalker and Stalked: Obsessed with Desire." I extend very special thanks to my friend and colleague, Harriet Basseches, who, as the moderator and discussant of that panel, helped me realize that I might make some important contributions to an area that initially I thought I knew nothing about.

I wish to extend my heartfelt thanks to the Membership Committee of the Cosmopolitan Club in New York City for calling my attention to the importance of stalking in their lives, and for encouraging me to pursue the subject further. My friend and fellow member, Ruth Turner, invited me to present my work on "Stalking" at one of the Club's "Members Only Luncheons." A professional editor, she volunteered to edit my drafts so that they would be free of the jargon of much psychoanalytic writing. She succeeded so well at paring down my style that when I did present a talk with film clips at a luncheon, people working in various fields appeared to understand many psychoanalytic nuances that they might not have otherwise. I was the first psychoanalyst ever to have presented at that Club. I wish to thank Ruth Turner for significantly turning around my style of and comfort in writing for people who would read more psychoanalytically themed work if it were presented in a form consistent with works in other disciplines in academia, the arts, the professions, and business.

Initially, my case material on stalking came largely from stalkees; that is, people who had been stalked, and not from stalkers, so I turned to film for illustrative examples of stalkers. Good luck brought me into contact with the superb talents of Krister Johnson, who created the DVD that contained clips I had chosen from the films that contained the most representative and compelling accounts and visual images of stalking. A consultant for routine problematic encounters with my Mac, Krister was not just an unusually competent computer expert, but was then developing a now fully realized interest in the theater and film world as both actor and writer that gave him a real feel for compiling the illustrations I had chosen. I could not have found a better person to provide me with the DVD I have been using ever since, and to which he has added the clips that I have been sending him all along as I come across additional examples of stalking in film. My job had been simply scrolling through my film DVDs, selecting the clips I needed, and indicating to him the places on the original disks for him to transfer to my trusty master DVD that he created for me. I have used that DVD extensively to translate the visuals and the dialogue into a form fitting for this book.

Representatives of various psychoanalytic groups have invited me to present my still expanding work in local, national, and international organizations (Gediman, 2008, 2009a, 2016; Gediman & Lieberman, 1996). I wish to thank Curtis Bristol and Sandra Hershberg of the American Psychoanalytic Association, Janice Lieberman of the Institute for Psychoanalytic Training and Research (IPTAR), Michael Stern as the representative of the Psychoanalytic Society of the NYU Postdoctoral Program in Psychotherapy and Psychoanalysis to the Joint International Conference on Psychoanalysis held in Vancouver, BC, Ruth Garfield of the Philadelphia Center for Psychoanalysis, and Fonya Helm of the Virginia Psychoanalytic Association. Most recently, and most importantly for the publication of my book, I have become indebted to the Confederation of Independent Psychoanalytic Societies (CIPS) of the International Psychoanalytical Association (IPA). I thank the Editorial Board of the CIPS Book Series for selecting *Stalker, Hacker, Voyeur, Spy* as a part of their book series, "The Boundaries of Psychoanalysis," in arrangement with their publisher, Karnac Books. I especially want to thank Phyllis Sloate, now the President of CIPS, and who was a member of the CIPS book selection committee at the time this book was accepted, for her confident support and encouragement. I thank as well Beth Kalish, Randi Wirth, and Fredric Perlman, all members of the CIPS book selection committee. Dr. Perlman was also the president of CIPS at the time I originally submitted my book proposal, and was the major liaison between CIPS and Karnac. I owe special thanks to Janice Lieberman, an outside-of-committee reader whose book, *Body Talk* (Jason Aronson, 2000) significantly influenced the sections of my book dealing with stalking and voyeurism, and whose general editorial comments have been invaluable.

A number of friends and colleagues called to my attention some of the most important films that I have used to illustrate the many facets of stalking. I owe a special debt of thanks to Jane Kupersmidt for suggesting *Red Road,* and *In Fear,* Isaac Tylim for calling to my attention Coppola's masterpiece, *The Conversation,* and Alan Sloate for sharing his early grasp of the apparently prophetic nature of *Enemy of the State* in its uncanny appearance of foreknowledge of Edward Snowden's forthcoming revelations about the then secret National Security Agency. The now closed Philoctetes Center at the New York Psychoanalytic Society helped me develop my ideas about "doubling" that I discuss in two of films about stalking, *Peeping Tom* and *Caché*. I owe a particular debt of thanks to my friend and colleague, K. William Fried, whose careful line editing of some early work, and constant presence and feedback during all phases of the writing process have been of immense editorial and supportive value. I am especially grateful to him for calling my attention to the term, "Stichomythia," or dialogue spoken in alternating single lines, as a process I could adapt for representing film dialogue with a corresponding written dialogue.

I wish to thank my editors at Karnac Books, Oliver Rathbone, Publisher and Managing Editor, Rod Tweedy, Editor, Cecily Blench, cover, Kate Pearce and the team at The Studio Publishing Services for their incredible patience with me during the production process. Without their prompt oversight this work would never have seen the light of day.

Finally, news media coverage of the disturbing *zeitgeist* of our day has been an enormous spur to my thinking about the critical issues of the ongoing conflict between privacy and civil liberties, on the one hand, and security and protection from terrorism, on the other. Like Edward Snowden, *The New York Times,* in particular, has provided invaluable information on governmental bulk collection of internet and telephone information that has alerted all Americans and others to myriad real and potential privacy invasions, particularly those that involve stalking in cyberspace.

To

Sarah Gonya Gediman and Elizabeth Ann Gediman

ABOUT THE AUTHOR

Helen K. Gediman, PhD, is Adjunct Clinical Professor of Psychology at the New York University Postdoctoral Program in Psychotherapy and Psychoanalysis where she is also a training and supervising psychoanalyst. She is a member and training and supervising psychoanalyst at the Contemporary Freudian Society in both its New York City and Washington DC Programs. She is also a member of the Institute for Psychoanalytic Training and Research (IPTAR), the International Psychoanalytical Association (IPA), the Confederation of Independent Societies of the IPA (CIPS), and the American Psychoanalytic Association (APsaA). Additionally, she is a Fellow and Diplomate in Division 39, Psychoanalysis, of the American Psychological Association, where she has served for fifteen years on the Board of Directors of its Section on Psychoanalyst–Psychologist Practitioners (Section I).

Dr. Gediman has published extensively in refereed psychoanalytic journals and in psychoanalytic books. A sampling of her over sixty-five papers and presentations will be forthcoming in the book *Building Bridges: The Selected Psychoanalytic Papers of Helen K. Gediman*, to be published by International Psychoanalysis. She is also the author or co-author of three other books: *Ego Functions in Schizophrenics, Neurotics and Normals,* with Leopold Bellak and Marvin S. Hurvich (Wiley); *Fantasies of Love and Death in Life and Art* (New York University Press); *The Many Faces of Deceit,* with Janice S. Lieberman (Jason Aronson).

Dr. Gediman is in the full-time private practice of psychoanalysis and psychoanalytic psychotherapy in New York City.

SERIES EDITOR'S PREFACE

Fredric Perlman, Series Editor

"Recent inventions and business methods call attention to the next step which must be taken for the protection of the person, and for securing to the individual . . . the right 'to be let alone.' Instantaneous photographs and newspaper enterprise have invaded the sacred precincts of private and domestic life; and numerous mechanical devices threaten to make good the prediction that 'what is whispered in the closet shall be proclaimed from the house-tops.' "

Samuel Warren and Lewis Brandeis (1890)

"Justice Brandeis taught us that privacy is the 'right to be let alone,' but we also know that privacy is about much more than just solitude or secrecy. Citizens who feel protected from misuse of their personal information feel free to engage in commerce, to participate in the political process, or to seek needed health care . . . Never has privacy been more important than today, in the age of the Internet, the World Wide Web and smart phones . . . One thing should be clear, even though we live in a world in which we share personal information more freely than in the past, we must reject the conclusion that privacy is an outmoded value. It has been at the heart of our democracy from its inception, and we need it now more than ever.

President Barak Obama (2012)

Stalker, Hacker, Voyeur, Spy is a book about privacy, about those who invade it, and those who must cope with the invasion. It is a book written by a master teacher and clinician, it is a product of psychoanalytic thinking, and it is animated throughout by a psychoanalytic attitude of inquiry. It is, to be sure, of signal importance for psychoanalysts, but it is intended for a much wider readership. It is light on jargon, free-wheeling in scope, enlightening and entertaining, and, with each passing chapter, more and more disturbing.

The author, Dr. Helen Gediman, is a most esteemed member of the psychoanalytic community, a prolific author who is widely recognized and respected for the breadth of her interests and the creativity of her thought. In this scholarly and timely volume, Dr. Gediman breaks new ground, initiating a pioneering study of stalkers and stalking, a subject that has received little prior attention in the psychoanalytic literature. With the publication of this book, it becomes evident that the paucity of the professional literature on stalking stands in dramatic contrast to urgency of the need for it.

The term "stalking" has historically referred to a specific pattern of behavior characterized by the obsessive, stealthy, and unwanted pursuit or harassment of another person, often motivated by sexual desires, vengefulness following rejections or hurt, and injured narcissism. In this conventional sense, stalking is an intensely personal activity, but it is one that may be pursued with a stranger that has assumed a place of psychological importance in the mind of the stalker. Unfortunately, people who stalk others do not typically seek treatment, although some patients seeking treatment for other problems, do stalk their therapists. As Dr. Gediman reports in this book, about ten percent of therapists have the very distressing experience of being stalked by patients. Few of those, including myself (unhappily, one of the ten percent), ever speak or write about it publicly.

Because detailed psychoanalytic case reports are rare and, of course, those that exist are subject to the strictest rules of confidentiality, there is little publishable analytic case material for a volume about stalking. Dr. Gediman, however, has overcome this problem by drawing extensively on films and, to a lesser extent, on published accounts of stalking experiences, to depict stalking conduct, and to explore and delineate the psychological forces at work in both stalker and stalkee. Throughout this effort, Dr. Gediman's employment of films is creative and disciplined. Not only has she selected films that aptly serve her psychoanalytic purposes, her discussions of these films is revelatory, even to the sophisticated cinemaphile. Some of the films are well known, others are less so, but each admirably furthers her exploratory effort.

Drawing on a wide body of theory, on her own clinical experience (mostly with stalkees), and on representations of stalking in films and literature, Dr. Gediman slowly builds up a new psychoanalytic framework for our understanding of stalking. Dr. Gediman characterizes stalking as a multidetermined behavior, that is, behavior that is driven by multiple motivations that have taken shape over the course of a person's childhood and subsequent life experience. As will be seen, Dr. Gediman not only deepens our psychological grasp of stalking behavior and the distress of stalkees, she also expands the hitherto narrow scope of behavior to which the term "stalking" has conventionally been applied. With each incremental step in this expansion, *Stalker, Hacker, Voyeur, Spy* grows in social relevance—and in its impact on the reader.

Dr. Gediman opens her volume with a discussion of stalking in the most conventional sense, that is, "sexual stalking." Sexual stalking is characterized by motivations related to sexuality, love, and rejection, and in particular, by erotomania, voyeurism, and sadomasochism. While these terms are, of course, familiar to analysts, readers with other backgrounds may find them a bit obscure. Each was employed by nineteenth century psychiatrists and remains in use today, albeit with more contemporary meanings. "Erotomania" refers to a person's delusional belief that another person, often a stranger or relative stranger, is in love with him or her. "Voyeurism" is the sexually motivated drive to look at others, especially others in states of undress, sexual excitement, or sexual conduct. "Sadomasochism" denotes a need to master or control another person—or—to be mastered and controlled by another person. Sadomasochism is often associated with feelings of rejection, hurt, and vengefulness in relation to another. While patterns of sexual stalking can take different forms, including syndromes driven primarily by voyeurism, erotomania, and revenge, the perverse quality of stalking behavior is primarily attributable to the sadomasochistic element evident in all stalking, that is, the aggressive pursuit of power, or the sense of power, over the other person. In Dr. Gediman's discussion, erotomanically driven stalking is illustrated by two popular films, *Play Misty for Me* and *Fatal Attraction*. In each of these films, a woman invades the life of a man she barely knows, believing that, whatever he says, he really loves her. Voyeuristic stalking is illustrated by Alfred Hitchcock's classic *Rear Window* and the lesser known film, *Peeping Tom*. In *Rear Window*, the protagonist, a temporarily disabled photographer, played by Jimmy Stewart, is more interested in the activities of his neighbors than he is in his beautiful and loving girlfriend, played by Grace Kelly. Dr. Gediman closes this section of the book with a discussion of the film, *Peeping Tom*, a movie that depicts a particularly sadistic and vengeful form of voyeuristic stalking, one that is fueled not only by voyeurism but by childhood hurts and persisting hate.

Despite the ugly character of some of the behavior described, especially in the discussion of sadistic vengeful stalking illustrated in the latter film, Dr. Gediman's discussion of sexual stalking is enlightening and engaging. Like the first chapter of Sigmund Freud's *Three Essays on Sexuality* (1905d), it is about other people—sick individuals and those unfortunate enough to cross their paths. It is not about us. We are relaxed in the reading experience. After all, we are neither stalkers nor stalkees. But this sense of ease must soon give way to other feelings, for the clinical and cinematic discussion of sexual stalking is only the thin edge of a widening wedge. As in *Three Essays*, considerations of the conspicuous perversions of others are prelude to examinations of perverse impulses that find expression in a widening scope of conduct and social life.

Drawing on ideas developed in the first part of the book, Dr. Gediman significantly expands the meaning of the term "stalking," conventionally applied to "sexual stalking," to include "surveillance stalking," a pattern of coolly motivated invasions of privacy, sponsored by the private sector or by the state, and carried out by professionals, by hackers, eavesdroppers, and spies who are just doing their jobs—or so they think. The case material is drawn from published reports and from four riveting films: *The Conversation* (a film that is also discussed in William Fried's 2016 volume, *Critical Flicker Fusion*, in this series), *The Lives of Others*, *Caché*, and *Red Road*. Each of these films depicts surveillance stalking, that is, stalking ostensibly motivated by impersonal objectives, yet each reveals that there is, as Dr. Gediman writes, no more than a thin line separating sexual and surveillance stalking. However impersonal the purpose, all surveillance is ultimately conducted by human beings whose desires, fantasies, and feelings can infiltrate and infuse the formal operations being carried out, with complex and very different consequences for both stalkers as well as for stalkees.

In the final section of the book, the focus expands the scope of stalking behavior yet again, now to consider the "macular level of stalking found in privacy invasions that have major national and global implications." Here Dr. Gediman focuses on two films, *Enemy of the State* and *Citizenfour*. *Enemy of the State* is a thriller, filmed in 1998, which depicts the murder of a senator opposed to a bill intended to expand the surveillance powers of the National Security Administration (NSA). The murder is committed on the orders of the director of the NSA, a man intent on securing passage of the bill and enlarging his own power. When the director and his agents discover that the murder was inadvertently filmed by a birdwatcher's automated camera, the sophisticated surveillance apparatus of the NSA is employed, not for the purposes of national security, but to track down the individual holding the incriminating photographs. The film, which is pure fiction, depicts advanced surveillance capabilities that are not. Three years after the release of the film, shortly after the 9/11 attack, Congress enacted the *Patriot Act*, a law intended to strengthen our national security, in part, by expanding the surveillance powers of the NSA. In 2011, these powers were again expanded to authorize massive programs of data collection on virtually all American citizens based on their telephone, email, and internet activities.

In 2013, Edward Snowden, a government systems analyst working for the NSA, secretly contacted Laura Poitras, an independent filmmaker, and Glenn Greenwald, a journalist for the *Guardian* newspaper, in order to secure publication of dramatic revelations about these NSA surveillance activities. *Citizenfour* documents their encounter. It focuses on eight days during which Snowden, Poitras, and Greenwald met secretly in Hong Kong to arrange for a series of publications laying out the content of Snowden's revelations and on the events surrounding these meetings. The content of the whistle-blower's reports is astonishing—warrantless surveillance and wiretapping, the accumulation of massive streams of data in huge databanks, the sense of a government operating outside the boundaries of consent. Early in the film, Snowden describes the overall situation to Poitras and Greenwald:

> Disturbingly, the amount of US communication ingested by NSA is still increasing. Publicly, we complain that things are going dark, but

> in fact, our accesses are improving. The truth is that the NSA has never in its history collected more than it does now. I know the location of most domestic interception points and that the largest telecommunication companies in the US are betraying the trust of their customers, which I can prove. We are building the greatest weapon of oppression in the history of man. (Poitras, 2014)

Perhaps most disturbing, however, is the real time footage of Wolf Blitzer, on television, reporting on Snowden's revelations—disturbing because it undermines any defensive "suspension of belief" based on the desperate idea that "this is just a movie."

Snowden's revelations are shocks to our sense of reality and, for some of us, more terrifying than the terror it is intended to prevent. However real the threat of terrorism, however benign the state's intentions, state surveillance is inexorably unsettling, upending to our assumptions of privacy and antithetical to our sense of freedom and democracy. "If we don't have a right to privacy, how do we have a free and open discussion?" asks Jacob Appelbaum, an encryptions specialist and journalist featured in *Citizenfour*. "When we lose privacy," he notes, "we lose agency because we lose liberty itself" (Poitras, 2014). Like sexual stalking, the idea of extensive surveillance engenders feelings of dread and vulnerability—of "justifiable paranoia," as Dr. Gediman writes. Indeed, such feelings of terror are the "red thread" that connects sexual stalking and surveillance stalking and justifies their inclusion in the same general category of behavior.

As I contemplate *Stalker, Hacker, Voyeur, Spy*, I am reminded of Bentham's odious 1787 *Panopticon Writings*, a series of letters in which the philosopher Jeremy Bentham sets out plans for an "inspection house," a building designed to ensure the perpetual surveillance of those individuals who live or work in it (Bentham, 1995). According to his design, the inspection house is a circular building, with an inspectors' tower at the center encircled by the living and working space of the inmates. From the tower, an inspector would have complete visual access to all surrounding areas of the building. The inmates would thus be subject to continuous observation but would not be able to see the inspectors surveilling them. This would ensure the sense of perpetual observation by invisible watchmen. Although Bentham initially presented it as a plan for a penitentiary, he suggested that the same design be employed for other institutions, including "houses of correction, or work-houses, or manufactories, or mad-houses, or hospitals, or schools" (p. 34). The orienting idea behind Bentham's design is the recognition that unremitting surveillance, or the belief in such surveillance, instills fear, expands the inspector's social control over the inmates, and inspires their submission and compliance with social rules. An individual stalkee is trapped in a private Panopticon, lives in terror because the stalker's gaze is ubiquitous. If the Snowden revelations are true, we are all, to one degree or another, living in a new Panopticon, under perpetual surveillance and unable to see those who watch us.

We, who are analysts, have another, very special and immediate concern, one that is beyond the scope of this book but not beyond the core interest of its readers. I am referring to the privacy of personal health information, including the privacy of psychotherapy records. In the case of *Jaffe v. Redmond*, the Supreme Court established the privilege of confidentiality in psychotherapy, noting that "the mere possibility of disclosure may impede development of the confidential relationship necessary for successful treatment" (*Jaffe v. Redmond*, 1996). The establishment of this privilege, however, has not ensured the confidentiality of treatment records. In the 1990s, many government leaders advocated the creation of a nationwide "interoperable" system of digital health care records to facilitate the advance of medical research and to support the development of integrated health care systems that depend on information sharing. In 2009, the government implemented the *HITECH Act* ("The Health Information Technology for Economic and Clinical Health Act) to incentivize the adoption and utilization of health information technology. Since then, the federal government has given more than thirty billion dollars to those who have adopted electronic health records. Over the span of these same years, nearly 160 million Americans have had their electronic health records breached (Andrews, 2016). More than 90% of health care organizations have had one or more data breaches, and 40% of these organizations have had more than five data breaches in the last two years (Ponemon Institute, 2015). According to a recent study reported in the online HIPAA Journal, "almost 45% of Americans have now had their personal information exposed in a healthcare cyberattack; and in some cases, more than once" (HIPAA Journal, 2015).

Even more insidious than the phenomenon of criminal hacking, however, are the so-called privacy policies of our own government. In

1996, the same year that the Supreme Court established the psychotherapy privilege, President Clinton signed the *Health Insurance Portability and Accountability Act*, better known as "HIPAA." While the initial intention of the HIPAA Act was to protect the continuity of health insurance coverage, the scope of the act was gradually expanded to regulate the use of information technology in health care. In 2001, President Bush implemented the HIPAA "Privacy Rule," requiring health care providers to obtain the patient's consent prior to using or disclosing protected health information. In 2002, however, the Department of Health and Human Services amended the earlier "privacy rule" to authorize the use and disclosure of protected health information for treatment, payment or health care operations"—without the patient's consent. Deborah Peel, founder of the privacy advocacy group, Patient Privacy Rights, observes that the amended regulations "opened the nation's sensitive health records to millions of providers, employers, government agencies, insurance companies, billing firms, transcription services, pharmacy benefit managers, pharmaceutical companies, data miners, creditors and more for any 'routine' use" (Patient Privacy Rights, 2016).

It may be that threat posed by terrorists to our national security may justify the massive surveillance operations described by Edward Snowden. It may be that the advance of medical research and the provision of medical services to an expanding population of patients warrants the adoption of electronic medical records and their free transmission through the health care system as described above. These are virtuous purposes. Jeremy Bentham also cited virtuous purposes, arguing that the societal crises of his time demanded the institution of the Panopticon. The opening words of his preface are filled with promise: "Morals reformed—health preserved—industry invigorated—instruction diffused—public burthens lightened—Economy seated, as it were, upon a rock—the Gordian knot of the Poor-Laws not cut, but untied—all by a simple idea in Architecture!" (1995, p. 31). To be sure, national security and health care and a host of other societal needs merit a measure of priority. But how much of our privacy must we yield to ensure their attainment? It is indeed possible that we may benefit from authorized invasions of our privacy. It is certain that we are also damaged by them.

Stalker, Hacker, Voyeur, Spy situates the experience of privacy and invasions of privacy at the center of our personal awareness and at the top of our scientific agenda. Psychoanalysts have long understood that privacy is a necessary condition for the development of our minds, for creative reverie, for the experience of "going on being" that D. W. Winnicott so sensitively described, and thus, ultimately, for the development of an authentic self-hood. At the same time, the privacy of our primal attachment experience is critical to the development of genuine relatedness and of our capacity to carry out intimate relationships in adult life. One might conclude from the foregoing that privacy is an essential condition for the development of social and psychological health—indeed, for the attainment and preservation of sanity. Dr. Gediman's book compels us to pursue new lines of inquiry that will deepen our understanding of the basic human need for privacy and of the professional, psychological, and societal implications of perpetual surveillance or, as described by Bentham, by the belief that we are subject to such surveillance.

The psychoanalytic community has a fundamental interest in the preservation of our privacy. We have the intellectual resources to understand why privacy is so important to our lives. And we have the organizational capabilities to more actively convey our understanding of privacy, and of the consequences of its invasion, to the wider public. We are all very much indebted to Dr. Gediman for giving us this important book and calling our attention to the challenges we face as a profession and as a people—while we can still do something about it.

Websites for reference

Health Information Technology for Economic and Clinical Health Act (HITECH). Available at: https://www.gpo.gov/fdsys/pkg/PLAW-111publ5/pdf/PLAW-111publ5.pdf

Health Insurance Portability and Accountability Act (HIPAA). Available at: https://www.hhs.gov/hipaa/for-professionals/privacy/

US Patriot Act. https://www.sec.gov/about/offices/ocie/aml/patriotact2001.pdf

PREFACE

People often ask me how my study of stalking and being stalked began. It was after a serendipitous invitation to speak on the topic at a time when I had no inkling that the varieties of sexual and surveillance stalking would become a major interest that led me to write this book. In 2006, Harriet Basseches asked me to present a paper on a panel that she was organizing for Section I, Psychologist–Psychoanalyst Practitioners, of Division 39 (Psychoanalysis) of the American Psychological Association for its forthcoming annual conference to be held that year in Philadelphia. I initially demurred because I thought I lacked clinical and other experience with the topic. I reflected a while and realized that at that very time I had been working with several patients who had been stalked, and one who had stalked me on the internet. My recovery of those recent, but apparently shelved, memories led me to think of stalking-related activity of others whom I had known personally, and of stalking themes in films.

Following my presentation at Division 39, I was invited to speak on the topic of stalking at the Cosmopolitan Club in New York. Some years earlier, during my interview for membership in that social club for women of accomplishment in the arts, professions, and business, I was asked to sit at a table at which all twelve members of the Membership

Committee were allotted five minutes each to start a dialogue with me on any topic they wished from among the items I had filled out in my membership application. In a process humorously reminiscent of speed dating, each of the twelve members, when her turn came to sit with me alone, opted to question me on, and only on, of all the many topics they found in my lengthy CV, my work on "Stalking." That topic was then a brand new area of interest that I had thrown into my resumé at the last minute. I was beginning to get an inkling that my social cachet among this group of women rested on their perceptions of my being an expert on the subject of stalking at a time when I was, in fact, only a novice. Only in retrospect do I realize that people, generally, are very strongly interested in, and fascinated with, the topic and that they turned to me as a source of enlightenment to satisfy their curiosity and to air their concerns about friends who had been stalked.

My assessors quizzed me about stalking so intensively that they piqued my interest in pursuing the topic further and intensively. So, I developed my psychoanalytically informed work in the years that followed and presented twice at the National Meetings of the American Psychoanalytic Association in New York City; once at the Institute for Psychoanalytic Training and Research (IPTAR) Conference on the Arts, also in New York City, once at an international meeting of psychoanalysts at the University of Vancouver, once at the Philadelphia Center for Psychoanalysis, and once at the Virginia Psychoanalytic Association. In all of my talks on stalking, I included some clinical treatment material, but the bulk of my presentations showed film clips organized on a DVD to illustrate stalking in many of its other clinical variations. As it turns out, some of the films I chose for their stalking content are considered to be masterpieces. That is how many would characterize Alfred Hitchcock's *Rear Window*, Michael Powell's *Peeping Tom*, Francis Ford Coppola's *The Conversation*, and Michael Haneke's *Caché*. Clint Eastwood, the director of *Play Misty for Me*, has certainly gained a reputation as a master director. Great directors and screenwriters had been drawn to the topic of stalking long before I had.

The Confederation of Independent Societies (CIPS), a national U.S. group of psychoanalytic societies affiliated with the International Psychoanalytical Association, invited me to submit a proposal for their book series, "On The Boundaries of Psychoanalysis," published by Karnac Books. When Karnac contracted to publish my work for the series, regulations of the publishing industry ruled out distributing the book along with the DVD of my selected film clips. A major task in preparing this book, then, has been to look at the films and selected clips again in order to translate the film imagery into words. I believe I have succeeded in my mission of achieving a close enough reproduction of screen images and dialogue so that my reading audience can experience the essence of stalking as well as my viewing audiences have been able to do.

In beginning to think about stalking, it certainly never occurred to me that I have ever been a stalker or been stalked. I had simply been invited to participate on a panel that happened to be on the topic of stalking. In gathering material for this book, however, I was able to think back to personal experiences I had had that I would regard as a variety of either stalking or being stalked myself, in both my personal and professional life. One that I would now identify in the class of stalker was a safari experience in South Africa. There, I was one in a party of tourists stalking their prey, not to kill or otherwise harm, but certainly to look at and to photograph with one degree or another of awed, aesthetic, and even voyeuristic interest. My knowledge of the field expanded from going in search of animals, originally a form of predatory stalking, to two more complex activities involving human beings that I am here calling "sexual stalking," the more familiar variety, and "surveillance stalking," the less familiar. The two activities have many common features.

Years into my preparatory work before actually sitting down to write this book to cover these two major forms of stalking, I realized that my clinical cases and film illustrations of sexual stalking were not so much about sexual stalking *per se*, but dealt with two very specific syndromes that translate into obsessional experiences that are well known in psychoanalytic practice. The first is erotomania, unrequited love, and revenge. The second is voyeurism. Erotomania is the false belief that one is romantically loved. The erotomanic sexual stalker, then, is often a jilted lover, who presumptuously and usually vengefully invades the stalkee's, or the victim's, privacy through unwanted pursuit. In cases of voyeurism, the invasive, obsessional following most usually occurs through visually tracking by eye, camera, or binoculars, the object of one's unwanted sexual and affectionate desire. Voyeurism is traditionally regarded as a perversion of sexuality, often sadistic, and, in that sense, the overall term "sexual" may be used to characterize it. As for erotomania, any observer would not be hard pressed to understand its vicissitude of unrequired love as a form of sexual stalking, so I am taking the liberty of returning the category "sexual stalking" to characterize both erotomania and voyeurism.

What I believe is truly new in my exposition are some underlying similarities between the erotomania and voyeurism of sexual stalking, on the one hand, and "surveillance stalking," on the other. I understand surveillance stalking to involve privately or state sanctioned unwanted pursuit of victims by keeping tabs on them, usually electronically. Both forms of stalking involve significant invasions of privacy, and distinctive reactions in the one being stalked, the "stalkee." Both forms, then, involve a stalker–stalkee couple that relate to one another in characteristic identifiable ways.

My topic is timely. It is nearly impossible to pick up a newspaper or tune in to a television newscast in this day and age without coming across an article, often a lead article or a discussion, on my subject of surveillance stalking. The topic is on everyone's mind, particularly in the context of the conflict between rights to privacy and individual freedom, on the one hand, and security, or protection, usually from terrorism, on the other. The psychoanalytic literature has very little to say about sexual stalking except in the cases of a few reviews of films, including several that I am covering in this book, and virtually nothing to say about surveillance stalking. So, I am taking advantage of a niche waiting to be filled on the topic of stalking that will cover the phenomenon in its two major variations, sexual and surveillance. I will contextualize my topic by emphasizing its central relevance to today's social, cultural, and political dilemmas with particular reference to stalking in cyberspace and its inevitable invasions of privacy.

This book was born at the same time that Edward Snowden blew the whistle on the National Security Agency (NSA), and The Patriot Act came up before the US Congress for renewal. Because these daily, headlined, and editorialized current events involved not just surveillance, but also surveillance stalking, I knew I had found my niche for presenting my ideas that might interest a large audience, psychoanalytic and otherwise. Soon, I had glimpsed, heard about, read about, or viewed on film the whole gamut of stalking, hacking, bugging, tapping, eavesdropping, surveillance, and spying, all of which involved, to one degree or another, terrorizing invasions of privacy. Once it became obvious to me that surveillance methods constituted a form of stalking, it was a small step forward to realize that stalking occurs in cyberspace as well as in life on earth. The myriad violations of privacy on the internet engendered the necessity to be very careful about what one writes online, particularly on social networks such as Facebook. The fact that there is no such thing as a private email has become all the more evident. I am increasingly conscious of being a potential victim of cyberstalking, mostly because of my internet searches backed by apparently innocent intent, like searching for websites of my favorite clothing designers. Any time I clicked on an item I fancied ordering some day, unbidden advertisements for dresses, jackets and so forth that appealed to me would pop up each time I tried to retrieve my email and continued to appear, especially if I had ordered the related items online. Who out there but a stalker of sorts could have been following my tastes so closely and would pick and feed back more of what met my tastes? Although helpful at times, the advertisements could certainly be harassing. The continuous pursuit of my patronage is a minor form of stalking with consequences for me that are mainly benign. However, the potential for much worse privacy invasions was disturbing and hit hard.

In assembling my thoughts and materials for this book, I came to notice the regular appearance in newspapers, particularly *The New York Times,* of accounts of hacking into people's telephone records and computers. The media coverage was intrinsically connected to the forthcoming action by Congress on the Patriot Act and the conflict between security and privacy that seemed to be on everybody's mind as never before. I had thought hacking occurred relatively infrequently, but technical knowledge and instructions on how to do it are now legion. Any one of us can get step-by-step instruction so that we can all be hackers and not just hackee victims of intrusions. Patients of mine, without any conscious and deliberate ill intentions that I know of, have also explained to me how well they have been trained in their technology education and in their jobs to hack into the computers and other related devices operated by business associates, family members, and total strangers.

Who knew that *The New York Times* would become my personal stalker by virtue of its regular reporting on hacking in cyberspace? That newspaper also became a major research source for my mission to develop a psychoanalytic perspective on cyberstalking. This form of stalking, which includes cyber attacks, is significant to the bulk of Americans and world citizens sharing the same global cyberspace because of the conflicts between privacy and security that the new technologies and their applications in communications industries have generated.

On June 2, 2015, as I was working on a draft of this Preface, I went to my computer in the afternoon when I had a break and discovered the following *New York Times* Breaking News Alert: "In a remarkable reversal of national security policy formed after the September 11 2001 terrorist attacks, the Senate voted on Tuesday to curtail the federal government's sweeping surveillance of American phone records, sending the legislation to President Obama's desk for his signature." Lawmakers had revoked amendments that would have rolled back proposed controls on government spying, a most pernicious form of stalking. The Freedom Act had replaced the Patriot Act. The news left me feeling that Americans would once again feel secure as robust counterterrorist surveillance activities against terrorists were resumed and indiscriminate collections by the government of every phone call made by everybody else would be discontinued. I had monitored a process in which stalking aspects of privacy invasion had been eliminated in favor of the security inherent in government surveillance activity, at least in the USA. Big Brother's stalking activities of 1984, if not significantly lessened in 2016, had been specifically identified and brought into the arena of potentially progressive conversation, dialogue, and debate.

After working for years on the subject of stalking, I finally had to choose a title for this book. Although my point of view is largely psychoanalytic, it is my wish that the book be of interest to the informed general public as well as my professional colleagues, film scholars, and film buffs. I settled initially on the title, *Stalking and Hacking: A Psychoanalytic Study of Erotomania, Voyeurism, Surveillance, and Other Invasions of Privacy*. I was concerned that my then favorite title, *Stalker, Hacker, Bugger, Spy,* because it contained the slang word "bugger" might be considered inappropriately salacious in some circles, as when the term evokes the British slang word, "buggering," a highly offensive term used to characterize the practices of anal intercourse or sodomy. The word does have connotations that are not at all included in what I have written about here, even though the word also captures, like no other, the defining characteristics of bugging–stalking activities of private investigators and other eavesdroppers. The word "bugging" here refers to intrusively investigative taping, tapping, listening in on, and keeping under surveillance. I will use the term "bugging," then, when it refers to the eavesdropping activity of planting an electronic device invasively on someone's person or property for the purpose of gaining information by this form of secret spying. The meaning of "bugging," in this instance, is exactly on point for my purposes, and I shall feel free to use it in the text when it means that and only that. Although I gave up the fight for the lilting title, *Stalker, Hacker, Bugger, Spy,* I am perfectly content with my present, unequivocal title, *Stalker, Hacker, Voyeur, Spy*. I fully credit John Le Carré (1974) for the format as well as the lilt.

Introduction and overview

My title, *Stalker, Hacker, Voyeur, Spy* extends the once limited context of "stalking" beyond its customary hemmed-in reference, which is to a stealthy, usually sexual, pursuit of another. I aim here to develop a wide-ranging and inclusive psychoanalytically informed view in four Parts, nine chapters and an Epilogue. Reading through the Table of Contents will present a better overview than any prose I could add at this point. The major varieties of stalking range from the historically limited notion of sexually related stalking to its present-day expansion to stalking in cyberspace. Invasions of privacy that produce extreme fear and terror in the stalkee create the "red thread" that runs through all forms of stalking.

The areas I cover are obsessional sexual stalking and the less often studied surveillance stalking. Sexual stalking involves two notable psychological syndromes. The first is erotomania, or the belief in a non-existent romance, which is permeated with unrequited love, loneliness, and vengeance. Vignettes from two clinical psychoanalytically oriented case histories, and two films, *Play Misty for Me* and *Fatal Attraction,* illustrate erotomania. The second sexual stalking syndrome is perverse voyeurism and sadomasochism. The films *Rear Window* and *Peeping Tom* illustrate the dynamics of voyeuristic and sadistic stalking and introduce the notion of "doubling" in filming, a process in which the ways of filming often parallel the content within the film when it comes to the subject matter of this variety of stalking. I end this section with a consideration of gender differences in sexual stalking.

I illustrate surveillance stalking through four films: *The Conversation, The Lives of Others, Caché,* and *Red Road*. Jointly, these films cover stalking that is sanctioned by state policy, as well as expert bugging, eavesdropping, peeping, tapping, and hacking. Psychological gratifications that sometimes overlap with those of sexual stalking are legion in the surveillance stalkers portrayed in these top-notch and award winning films.

Part IV of the book, "Stalking and Hacking in The World We Live in: The Planet Earth and Cyberspace", takes off from the relatively molecular content level of the preceding parts on sexual and surveillance stalking and moves on to consider a present-day macular level of stalking found in privacy invasions that have major national and global implications. I begin with celebrity stalking, a subject covered in our news media, both the tabloids and the major respected news organizations. I then develop my ideas on the epidemic of internet and telephone stalking, promoted by giant step high-tech developments. Although the media is rife with stories of cyberstalking, coverage of that subject matter is extremely sparse or perhaps non-existent in the psychoanalytic literature. I begin with some case vignettes, and then devote major space to discussing the psychology of those who hack into emails for primarily personal reasons. I reserve my last chapter for the larger major invasions of privacy on national, international, and global scales, with illustrations from two films: the prophetic *Enemy of the State* and the more recent *Citizenfour,* the real time documentary about Edward Snowden's leakage of top-secret material to expose the abuses of too much internet and telephone surveillance. The book ends with increasing emphasis on stalking at a global level in the current debate over the conflicts between the two vitally and equally important world goals of security and privacy. The Epilogue, "On learning that one's privacy has been invaded by stalking", aims to wind up the red thread to be found in a psychoanalytic understanding of what it feels like to stalk or be stalked in all of its varieties discussed in this book.

* * *

Now that I have presented an extremely condensed overview of my book, I should like to offer some general introductory commentary that sets the tone and offers a small taste of varieties of stalking in today's culture that I have outlined and developed more in depth as I move along. A typical stalking scenario involves unrequited love that sets off intense feelings, ranging from vulnerability to rejection, abandonment, and humiliation, up to pathological erotomania accompanied by murderous rage. Male and female sexual stalking are both motivated by a perverse scenario, usually sadomasochistic, and often voyeuristic. It should come as no surprise that stalker and stalkee often share attributes in common: conscious and unconscious identifications in fantasies involving sex and aggression, love and hate, shame and revenge, which bind them together, often symbiotically or co-dependently as a couple, albeit a highly dysfunctional one.

As early as 1943, C. D. Daly presented a psychoanalytic account, one of the few, and perhaps the earliest ever published, based on Edward Thompson's novel, *An Indian Day* (1927). In Thompson's fictional account, an insane European missionary named Findley believed, in his insanity, that Padalsini, a woman stalker, was terrorizing him.

> She was seeking him now, she was persecuting him. . . . Findlay was mad and Padalsini was seeking him—stalking him, his soul and body would be hers, and his gallant spirit, that had never cried for help before, cried for it now. . . . As the night took visible menacing form, and towered above him with burning unpitying eyes, Findlay called out—he stumbled and felt the hands of the jungle across his flight. The demon queen had caught up with him; she was lying in his way and had gripped his foot. He cried again terribly and all was blankness. (Thompson, 1927, p. 160)

Thompson certainly conveyed that stalking is a form of terrorism that appears in many guises. At its most extreme, stalking is a criminal or quasi-criminal activity, usually involving sexual harassment, in which one person, usually a male, stealthily follows another, usually a female. The only recourse available to most stalkees is to take out a court order of restraint against the stalker, who may then be arrested upon report to the police of any additional stalking activity. These days, it is not unusual for a woman to stalk a man when she feels immensely vulnerable to rejection and abandonment. Terror, dread, and other forms of affectively negative excitement are bound to accompany the experiences of both stalking and being stalked. In addition to sexual stalking, surveillance stalking has become exceedingly common in connection with the current increase in computer hacking and widespread invasion of privacy by the government, by start-up companies, and countless others. Surveillance stalking ranges, then, from everyday cyberstalking, up through state-sanctioned stalking in the interest of both terrorism and counter-terrorism.

We get to know about stalking from case studies and film, experiences in the private realm, and by working as a professional psychotherapist and psychoanalyst. A very small body of data now exists on psychoanalysts and other psychotherapists who have been stalked (Ainslee, 2006; Basseches, 2006; Gottlieb; 1994). Several patients of mine have confessed, or simply disclosed, outright, that they once secretly web-stalked me, aided and abetted by Google. I am certain that still others have pursued me on the internet but have not acknowledged their activity because they feel guilty or shameful about it, or because they prefer to keep their activity infused with a degree of illicitness, short of the illegality of the harassing *bona fide* stalker. Today, many patients, perhaps most, Google their analysts simply to check out their credentials or to conjecture if they would be a good match. I know for sure that increasing numbers of my patients have Googled me. In learning directly from patients that they stalk people other than their analysts, it is a good idea for analysts to assume that they will be stalked at some later day by that patient, if they have not been stalked already. Such internet investigations are an acceptable thing to do in our current *Zeitgeist*. Googling is so common today that nearly everyone Googles others, in manners that would usually not raise an eyebrow, but that might lead, in those so disposed, to cyberstalking. Internet dating services, various blogs, and social networks are frequently used for purposes not only of harassment but also of other common forms of stalking. In fact, stalkers, gangsters, and others, including spies employed by organizations of our own government, such as the CIA and the NSA, and those of other countries, such as Interpol, do make use of online data brokers for state-sanctioned purposes.

To stimulate your curiosity about other examples yet to come under their appropriately delineated rubrics, I now offer a foretaste, in vignette form, of my experiences with two male stalkers from my own practice. The first, a voyeuristic stalker, whom I shall call Tom, identified himself explicitly as a "peeping Tom." The second, whom I shall call "Don" was stalked by his partner during an extramarital love affair. Primal scene traumata figure for Tom as importantly as they did for the famous *Peeping Tom* of filmdom, to be discussed in Chapter Four. Tom sought psychotherapy when his girlfriend learned of his perverse voyeuristic activities, regarded him as cheating on her, and issued an ultimatum that he get treatment or she would leave him. Early on, he disclosed to me that, as a child, he had devised multiple strategies to spy on his parents while they were alone in their bedroom, and thus habitually witnessed their sexual activities, the "primal scene." For nearly a half a year, he dutifully reported to me his current obsessional stalking activities, such as following the women flight attendants he met on his business trips to their motel rooms and peeping through the keyholes to watch them undress. In the sixth month of treatment, he had begun to talk about his strategies of ascending to rooftops with binoculars to spy on particular couples whose most intimate acts he would watch from beginning to end. I think of binoculars along with present-day electronic methods as the stock-in-trade tools as well as symbolic representations or logos of sexual stalkers, surveillance stalkers, and even ordinary stalkers on safaris. Very shortly after this disclosure, Tom failed to show up for a session, and never returned. I imagined he had found out where I live, which is a thirtieth floor apartment with wall-to-wall and floor-to ceiling glass windows. I had to consider the possibility that I had become the newest object of my peeping Tom's stalking perversion and that he had been stalking me voyeuristically from nearby rooftops. I have decided not to report to you any more of my work with him in the interests of confidentiality and of minimizing prurience. As my reading audience, however, you might decide to speculate on and to imagine what he revealed to me, and what transpired between us before termination overtook further treatment opportunities.

When I disclose that I, as an analyst have been stalked, I mean to say that not only have I been stalked by patients, but also by significant people in their lives who might want to obtain material they think I have, or to influence me to say certain things to their significant others. Don, another patient, whom I discussed at length in a presentation (1992) and in my book, *Fantasies of Love and Death in Life and Art* (1995), yearned, in his late sixties, to "die in the saddle." He had a lifelong pattern of compulsively driven, extramarital, "dangerous" sexual liaisons with women he regarded as *femmes fatales*. Versions of the *femme fatale* theme, so common in romantic literature, also play out in the real lives of actual stalkers and those they stalk. Don came to me because he could not extricate himself from a painful relationship with his latest mistress, Victoria, who was an erotomanic stalker. Victoria's obsessional sexual pursuit of Don bore uncanny similarities to Glenn Close's portrayal of Alex, the seemingly surreal "vampire" style stalker in the film, *Fatal Attraction*, to be discussed in Chapter Three. Don's mistress stalked not only him, but also *me* as his analyst, harassing both of us, and Don's wife as well. Victoria wrote me letters, made phone calls, and left voicemail messages with suicide threats and persistently made "hang-up" calls in her driven efforts to verify Don's whereabouts and to tell me how to advise him to cast his romantic lot with her. She pleaded with me to be her supportive ally, and to let her join him in sessions. On a couple of occasions, she stalked him right into my office and stayed on for a session during which, in a typical erotomanic mode, she tried to intimidate me into persuading him to leave his wife. Victoria thought that if she could convince me that Don loved her more than he loved his wife, then I would convince Don to leave his wife for her. Don felt helpless to deal with these pressures and tactics. We might easily think of them as the quintessential stalker–stalkee couple, in that he definitely had something at stake, related to his rather grandiose goals of boosting his body ego, in permitting himself to be pursued, relentlessly. A sense of manic excitement during his frequent episodes of infidelity motivated Don as the apparently passive stalkee of the couple. The excitement of extramarital affairs helped him to regulate dysphoric feelings connected with his fear of dying. Eventually, he was able to resist the temptation to submit to the sexually exciting pull of their liaison, and I was able to refuse Victoria admission to my office.

I am certainly not alone as a stalked psychoanalyst. Ainslee (2006) has noted the absence, in the psychoanalytic literature, of any notable coverage of that topic, and has filled the breach with her own research and clinical commentary. One patient from another practice tracked her analyst's movements in and out of her office. Another performed an internet search that yielded information about her analyst's financial contributions to political causes that the analyst had no idea were made public (Basseches, 2006). Another left voicemail messages for more than ten years after the analysis had been terminated. Yet another patient imagined herself as a vampire/ghoul stalking her male analyst as prey, but never enacted much more than her fantasy of visiting his summer home and of repeatedly telephoning him (Gottlieb, 2000). Erotic "hunter–stalker" transferences toward the analyst occur more frequently than we realized. Statistics vary, but generally show that 10% of therapists have been stalked. Of these stalkers, 68% are women, 32% men. These numbers seem to be at odds with the male to female ratio of stalkers in the general population. These stalker patients tend to have experienced a recent divorce or breakup of an intimate relationship, and displaced their attempts to restore the lost connection via obsessional perverse stalking of their analyst (Ainslee, 2006). That is, their erotomania that had been directed toward rejecting partners becomes displaced in erotomanic transferences toward their analysts.

Quite a few men and women patients who are curious about whether their partners have "cheated" on them have perused cell phone logs, web-stalked the habits of their spouses or paramours to investigate which pornographic and other web sites they have visited regularly, and which emails and text messages have been exchanged on the sly with which "other" women or men. Cyberstalkers use this information for purposes that are sometimes suspicious and verge on the illegal, perhaps for perverse excitement and/or in pursuit of revenge for unreciprocated romantic, usually idealized, love. Some patients terrorize or have been terrorized by their exes, once they discover these incursions. The internet, then, these days, provides fertile ground for "closeted" sexual stalkers. Katha Pollit (2004) confessed in the *New Yorker*, after her lover left her, " I was like Javert, hunting him through the sewers of cyberspace, moving from link to link in the dark, like Spider-man flinging himself by a filament over the shadowy chasm between one roof and another" (p. 24). In the throes of romantic love, some people, when rejected, "contemplate stalking, homicide, suicide. This drive for romantic love can be stronger than the will to live" (p. 32).

In this attempt to put forward and reflect upon forms and variations of stalking in real life, films, and fantasy, it has become apparent to me that stalking is a multi-determined phenomenon, certainly an aberration that both stalking *enactments* and stalking *fantasies* serve in both film representations and in patients; that is, in art and in life. I present now an additional foretaste from major illustrations from the films about stalking that I shall be discussing in detail further on. In the realm of sexual erotomanic stalking, Clint Eastwood's 1971 *Play Misty for Me* has usually been considered the first notable film about sexually perverse obsessional stalking. Adrian Lyne's *Fatal Attraction* followed in 1987 and is arguably the more famous because of Glenn Close's iconic portrayal of Alex, the "bunny-boiling" lethal *femme fatale* of obsessional sexual stalking. Both *Misty* and *Fatal Attraction*, to be covered in Chapter Three, deal with the lonely woman stalker trying to cope with the torments of erotomania and unrequited love. Images of the presumably promiscuous *femme fatale* sexual behavior that is often considered a sexual perversion pervade both films. By "sexual perversion," I do not mean a gender-based sexual stereotype or deviation from any so-called sexual norm. I consider the perverse elements in stalking as a fusion of love and hate—a particular form of sadomasochism—that can culminate in a romantic agony. Engaging in perverse stalking behavior, then, dehumanizes and *uses* others as objects of sexual desire in order to provide the reality or illusion of empowerment over another.

Rear Window (1954), which portrays voyeurism in sexual stalking, in this instance, of suspicious looking sexually involved neighbors, was probably the first of that genre, followed by *Peeping Tom* (1961), a film that focuses on male stalking. Both films will lead to a thorough consideration of parallel levels of voyeurism in stalking, in filming, , and in viewing films. I devote Chapter Five to gender differences between male and female erotomanic and voyeuristic stalkers.

Four surveillance-stalking films that are reviewed in Chapter Six either foreshadow or echo the "Orwellian" turn of events in the world at large since 9/11: *The Conversation* (1974), *The Lives of Others*, from Germany (2006), that takes place in Orwell's fateful year, 1984, and the relatively unknown Scottish film, *Red Road*, also 2006. While I include these films under the "surveillance" rubric, they depict important aspects of sexual stalking as well. The line between sexual and surveillance stalking is a fine one, particularly in the film *Red Road*. I end Part III on "Surveillance stalking" with *Caché*, (2005), about a couple who are terrorized by a stalker who delivers to their very doorstep surveillance videos of them leaving and entering their home at various times. In the film itself, we suspect that the terrorism is perpetrated by a man who, as a young boy, felt ostracized by his stalkee's family. In the end, however, sharp-eyed viewers and film buffs notice someone else in images that accompany the final rolling credit lines of *Caché*, whom they identify as the culprit.

Fiction, most particularly in film, is replete with examples not only of men stalking women, but also of women stalking men. We are probably most familiar with the stalker Alex Forrest (Glenn Close) in *Fatal Attraction* (1987). A married man's one-night stand comes back to haunt him when that demented seductress to whom he had yielded begins to stalk him and hunt down his family. Who can ever erase the image of Alex, clinging, clawing, and going endlessly in search (see Hermann, 1976) of her prey, Dan Gallagher (Michael Douglas)? Dan was like "everyman," yielding to a seductress for what he thought was a simple one-night—or, more accurately—one-weekend stand. Alex, hooked, psychotically stalks, slits her wrists, boils Dan's daughter's bunny to death, and tries to stab his wife, who, in turn, kills Alex as she defends Dan who, in his own life defense, is trying to drown Alex in the bathtub. And who can forget a similar, but not as terrifyingly vengeful, stalking in Woody Allen's (2005) *Matchpoint*. The hero, Chris (Jonathan Rhys Meyers), kills his sensuous woman stalker, the *femme fatale* Nora (Scarlett Johansson) rather than allow her to reverse the course of his charmed life. By 1987, it was clear that films about stalking belonged to the horror film genre. By 2016, films about stalking extended to cyberstalking and highlighted general issues of security and privacy invasions. They included terrorism along with horror. *Stalker, Hacker, Voyeur, Spy* seeks to expand the extent and the depths of a psychoanalytic exploration of stalking.

PART I

DEVELOPMENTAL ROOTS

CHAPTER ONE

From psychoanalysis, neuroscience, and attachment theory

Scant references to the words "stalking" or "stalker" from the now standard source, Psychoanalytic Electronic Publishing (PEP CD ROM) fall into three main categories: neuroscientifically based stalking—usually genetic patterns in animals, stalking based on mother–infant attachment patterns, and stalking in aggressive and sadomasochistically charged object relationships. My account is brief because the findings are sparse.

Predatory animals and human beings stalk their quarry

In the psychoanalytic literature on neuroscience and neuropsychoanalysis, authors identify stalking in animals and, to some extent, humans, as brain mediated normal behavior. One animal will stalk another animal to kill and eat it for purposes of survival. A genetic code governs the timing of stalking that avoids danger and promotes survival (Bloomfield, 1987). "Kairos," an experiential sense of time, governs and enables the stalker to wait for the right moment to mobilize a range of aggressive actions: to make a sexual advance toward a selected mate, to attack a foe, or to spring while stalking prey for food, These behaviors enable or even guarantee an animal's survival. Zellner (2000), in his review of Panksepp's (1998) work on anger and aggression, notes some neuroscientific bases for stalking in animals that could promote psychoanalytic consideration of stalking in humans. Panksepp's investigators have unearthed evidence for at least three different kinds of aggression typical for animal stalking behavior: predatory aggression—or "quiet-biting attack"; internal aggression; and affective attack—"defensive attack or rage." Zellner maintains that quiet biting-attack entails "methodological stalking and well-directed pouncing" (p. 194). Behaviorally speaking, affective attack in animals, which involves hissing and growling while attacking, looks like anger in humans. These two states have been linked, in animals, to different brain structures: quiet-biting attack is elicited by stimulating the dorsolateral hypothalamus, and affective attack by the ventrolateral and medial hypothalamus. However, these two forms of aggression are not absolutely disconnected. Of course, the brain linkage has not been established in human stalkers.

My personal experience on safari has encouraged me to indulge in a speculative attempt to translate some of the neuroscientific knowledge of animal stalking to human stalking of animals. Each and every game ride through the bush in a Land Rover may be considered a stalking expedition, because safaris inevitably involve humans stalking animals that are stalking other animals as prey. Human tourists who stalk animals are now generally no longer animal killers, so they might not fit very well into Panksepp's classification. Vacationing tourists tend to be amateur photographers or else non-photographing viewers who use binoculars to search and gaze for pleasure and wonderment. On a photographic safari in the Mala Mala game reserve abutting Kruger National Park in South Africa, I was the only one in my group who did not bring a camera. I feared that if I were to focus on getting good shots of the animals, I would be distracted from looking at them and from deeply taking in the scene. So, I used my high-powered binoculars instead, eating and drinking them in with my eyes. Stalking and voyeurism are indisputably involved on safaris. And, as we shall come to discover from many film images of both sexual and surveillance stalking, binoculars serve as an apt logo that frequently precedes or accompanies voyeuristic stalking activity in films.

The Mala Mala game guides have a reputation for being among the best in South Africa, and the animal spotter, who sits on a high perch at the rear of the Land Rover, directs the driver–guide at the wheel to head for areas on the reserve where one would be most likely to find the prey of the day or night. One starry night, we paying guests found ourselves on a dizzyingly driven search for what we did not know at first, but the object of our guide's stalking frenzy turned out to be an exquisitely beautiful leopard who had found sanctuary up in a tree after the professional safari-stalkers had intensely followed his own stalking behavior. On and on we went in pursuit, seemingly for hours, until, lo and behold, there he was. The cameras were all poised to shoot. I peered into my binoculars and could imagine what it felt like to be up in the tree as prey to satisfy another's pleasure, if not survival. Before you knew it, our guide shared, via up to date electronic walkie-talkies, cell phones, and other devices, his stalking success with the several other guides from nearby camps who were out competing on their own similarly motivated stalking safaris. Several Land Rovers converged with their enthralled guests, all in love both with the animals and the thrill of the hunt. The safari professionals in the Land Rover that carried me emerged as the macho heroes of the night because they got to the site first to corner the prey. I suddenly understood, at least in my gut, some of the excitement of stalking, and I have been processing the experience since that lucky starry night. We were mesmerized by the sight of the beautiful animal, as well as overcome by our own instinctive urge to pursue our stalking mission until accomplished.

Still keeping in mind the primal hunter–prey model of animal stalking, I turn to possibly derivative parallel examples of human stalking. The ones I choose are, not surprisingly, stalking of and by the analyst, which, as I noted in my Introduction, have been the subjects of several psychoanalytic studies. Gornick (1994) studied stalking driven by erotic transferences by men toward the women treating them. He offers an example of a therapist who worried at first that she had elicited a male patient's sexual feelings toward her by acting in a seductive manner. Specifically, she was concerned that her patient would "get erotically attached and would not be able to find other people," and that he would then intrude on her and "start stalking . . . find me in personal life." This therapist seemed to sense potential erotomania and erotic transferences as a prelude to stalking of the analyst, and, of course, others as well. Gottlieb (1994), in his work on vampirism, wrote of a woman patient who literally stalked her male analyst. Prior to transforming fantasy into action, this particular patient had imagined herself as a vampire/ghoul, "stalking me as prey (the 'deer') and feeding upon me as carrion. Her necrophagic interests . . . I believed, had found expression in her fantasy . . . of visiting my summer home and of repeatedly telephoning me" (p. 476). In a later work (2000), Gottlieb states that, from an object relations point of view, the central narrative of a manhunt centers on a description of an object relationship between hunter and quarry. He believes that the special relatedness of hunter and quarry is more frequent as a transference manifestation in analysis than is commonly appreciated. He wonders just how many psychoanalysts have experienced a patient tracking us to our homes, stalking us, learning about our habits, lying in wait for us—or as warding off such enactments? When associated with other ideas of analyst-as-food, the stories in which such vampiristic actions actually appear can be expressions of cannibalistic fantasy.

Miller and Twomey (2000) also refer to stalking and stalking fantasies in the analytic relationship. A male patient who was interested in finding out where his female analyst lives and goes on vacation, for example, expressed the belief that his therapist might call the police to report her fears that he was stalking her menacingly. The patient simultaneously imagined that should he actually appear on her doorstep, she would casually dismiss him as an annoying nuisance, a "mere fly." This account reminded me of my "peeping Tom" patient, to whom I referred in my Introduction. After he regaled me with grand stories of how he followed any woman, indiscriminately, he suddenly stopped treatment after a few months. I was reasonably certain, then, that he had started secretly to stalk me, but anticipated he would not be able to bear the shame of me learning that he wished to be a fly on the wall who could see all and then be sent off on petty harassment charges.

Stalking as disorganized attachment in mother–infant dyads

The second broad category of neuroscientifically relevant developmental roots of stalking involves human parent–infant dyads characterized by disorganized and other poor early attachment patterns in which mothers stalk, or "sham stalk" their babies with regular and describable patterns. Some of the findings are remarkably consistent with the neuroscientists' observations of stalking in animal behavior. Hesse and Main (1999, 2000) discovered that some parents in interaction with their infants exhibit serious, as opposed to playful, movements that resemble the predatory stalking behavior of animals in a hunt or pursuit sequence. In one study, a mother was observed suddenly crawling, silent and catlike, toward her infant. Then, simulating "mauling" behavior, she turned the infant over with her fingers extended like claws. Other parents engaged in hissing, deep threatening growls, teeth baring, and even one-sided lip raising; in essence, one-sided canine exposure, a well-known primate threat gesture. Again, none these expressions appeared to be playful, as we might see in affectionate mimicking of mother-bear to baby-bear threats, or other familiar threats from beloved fairy tales about primitive animals. Most of them seemed to arise out of nowhere, and then to disappear. The crucial importance of what might have been on the minds of these mothers that could be of interest to psychoanalysts in their quest for the meaning of stalking behavior in human interactions was not mentioned in this very sparse coverage of the literature.

Attachment theory, added to older psychoanalytic perspectives on stalking, might help to clarify adult interpersonal behaviors that otherwise could remain obscure. The disturbed, complex, later object relationships that are based on earlier neuroscientifically based observations range from the avoidance of intimacy characteristic of a detached personality style to its phenomenological opposite: an obsessional and even perverse preoccupation with the attachment figure that, in one extreme form, might result in stalking as a manifestation of an inability to leave an abusive relationship. "Don't make that call" or "don't mail that letter" are prototypical warnings against perpetuating stalking in many sorts of abusive attachments. Using the developmental insights of attachment theory in conjunction with other object-relational theories has potential for advancing the psychoanalytic thinking of internalized self and object representations in the stalker–stalkee couple.

From "clinging and going in search" to perversion, internalized object relations, and object relationships

Stalking gratifies not only survival and attachment needs, but also sexually and aggressively charged internal object relations in adults who have suffered humiliating losses or shameful rejections at the hands of loved, yet abusive, others. This psychoanalytic literature on stalking, *per se*, to repeat, is very sparse, a major reason for my motivation to fill it out somewhat in this book. The few referenced contributions in this category are most consistent with my views on sexual stalking as a perversion of the search for idealized romantic love. When writing up this latest draft of my work, I looked particularly closely for references of work written after 2005, when I did my initial PEP CD ROM search. To my amazement and delight, I came upon an article written by Eileen McGinley and Andrea Sabbadini, published in the *International Journal of Psychoanalysis* (2006). Its title, "'Play Misty for Me' (1971): the perversion of love," captured subject matter that stunned me because it was so similar to what I had already extensively written and reported on (Gediman, 2005, 2006) and expanded in Chapter Three of this book in the section on film portrayals of erotomanic sexual stalking.

Several writers (Ogden, 2002; Shelby, 1997; Solomon, 1997) refer to stalking and extreme sadomasochism, a frequent component of erotomanic and voyeuristic sexual stalking. The sadism in melancholia (generated in response to the loss of, or disappointment by, a loved object) gives rise to a special form of torment for both the subject and the object—that particular mixture of love and hate between predator and prey encountered especially in relentless, crazed stalking. Such relational problems suggest that stalking might imply serious narcissistic tensions, often embedded in a borderline personality organization. Goldberg, in his important 1995 book, details how behavior such as the sexualization found in telephone stalking can aid in self-cohesion. Splitting mechanisms are used extensively, so patients with narcissistic behavior disorder experience a reality self alongside a more archaic, primitive self. Different self-states develop from both sides of the split. The erotomanic stalker's idealized love object could then be a selfobject who, in reality, does not reciprocate the stalker's desperate erotic cravings despite the stalker's belief, at times quasi-delusional, that he or she does reciprocate. Today, we must not fail to add a degree of terrorism to the sadism found not only in internal object relations, but also in the external reality contexts of aggressive stalking.

I end my brief overview of psychoanalytically relevant developmental contexts for stalking, and now continue with the bulk of my ideas on sexual and surveillance stalking as illustrated clinically, in film, and in today's real and virtual world at large.

PART II
SEXUAL STALKING

Introduction

Part II covers, in four chapters (Two to Five), two forms of what I refer to as broad sexual stalking. I begin with stalking that involves erotomania, unrequited love and revenge, and the move on to voyeuristic stalking. There are two chapters on erotomania: Chapter Two, which contains clinical vignettes, and Chapter Three, which covers film portrayals. Chapter Four, on voyeuristic sexual stalking, covers two film portrayals, *Rear Window* and *Peeping Tom*. Chapter Five is devoted to gender issues in sexual stalking.

CHAPTER TWO

Erotomania and unrequited love: case vignettes

As interesting as my clinical encounters with erotomanic stalkers and stalkees may be, I cannot do justice to the phenomenon as well as those who have portrayed the stalker–stalkee couple in film. So, I begin with case examples and lead up to the more gripping film presentations of erotomania, unrequited love, and revenge.

In 2008, a woman writing under the assumed name of Kate Brennan published a memoir, *In His Sights*, of her experience as a victim of erotomanic stalking for more than a decade by her former boyfriend, Paul, whom she had rejected. According to the *New York Times* article (Newman, 2008) that reviewed her stalking history and that of others, most stalkers are driven by a need to control others in order to prove that they cannot be excised from life by a simple "Dear John" or "Dear Jane" letter of rejection. Paul enlisted the help of hackers and others to break into Brennan's computer and house to "psych her out" online, by misplacing items in her home, and by manipulating her mind and baffling her in other eerie ways. His aim was to relentlessly torment and terrorize, all the while loudly protesting his love for the woman who rejected him. Clearly, surveillance stalking was a way to avenge his rejection. He made so many extremely harassing invasions into her private life that she moved her residence sixteen times in sixteen years. I have not had the opportunity to treat such vengeful reactions as this to unrequited love, but I can present some of my work with two stalkees who have deepened my understanding of erotomanic stalking.

Charity: stalking excitement wards off dread of aphanisis

Aphanisis (Jones, 1927, 1929) is the fear of total extinction of the capacity and opportunity for sexual pleasure and excitement. Not only was that fear paramount in the patient I am about to discuss, but is, I believe, very commonly found in men and women who are involved in erotomanic sexual stalking.

A thirty-one-year-old married woman patient, whom I shall call Charity, was a high level executive, well educated, intelligent, attractive, and privileged. She spent her childhood in the late1960s and 1970s with a free-thinking, hippie, single mother who seemed to be as highly devoted to the welfare of the poor and underprivileged as she was to that of her only and out-of-wedlock child. In the name of protection, Charity's mother made sure that Charity's biological father, who had left her shortly after their baby was conceived, never had any contact with Charity, an action whose meaning to Charity had life-long effects on her choice of men. An unforgettable bit of family lore that mother told daughter when she was about six is that father did attempt to maintain a connection with his daughter. Mother refused father's request and succeeded in her efforts to keep Charity's father at bay. Charity has harbored a grudge against her biological father ever since. Although she focused on her father's abandonment of her, I understand her chronic anger and the chip on her shoulder as indirect resentful expressions toward her mother for forbidding any encounter in the name of "benevolent" social intentions toward strangers above family. Charity was nursed until four and slept in her mother's bed until she was eighteen. She developed an overly close primary erotic tie and symbiotic attachment to her "preoedipal" mother that intertwined with her life-long "oedipal" paternal search for men who were hardly suited to gratify her as a woman of accomplishment.

Charity had become sexually enthralled with a sixty-two-year-old homeless man, Hank, a drug addict who had been convicted of, and imprisoned for, the manslaughter of his wife. On parole, he started, during their trysts, to physically abuse her, and threatened to destroy her marriage to a man who was, not surprisingly, given mother's predilections for the poor and downtrodden, her educational, economic, and social inferior. Frightened by the parolee, who had begun to stalk her, and by her own inexplicable, obsessional attraction to him, she sought treatment and an order of restraint against her stalker. Hank was jailed and then released again on parole. Instead of checking in regularly with his parole officer, he went into hiding, stalked Charity around town, phoned ceaselessly, and suddenly stopped his frightening pursuit. Charity then felt abandoned, unattractive, and jealous of other women she imagined he had begun to stalk. She began to seek him out, reversing the stalker–stalkee pattern fairly successfully, and when she could, made sure he discovered her whereabouts.

Before treatment began, and during its early phases, Charity developed a theory that her ego-alien sexual obsession with this homeless, older man who was addicted to drugs was a symptom that represented a search for her now deceased father, whom she never knew. She bolstered her theory *ad infinitum* and argued that her incestuously based search for her now dead father must be the psychological root of her troubles. Charity reminded me that she had never been involved sexually with a man her own age or even a bit older, but only with men twenty or more years her senior. She was attempting, in these protestations, to prove that her enthrallment was a helpless and hopeless condition that she felt doomed to repeat. At the height of her irresistible attraction to this stalker, she had been married for eight years to a sixty-year-old divorced man—the same age as her stalker—who is the father of two children from a former marriage. He was extremely caring and protective of her and she saw him as a compensation for her fantasized creation of her lost father. I thought she also imagined that her stalker satisfied her perverse version of maternal nurturing and safety. Although she focused on her father's abandonment of her, I thought about the chip on her shoulder about her father as displaced anger toward her mother for preventing any relationship whatsoever between Charity and her father, and her strange object choice as a mockery of mother's 1970s exclusionary social values.

Charity's sexual obsession, thus, rings both of oedipal rivalry and of preoedipal fixations and "disorganized attachment" to her mother during her early years.

During the course of treatment, Charity came up with the idea that she obsessively and repeatedly sought out dangerous relationships to keep her level of sexual excitement as high as possible. In fact, one reason she sought treatment was because she had knowingly exposed herself to AIDS some twelve years before she began treatment with me, in a sexual encounter with another socially marginal man who was HIV positive. After that enactment, she was beset by a paralysis of will and action in which she refused to get an AIDS test. She lived in dread of being HIV positive all those years and even went into cognitive–behavioral treatment for help in "being forced" to go for testing. Once, accompanied by several supportive friends, she went so far as to have the test done, but never asked for, or learned, the results. So, she kept herself at the edge of the excitement of terrifying dread, just as she later kept herself at the edge of sexual excitement by choosing a partner who stalked her. She was, so to speak, "stalked" by the specter of AIDS, a specter she refused to give up. Charity begged me to take her by the hand and take her to an AIDS clinic to get tested. She earnestly wanted to hear she tested negatively because she wanted a child of her own with her current husband, or, if she decided to leave him, as a single woman, repeating in fantasy the story of her own birth and early rearing by a single hippie mother.

In sum, when Charity was stalked, she no longer felt bored, empty, disenlivened, and deadened. She yearned to resume her dangerous liaison, believing and theorizing elaborately that she had a "monstrous" sexual addiction that was the bane of her existence. Her search for excitement and danger served to regulate dysphoric affective states. One major motive for Charity's self-endangering repetitive attempts at object seeking and object refinding by maintaining a high level of sexual excitement from being stalked is a variant of what Ernest Jones (1927, 1929) called "aphanisis." Jones, basing his idea on the Greek translation of the word, defined aphanisis as the fear of total extinction of the capacity and opportunity for sexual pleasure and excitement. In men, according to Jones, this specific fear takes the form of castration; in women, of separation, which can be fantasized and/or, as in this case, actually realized, as "coming about through the rival mother intervening between the girl and the father" (1927,

p. 462). This is precisely the situation that Charity believed to underlie her urges for dangerous sexual encounters that included stalking, and her shaky motivation to contain them. She never abandoned her theory that mother's attempt to disemparent her father accounted for her misery. Both oedipal longings to refind the fantasized father and a primary maternal erotic tie have primed this woman to live her life around seeking and then dreading situations in which her craving to be alive sexually and in every other way have misfired. As a stalkee, she has put herself at maximum risk: by realizing her sexuality, she has maximized her excitement.

Hester, a stalkee: a woman from a patriarchal culture fantasizes being stalked

Whereas Charity actually and actively sought stalking and being stalked, Hester tormented herself with fears, fantasies, and quasi-delusions of being stalked, which she elaborated excessively. Weeping histrionically, she would report endless fantasies of being stalked by Charlie, an older cousin, and John, his sidekick and her ex-lover. She believed they stalked her malevolently to prove to her morally traditional extended family that she was, at core, a whore. Her weeping expressed her rageful conviction that she was a vulnerable woman in a phallocentric Asian-American cultural milieu, in which many of the men had achieved great wealth and professional success, and thereby wielded power over women. They chose to make her the laughing stock of the family by stalking her and scaring her. Initially, I had to work hard to suspend my disbelief that Hester's cousin represented any real and present stalking danger, convinced that the patient's desperate need to stay out of harm's way was largely based on fantasy. I soon learned that her fears were rooted in real, socially based inequalities. The patriarchal Asian-American culture in which she lived nourished her pathological feelings of sexual guilt and mortification.

Hester's fears were revived, inconsolably, whenever there was an upcoming family gathering, in which cousin Charlie was bound to be present. She was constantly on the alert for harassing, harrowing behavior. She felt threatened by the male bonding between cousin Charlie and John, her ex-boyfriend, convinced that the two men flaunted their bonding in a conspiracy against her as an excluded woman. Hester believed, and came to dread, that the men were exchanging lascivious ideas about her, which they then spread on to the family at large. She was convinced that they were engaging in male chauvinist teasing in order to humiliate her sexually. Hester reported that John also stealthily followed her to the places that she frequented with friends, where he would leer at her as he circled around her group in order to embarrass her publicly and to insinuate to everyone that he and she had once had a sexual relationship. Additionally, John often showed up on the same subway train she rode, getting on at the stop before she did. After she got off, she would see him though the window, grinning at her with his teeth bared, like a stalking animal. Her image was so reminiscent of Hesse and Main's (2000) description of the teeth-baring stalking behavior of certain mothers involved in disorganized attachment dyads with their babies that it was easy to believe that Hester's psychic reality corresponded to the "objective" or material reality of this stalking pattern.

Once, when her cousin Charlie invited John to a family party, John came on to Hester sexually and she did nothing to discourage him but "went along" with the sex, despite fearing that everyone in the family, if they knew, would think her a whore. She rationalized her sexual submission as a way of staying in control. That is, if she did not pretend willing submission, the act would be regarded as a rape rather than submitting to the male–female power differential that was expected in her cultural milieu. Hester opted, she said, to "sleep around" just to prove that she, a woman, could be in control of her sexuality. By rationalizing her sexual submissiveness as a product of her own authorship, she denied her vulnerability to both condemnation by, and power of, others. Although Hester presently lived in morbid fear of being shamed sexually in the eyes of her family and the world at large, most of these potentially shameful events had occurred many years before treatment began. However, they were told to me every session as though they had just occurred, always accompanied by tears that appeared several minutes after the session began and continued until the very end. It was as though Hester was displaying to me a state of constant trauma of being stalked sexually. Her plea served both to justify her sexual gratifications that she experienced as immoral transgressions and as life punishment for indulging.

Fortunately, Hester came to understand that her major danger lurked within and not without. Nonetheless, sometimes I was so amazed at the way this patient jumbled remote past with recent present and seemed so out of the times that I wondered if I were dealing with something that is so specifically sub-cultural that it is alien to me, or if I were dealing with severe psychopathology of a sort that I had not encountered before: the psychology of the stalked woman. So, what are the internal and internalized dangers Hester fears? The role of shame is clear. The role of prostitution fantasies is clear. The defensive nature of her projections and rationalizations to defend against the prostitution fantasies is clear. And the role of the culture of her family's country of origin is clear. A few words are in order, here. Hester has access to many empowered female role models that contradict the cultural stereotypes that pervade her stalking fantasies. But she found it quite a challenge to let go of the images of oppressed women, despite consistent attempts to get them into perspective in the therapeutic setting. Maternal family members of her mother's generation still look on girls as not as valuable as boys. These socio-cultural facts captured my patient's imagination and contributed to her constant fear, verging on terror, and repudiated sexual excitement every time she believed that she was being stalked, whether on the subway, social gathering places, the bedroom, the family gatherings, or on the telephone. Perhaps the only way she can justify her sexuality is to think of it in these settings as a forbidden, exciting, yet dreadful, perverse form of activity. She is stalked as passive victim but does not find the danger of her position to be as overtly exciting as Charity did. What she sought out more covertly is another story.

Hester fancied herself a degraded, fallen, kept woman in the eyes of her compatriots, vulnerable to inevitable mockery and domination by men; entrapped, paralyzed, and unable to proactively end her victimhood. Unlike my patient, Charity, and Jacqueline Kennedy Onassis, to be discussed in Chapter Seven, she did not go to court to seek a protective order to require her stalker to remain twenty-five to fifty feet away. Hester's unconscious fantasies of being a protected woman of rich and powerful men resonated with more universally and cross-culturally based prostitution fantasies. These fantasies contributed to her submissiveness and got in the way of her seeking a legal order of restraint against her tormenting pursuers. These very fantasies are the symptoms that became the major focus of the analytic work.

These two case presentations, Charity and Hester, are extremely abbreviated and disguised for reasons of confidentiality. I am grateful that I can move on to illustrations from films of erotomanic and voyeuristic sexual stalking, where I feel free to go into all the detail I need to expand our psychoanalytic understanding of the phenomena.

CHAPTER THREE

Erotomania and unrequited love: film portrayals of sexual stalking

Erotomania is a type of illusion, or, more often, delusion, in which the affected person believes falsely that a person whom he or she idealizes is in love with him or her.

Two horror films, *Play Misty for Me* (1971, Clint Eastwood, director) and *Fatal Attraction* (1987, Adrian Lyne, director) give us iconic portrayals of erotomanic, vengeful female sexual stalking. The films have intrigued feminist scholars because, in them, patriarchal values appear to disintegrate and give way to portrayals of the torments of unrequited love and erotomania in lonely, obsessional, romantic women stalkers whose appetitive and often phallic hunt for men appears to rob those men of their gendered sense of pride and power. Each of these two films presents the deconstructed image of stalked man as castrated and stripped of self-agency, one whose initial image as an active man is destroyed. In both films, the erotomanic woman stalker assumes a relational intimacy between her and her stalkee that exists only in her mind. Evelyn, in *Misty*, and Alex, in *Fatal Attraction*, turn out to be morbidly jealous and murderous, psychotically obsessed, erotomanic women.

I begin with Clint Eastwood's *Misty*, the very first of the genre of sexually perverse erotomanic obsessed stalking, and a template, I believe, for *Fatal Attraction*, the more well known and prototypical film on female stalking, because of Glenn Close's iconic portrayal of Alex, the "bunny-boiling" lethal *femme fatale* of obsessional sexual stalking.

Play Misty for Me

Clint Eastwood both directed and starred in the 1971 *Play Misty for Me*, a film in which Evelyn (Jessica Walker), a woman stalker, is smitten by romantic love which, when unrequited, morphs into the excessive emotions of fused sex and aggression that climax in over-the-top aberrations with fatal outcomes. Eastwood plays an all-night disc jockey, Dave Garver, a philanderer who has two-timed and jeopardized his relationship with his girlfriend, Tobie (Donna Mills). Just as Dave tries to re-establish his relationship with Tobie, Evelyn begins her obsessional persecutory stalking of him. Night after night, she requests that Dave play the ballad "Misty" and assumes a romance and relational intimacy developing between them that in his mind never existed. One night, Evelyn stalks her idealized lover to a bar and successfully picks him up. She has little trouble getting him to agree to a one-night stand with "no strings." She forms a delusional idea that Dave is in love with her, a hallmark of erotomania. Evelyn turns out to be morbidly jealous, murderously violent, and psychotic.

This film, about a brief fling between a male disc jockey and an obsessed female fan, which takes on a deadly turn, sounds to me so similar to *Fatal Attraction* that I wonder if we are looking at a sure-fire film script success based on a characterization of female sexual stalking as an erotomanic perversion gone astray. *Misty* could easily be a template for a genre depicting erotomanic women stalkers as having a devastating effect on the complacent security that was so essential to the male persona when patriarchal values reigned. On first reading the script of *Misty*, Eastwood (McGinley & Sabbadini, 2006) recalled an incident that occurred when he was about twenty. An older woman became obsessed with him, and threatened suicide when he tried to end the liaison. He took an option on the script and sought to film it. Universal Studios at first refused, but later agreed. The studio might have feared that his performance in the starring role would undermine his erstwhile macho persona and make him lose his box office appeal. Perhaps they were anxious about promoting his image as a male stalkee pursued by an erotomanic woman. This film contains scenes that are emblematic of erotomania: Evelyn behaves and talks as though she and Dave have a mutual love relationship even, and especially, in the face of Dave's insistence that they have no relationship at all. He tells her he has a viable relationship and that he rejects her attempts to imply that he loves her and only her. His explicit rejections of her erotic advances toward him provoke and escalate her stalking behavior. From the start he discloses that he is hung up on a very nice girl and does not want to complicate things by further involvement with Evelyn, who responds, "Who needs nice girls." She says that she doesn't want to complicate things, either. "But that's no reason we shouldn't sleep together tonight if we feel like it." He succumbs, having had quite a bit to drink, but that's it for him as he unknowingly eggs her on further and further into her cruel teasing and vicious stalking. In contrast to earlier roles, here he is entrapped in a threatening and terrifying nightmare and unable to find a way out of the *impasse.* As star and film director, Eastwood deconstructed the male supremacist patriarchal image that he had developed in his previous films. Film scholars have studied this shift in Eastwood's screen persona.

Evelyn invades Dave's life with ever-increasing intimidation and violence: verbal abuse, stalking, public humiliation, and any castration equivalent at her disposal. In the first scene after their one-night stand, Evelyn presumptuously situates herself inside Dave's car. As he stands outside looking helpless, she jangles his car keys at him. His disgusted facial expressions clearly indicate that he has had it with her.

> DAVE: What are you doing here?
> EVELYN: Why didn't you take my call?
> DAVE: What does it say that I've got to drop everything I'm doing and answer the phone every time it rings? . . . Come on, Evelyn, I've got to go.

Perhaps this interchange introduces a most important film reference to telephone stalking, along with Evelyn's persistent calls to Dave as a semi-celebrity disk jockey with her ploy of asking him to play the song, "Misty."

EVELYN: Come on, you don't work tonight.

DAVE: [*defensively, and assuming incorrectly that making his getaway will be a cinch, as he is trying to squirm away from her*] I've got this show that I've got to set and it happens to be a very important show to me. That means I've got to find some music, pick the lead-ins and find some poetry. Now come on, will you? [*He is beginning to beg*]

EVELYN: Poetry? [*Intimidatingly*] Let me help you. I'm terrific with poetry.

DAVE: [*raising his voice and gritting his teeth*] Not tonight!

[Looking jilted, she steps out of the car to be on a higher level than he, and tauntingly dangles the keys in front of him.]

EVELYN: [*provocatively*] Does he want his key?

DAVE: [*still not aware of her erotomanically increasing fury*] Come on Evelyn.

EVELYN: [*stepping up the dangling pace*] Good boy. Let's hear it. Come on.

DAVE: [*approaching Evelyn with outstretched hands, as though to an innocently teasing girl*] Come on, give me my keys. [*Then, starting to angrily grab at her*] Come on. Give me the keys!

Evelyn laughs with increasing menace. They begin a physical struggle, truly hand-to-hand combat by now. Dave turns his back on her and walks away as she plasters a saccharine-sweet expression on her face and says, "Bye." She is still deluded that she has him in the palms of her hands, stepping up the violence that he just tried to subdue. The film is a psychological study of the different forms of madness that can result from the condition of "being in love" (McGinley & Sabbadini, 2006). In this case, the mad person is a woman who idealizes and covets stereotypical male power, aggression, and destructiveness over stereotypical feminine receptivity, compassion, and concern. Evelyn denigrates these "feminine" qualities while Eastwood has Tobie embody them.

Clint Eastwood's performance in *Misty* took him from his established role of arch male chauvinist and secure representative of male supremacy to that of a helpless, confused, anguished, distraught man, terrorized by his murderous, psychotic stalker. In contrast to earlier roles, here he is entrapped in a threatening and terrifying nightmare, unable to find a way out of the *impasse*. Eastwood's screen persona deconstructed the stereotypical male patriarchal image of refractory, ferocious, and seemingly invulnerable macho masculinity that he had projected in previous roles. Nowhere is Dave's undoing better illustrated than in an early scene, after the incident of the dangling keys, when he visits Evelyn's home where she is trying to seduce him with food and drink. With "Misty" playing in the background, Evelyn, dressed to kill, comes on to him, as Dave unambiguously registers disgust in his facial expression, but to little effect.

DAVE: Look, Evelyn, there's something we're going to have to get straight.

EVELYN: [*dreamy-eyed, and undeterred in her scheming wining and dining*] It's amazing what a man will go through for a hot pastrami sandwich.

DAVE: Now look.

EVELYN: [*pirouetting around*] Wait a minute, you haven't yet told me how nice I look.

DAVE: [*still trying to be civil, yet obviously feeling emotionally distant and disconnected from his predator*] Now listen, can we talk?

EVELYN: [*tantalizingly*] Wait.

[She caresses his shoulder, pulls him to sit down next to her, and presents him with a gift of "sexy" slippers. He looks overwhelmed and determined to stand firm despite her increasingly persistent efforts to seduce him.]

EVELYN: Don't you like them?

DAVE: Yes, but . . .

EVELYN: Oh my darling I love to give you things.

[He finally cannot stand it any longer, and roughly pushes her away and down.]

DAVE: Now we've got to talk.

EVELYN: Have I done something wrong?

DAVE: I'm just trying to be straight with you, that's all.

EVELYN: [*rising and slithering her hands around him*] Be nice to me instead.
DAVE: Jesus Christ.
EVELYN: I don't understand. Are you trying to say you don't love me any more?
DAVE: I never told you that I loved you.

With these words, Eastwood alerts us to the quintessence of erotomanic vengeance following unrequited love, a theme that continues as the film progressively mounts one horror scene after another. By now Evelyn is on her knees in a pseudo-begging position, and starts to rise.

EVELYN: Not in words maybe but there are lots of ways of saying things that have nothing to do with words.
DAVE: [*in response to her erotomania*] I'm sorry you read it that way.
EVELYN: [*with teeth gritted and eyes flaming*] It's that other bitch, isn't it?

As she brings Tobie into their dialogue, Dave denies Tobie's involvement in an attempt to protect her. His new mission is to escape from Evelyn's stalking. He turns his back and walks toward the door as she just as quickly counters by placing herself between him and the door so that he cannot get away. He finally pushes her away.

DAVE: Get off my back Evelyn [*he starts to leave her apartment*].
EVELYN: [*screaming*] What, are you waiting for me in my little whore suit waiting for my Lord and master to call? You're nothing. You're nothing at all. You're not even good in bed. I just feel sorry for you. Bastard. You poor pathetic bastard.

In the very next scene, Dave and his girlfriend Tobie are on the beach in a very intimate true love scene. Then we, the viewing audience, see Evelyn in the bushes behind coming forth in one of the best imaginable visual stalking images depicting primal scene intrusion.

This melodramatic thriller about a brief fling between a male disk jockey and an obsessed female fan takes a deadly turn. When Evelyn finds her love for Dave Garver is unrequited, deadly, vengeful violence and murderous horror ensue. She invades Dave's life with ever-increasing intimidation and violence, including verbally abusing him, stalking, and, when she realizes how earnestly dismissive he is of her, humiliating him in public. She slashes her wrists, tears his house apart, attacks him with a knife, severely injures his house cleaner, and murders a police officer investigating the case. When Evelyn is caught and imprisoned, Dave and Tobie negotiate a brief reconciliation. When Evelyn is unexpectedly released she resumes her pursuit and terrorizes all along the way. She calculatedly, in a ruse, moves in to live with Tobie, who had not met her previously, ties her up, threatens to murder her, and stabs Dave when he tries to rescue Tobie. As the struggle escalates, Dave punches Evelyn over a balcony and she falls to her death in the ocean. The final scene of *Misty* shows Dave bleeding, shaken, and leaning dependently on Tobie, who helps him to the car. This image, more than any other, captures the effect of a man beaten down by the terrorism of erotomanic sexual stalking.

Fatal Attraction

As I have mentioned, Adrian Lyne's (1987) *Fatal Attraction* is the most well known film portrayal of all time of a vengeful, crazed, erotomanic sexual stalker. In many ways, the film presents a caricature of psychopathology rather than a gripping portrayal of one woman's psychic pain. That said, Alex Forrest (Glenn Close), epitomizes the erotomanic sexual stalker as a professional woman romantically obsessed with the man she is determined to have and to ruin. Unrequited love propels her to self-abasing, uncivilized, and terrorizing destructive psychotic behavior. The image stays with us of Alex, driven, enthralled, clinging, clawing, and seeking out Dan Gallagher (Michael Douglas), the lead male character, who was her prey. Alex also hunts down Dan's wife, Beth (Anne Archer) and daughter, and to begin her reign of terror, telephone stalks the married couple via hang-up and other frightening calls. She is grimly determined to intrude on the Gallagher family "primal scene" and to destroy its intimacy that excludes her and drives her to madness of gothic proportion. It is no accident that many of Alex's calls are delivered when Dan and Beth are in bed together. Dan, like Dave Garver in *Misty*, was yielding, in a classically sadomasochistic relationship, to the *femme fatale* seductress for what he thought was a simple one-night stand. Both Dave and Dan relied on male prerogatives of the time: they could have a long-standing marital relationship while engaging in a non-committal fling on the side. Alex, like Evelyn in *Misty*, projects the *femme fatale* image of erotomania, a perversion of idealized but unrequited romantic love commonly found in sexual stalking.

Alex's unrequited love and erotomania, like Evelyn's, drive her to self-abasing, uncivilized behavior, and, ultimately, her death. She eventually slits her wrists, boils Dan's little daughter's bunny to death, and tries to kill his wife. Dan, her prey, in his own defense, tries to drown his murderous stalker and Beth delivers the final murderous blow. "Bunny boilers," as I have suggested earlier in references to *Play Misty for Me*, has come to be the signature shorthand signifier of many present-day fatal sexual stalking scenarios, in which the stalkee's family intimates become victimized as much as the thwarting idealized lover. Alex's demise follows an initial one-weekend stand with Dan while his beloved wife and daughter are out of town, a traditional prelude in depictions of illusory romantic, idealized love gone sour. We watch the thwarted erotomanic Alex go to pieces, counterpointing Dan's undoing as he loses confidence in his male prerogative to engage in a weekend fling with the woman who pursues him sexually in wild abandon and with desire in excess of his.

Alex and Dan's one-weekend affair starts with a classic seduction scene in a restaurant where the intimate gestures are mutual at that time. Thereafter, Alex initiates all contacts and Dan responds reactively: her erotomanic fantasies take charge of the interaction and the dialogue. In the scene of their second sexual encounter of the weekend, Dan hurries out of bed while Alex plays out the enraged victim of his abandonment, setting the tone for every other stalking interaction in the film. Dan leaves the bed and puts on his shirt while Alex lounges back and exposes her nudity a bit more. Dan says he has to go and Alex gets edgy. She accuses him of running away every time they make love. As he starts to go, Alex fiercely rises, naked, from her position in bed, grabs Dan, starts to punch him hard, and falls back, while he is still buttoning up. He pleads with her to stop, and Alex taunts him not to justify himself so pathetically: "If you'd tell me to fuck off, I'd have more respect for you." When Dan says, "All right then, fuck off," Alex ragefully raises her voice and then breathes loudly, as if to announce that she is the rejected victim: "Then you get out!"

Alex's hurt feelings transform into actions as she initiates her stalking, proper, which begins with an uninvited trip to Dan's New York City office where she vainly attempts to restore what she believes is their mutual love relationship. She makes herself known to his support staff so as to make them assume she belongs with him in some erotic way that grants her *carte blanche* admission any time she appears. As she deludes herself that they are sympathetic to her unannounced visit, Dan is hardly an inviting presence. In fact, he indicates to his staff that he feels hounded and instructs them to deny her future admission. With this equivalent of an order of restraint, Alex's *modus operandi* for stalking her prey then changes to telephone stalking, a most common means for unrequited lovers to try to keep up their illusional or delusional contact with the one whom they fantasize loves them. Alex now ceaselessly calls Dan at his office. The telephone stalking scenes in *Fatal Attraction* are as evocative as they come. Dan, distraught, and obviously now an unwitting party to the stalking, allows his administrative assistant to put Alex's call through. We listen as the intensity of his anxious breathing increases. Containing his rage, he patronizingly but anxiously reminds her that they had agreed that continuing on was not a good idea: "I apologize. I don't think it's a good idea for us to talk to each other any more. OK? Goodbye" and hangs up on her. He tells his assistant to tell Alex he is not in if she calls again. Failing at the office telephone stalk ploy, Alex shifts her MO to hang-up calls to Dan's home, especially when she knows he is with his wife, Beth, and especially when he is with her in some romantically intimate setting. We get our first taste of primal scene intrusions of the stalker, in this instance, the screeching note of a phone ringing. We get an idea of what is to come in a scene in which Alex invades the Gallaghers' privacy by ringing them up at a dinner party at their home. The jangling notes of the telephone interrupt Dan, Beth, and their guests. Beth picks up the phone, and we hear the phone at the other end put back on the receiver as Alex hangs up on her quarry. That night while Dan and Beth are in bed together, the phone on Dan's night table rings, jarring the viewing audience's nerves as well as Dan's in this perfect cameo of a primal scene stalking intrusion.

By now, we know that Alex is crazily obsessed and that the stalking will escalate. In a famous stalking scene, she walk-stalks him to the subway, having been thwarted in her attempt to get him back by phone. Their dialogue might contain the best example ever of an erotomanic revenge for unrequited love.

DAN: This has got to stop.

ALEX: If you had agreed to see me I wouldn't have called you.

DAN: You get it right. It's over. There's nothing between us.

ALEX: You mean you've had your fun, now you just want a quiet life.

DAN: [*Turning to face her at his side while angrily recoiling*] What are you doing? You need . . .

ALEX: No! Don't tell me what I need.

DAN: You need a shrink. [*He pulls ahead of her thinking he is free of her, but, alas*]

ALEX: [*Catching up as they descend the subway stairs*] Why are you so hostile to me? I'm not your enemy, you know.

DAN: Then why do you want to hurt me?

ALEX: I'm not trying to hurt you, Dan. I love you.

DAN: You what?

ALEX: I love you

[Dan pulls ahead in a gesture of eluding her verbally threatening grip on him. She catches up as he sets the pace for running down the subway stairs to outrun her stalking pusuit.]

DAN: You don't even know me.

ALEX: How can you say that?

DAN: Alex, we spent a weekend together, that's all.

ALEX: What you said that second night means you must love me.

DAN: Because I was concerned about you. Jesus Christ, why do you read so much into everything? I mean, can't you understand, I have a whole relationship with someone else. I am very happy.

ALEX: All needs complete. If your life is so complete, what were you doing with me?

DAN: Is this what you want to talk about? Our imaginary love affair?

ALEX: I'm pregnant.

From here on we know we are in for a horror film. In her next stalking endeavor, Alex barges into Dan and Beth's apartment, her first in-person intrusion into their blissful primal scene, while Dan glowers. In the scene that follows, Dan visits Alex's apartment. Alex, dressed in a revealing negligee, offers Dan a drink as though her feelings were reciprocated, and as though they were a mutually committed couple. He counters: "CUT THIS SHIT! WILL YOU. JUST CUT IT! I don't know what you're up to, but I'm gonna tell you, it's gonna stop right now." Alex, with saccharine sweetness, tells him "it" is not going to stop but will go on and on until he faces up to his responsibilities. Dan, yelling and increasingly infuriated, then screams, "WHAT RESPONSIBILITIES?"

ALEX: I JUST WANT TO BE A PART OF YOUR LIFE.

DAN: So this is the way you do it, huh, showing up in my apartment?

ALEX: [*Sounding innocent and bewildered*] What am I supposed to do? You won't answer my calls, you change your number, I mean, I'm not going to be *ignored,* Dan.

Glenn Close delivers this line, "I'm not going to be *ignored,* Dan," so effectively that it is to become the hallmark representation of the humiliation felt by erotomanic stalkers when it begins to dawn on them that their love is unrequited. Alex's erotomania is clearly delusional, and her sweet, beguiling, self-confident attempts to tempt have begun an irreversible transformation into vengeful hatred. The couple's relationship has totally deteriorated into a battle between his agitated sanity and her delusional revenge at his real, no longer idealized, person. Still in her apartment, Dan is drawn into a fight just as he tries to leave. He finally understands the chasm between what she wants and what he feels, and then mutters to her that she just doesn't get it. Alex counters, as though the two shared fond memories of their weekend, insisting it was wonderful, that he must certainly agree and want to continue with her. As she brings her misty-eyed face close to his in presumed intimacy, he violently pushes her away and tells her not to flatter herself. Alex, in her growing attempts to shame him, spits out, "Go ahead, hit me. If you can't fuck me, why don't you just hit me?" In an attempt to pander to her mental fragility, Dan tells her she is very sad, lonely, and sick. She begs him not to pity her and calls him a bastard. Then she pulls away in an attempt to control him with some physical distance and he counteracts by grabbing at her. Escalating the feud, Alex accuses Dan of wanting to treat her like some slut that he's banged some times and wants to throw in the garbage. She reminds him that she is going to be the mother of his child and asks for a little respect. Dan, disgusted, moves away and prepares to leave her apartment. This is the last straw for Alex who attacks: "Please don't go, I'm sorry. I'll tell you what I'm going to do. I'll tell your wife." Dan pins her against the wall and grabs her throat: "You tell my wife, I'll kill you." Alex gloats with the last threat for now: "It only takes a phone call." This scene is so incredibly reminiscent of the dangling key chain scene, discussed above, between Dave and Evelyn, in *Misty*, that it must be one that has led film critics to regard *Misty*, as I have noted earlier, as the template for *Fatal Attraction*. The scene ends with Dan slamming the door as he leaves, and Alex rushing to the phone to resume her phone stalking with his wife, Beth. She picks up the phone, decides not to proceed as her fury mounts, and then slams it against the wall.

The famous car-stalking scene follows. Alex, in her car, follows Dan in his as he drives from work in the city to his new home in the suburbs. We see Dan looking through his rear-view mirror at Alex in her car hard behind him as he picks up the tape that Alex has deposited in his car. We see Alex looking, stretching her neck to get a better sighting through her windscreen as Dan places the threatening stalking tape, labeled "PLAY ME–Alex", in his player. The camera toggles back and forth between Alex's face, which looks obsessively determined to get him, and Dan's, which looks as though he is mesmerized and hooked, yet done in. We watch Dan listen to the tape on which Alex harangues him for reducing her to a stalker. She taunts him with her present wishes to touch him, feel him, and taste him. Dan puts his hand to his head and closes his eyes but makes no move to remove the tape. He simply listens on with her in the next car behind him in a tunnel, a symbol for the trap he is in. Arriving in the driveway of his new suburban home, Dan stops his car, sits still, and listens as Alex continues to "pussy-whip" him. "You know who you are, Dan, you're a cock-sucking son-of-a-bitch. I hate you. I bet you don't even like girls, do you?" Instead of leaving his car at this point, Dan puts his head in his hand and listens on as we wonder what kind of weird or perverse attachment allows this stalkee to permit this stalker to invade his private space so terroristically. With the last word once again, Alex calls him a "fucking faggot." At last, Dan turns off the tape and leaves his car as the camera switches to Alex who sits for a moment and visually stalks him as he walks into his home. From this point on, the film is a gothic horror tale. Having witnessed a domestic scene of bliss among mother, father, little girl, and the bunny, Alex begins her reign of terror. She steals the bunny, boils the bunny, and enters the final, wildly surrealistic fight in the bathroom where they all try to kill each other and Dan ultimately kills Alex in the bathtub filled with water. This scene is strikingly similar to the last horror blow in *Play Misty for Me* when Dave punches Evelyn over a balcony and she falls to her death in the ocean. One wonders if the watery grave that awaits both Evelyn and Alex in the later film is of any significance. In both *Play Misty for Me* and *Fatal Attraction*, the erotomanic female protagonist attacks and tries to kill not only the man who frustrated her fantasies of idealized romantic love, but everybody close to him as well: in *Misty*, Dave's maid, the police, and his girlfriend Tobie, and in *Fatal Attraction*, Dan's wife, daughter, and the daughter's bunny. Thus, the term "bunny boilers" has been used to characterize films about female stalking. Eastwood, himself (in McGinley & Sabbadini, 2006), regarded *Fatal Attraction* as a pale replica of *Misty*. Both films climax with an outrageous, unsubtle horror scene that terminates an illuminating psychological tale of erotomania, unrequited love, and murderous revenge that provides informative insights into the psychology of stalking. The juxtaposition of horror and psychological truth jars and disturbs enormously.

It is hard for any viewer to dispel the image of Alex, driven, enthralled, "clinging and going-in-search" (see Hermann, 1976), and seeking out Dan Gallagher, her prey. The images of stalking in this film are unforgettable, especially the one I just described, an iconic car-stalking scene of the menacing Alex driving her car behind Dan's as she stalks him from his workplace all the way to his new home. She projects the image of a detestable *femme fatale* that is often crucial to a stalking scene scenario in which a perversion of romantic love and erotomanic revenge underlies stalking behavior. The idea that her brief sexual encounter with Dan was a true love affair existed only in Alex's mind. Dan is entrapped in a terrifying nightmare and unable to find a way out of the *impasse*, short of a murderous blowout that truly terrifies all involved, including the film's audience.

As the film *Misty*'s director and male lead, Eastwood, as Dave Garver, countered the patriarchal image of arch male chauvinist and secure representative of male supremacy with one of a helpless, confused, anguished, distraught man. Douglas, as Dan Gallagher, continues the tradition. These two films each tell a story of a machochistic stalked man now stripped of self-agency, whose image as a once active, potent man is deconstructed as it gives way to impotent despair. Married men who have strayed are often terrified, if not terrorized, by this film.

CHAPTER FOUR

Voyeurism, sadism, and the primal scene in film portrayals of stalking and in filming itself

It has been said that watching a film sublimates watching a primal scene: If that is so, watching a film about voyeuristic stalking might very well sublimate the voyeurism of viewing the primal scene. Psychoanalysts have defined the primal scene as the young child's observing the sights and hearing the sounds of sexual relations between the parents. Very young children make their own sense or nonsense of the scene, which remains enigmatic and provokes sexual and aggressive excitement (Freud, 1918b). Many film images touch on the centrality of the primal scene in the fantasy and real lives of stalkers. The two films that I have just used to illustrate erotomania in sexual stalking, *Play Misty for Me* and *Fatal Attraction*, are replete with primal, voyeuristic visual images. We look at a most exemplary one in *Misty*, where Evelyn stalks Dave and Tobie on the beach. Hidden behind the bushes, she furtively stares at the primal scene with her stalkee and his beloved, as we look at her voyeuristically stalking them. Evelyn, now excited, makes maximal mayhem in their lives. Primal scene imagery also features prominently in the two films I cover in this chapter: *Rear Window* and *Peeping Tom*.

Sabbadini (2000; McGinley & Sabbadini, 2006) in his psychoanalytic commentary on *Misty*, considers sedentary or non-mobile stalking as covert voyeurism because it involves secret, furtive, intrusive watching of the primal scene: the couple, unaware of being looked at, is, therefore, not exhibitionistic. Interestingly, Sabbadini identifies two types of covert primal scene sexual voyeurism that are, I believe, significant precursors to the observations that I am emphasizing in this book. The first type involves the persons who hide in the dark as they follow their prey—an example of sexual stalking, while the second involves the targets of professional spies and private eyes—an example of surveillance stalking. Evelyn of *Play Misty for Me,* and Alex of *Fatal Attraction* would be quintessential examples on point of film portrayals for Sabbadini's covert, primal scene, voyeuristic *sexual* stalking. Private investigator Harry Caul of *The Conversation,* and Stasi operative Gerd Wiesler of *The Lives of Others,* whom I will discuss in Chapter Six, each correspondingly represents covert *surveillance* stalking. Sabbadini identifies a second category of primal scene stalking that is not covert, which he calls "collusive voyeurism." Here, the stalkee is aware of being voyeuristically looked at so that the stalking of voyeuristic gazing gratifies his or her exhibitionism. My corresponding examples here are Mark from *Peeping Tom,* in which the actress Viv's exhibitionism is so gratified by dancing for her photographer that she has no inkling that he is preparing to kill her, and Jackie of *Red Road*. Sabbadini considers covert voyeurism as the more predatory and, therefore, primitive form, while collusive voyeurism is a more complex, "higher level" perversion that involves the interaction of the stalker and stalkee as a couple. Each of the two participants complements the other in their co-dependency. Sabbadini also believes that collusive voyeurism is probably modeled on the earliest exchanges of glances, or mutual gazing, between mother and baby. Although he makes an important distinction, I would question the notion that if something like mutual gazing were developmentally beneficial, it would be the precursor of a more highly developed level of *pathology*. Additionally, I believe, in keeping with Sabbadini's ideas, that, in viewing many of the films I comment on in this book, we are inevitably "voyeurs at the cinema—or, more appropriately, *film-lovers*" (2000, p. 810). If we are all voyeurs at the cinema, are all of us potentially stalkers? We should not confuse pathology with inevitability.

I will develop my ideas about doubling, a term introduced by film studies experts, as this chapter progresses. Dunn (2014) has referred, recently, to doubling as a hallmark of *Rear Window*. He also develops the important idea that the problem of voyeurism is clinically relevant in the age of the internet, in the hope that more psychoanalytic attention will be devoted to the issue. This is precisely what I am attempting clinically by designating sexual voyeurism as a form of stalking. Other than Dunn's work on *Rear Window*, Mulvey's (1975, 1989) on the "male gaze," Lieberman's (2000) *Body Talk*, and Sabbadini on *Peeping Tom* (2000, 2014), not much has been written, psychoanalytically, on voyeurism since Freud (1918b) and Fenichel (1946) wrote that sexual voyeurism emerges from a primal scene trauma at the oedipal stage of development. The young child's exposure to sexual intimacy between his parents might lead to a central unconscious fantasy of sadistically violating the privacy of a couple or an individual, as in adult voyeuristic stalking, sometimes with long-term noxious sequelae but at other times with a sense of control and mastery of the original trauma. Similar dynamics dominate themes in *Rear Window* and in *Peeping Tom*, to follow.

I introduce here my own ideas about the parallel or layering process in doubling and voyeurism with reference to illustrative films. Traditionally, psychoanalysis has regarded voyeurism, like sadomasochism, as a variety of perversion. Film portrayals of sexual and surveillance stalkers' voyeurism, and that of the viewers and reporters of those portrayals, reflect psychological processes that parallel each other in many significant respects. In the granddaddy of these films, the 1954 *Rear Window*, which I shall be discussing in the following section of this chapter, Hitchcock makes us all accomplices in the injured photographer Jeff, or L. B. Jeffries' (James Stewart) voyeurism as Jeff sits immobilized by a broken leg and uses binoculars to peep over at what he cannot walk to. The films *Peeping Tom* and *Caché* are inspirationally dedicated to explicate the voyeurism inherent in the parallel activities that film studies experts call "doubling." Doubling has also been used to refer to the process in which the cinematographers' cameras voyeuristically record the voyeurism of the camera action of the film protagonists who portray camera operators. In the films I have chosen, the photographers are cast in the roles of sexual and/or surveillance stalkers. In a prime example of doubling, director Francis Ford Coppola says of his 1974 film, *The Conversation*, that his crew's camera behaved like an automatic surveillance camera. He regarded himself as a professional film-making eavesdropper who was eavesdropping on his fictional representation, the eavesdropper

Harry Caul and his obsessional, voyeuristic, personally disassociated, albeit professional, private-eye eavesdropping.

Arguably, filmmakers, cinematographers, editors, and filmgoers inevitably become voyeuristic as they watch the actors who portray surveillance operators in films about stalking and surveillance. That is, fans of these films, such as you and me, could be construed as the voyeuristic and surveillance stalker's counterparts. There are other parallels as well. For example, the voyeurism of someone like me who studies filmed portrayals of stalking parallels the voyeurism of my audiences that watch "stalking" clips or read verbal "stichomythic translations" of the clips. I think of these parallels as "layers of voyeurism", or at least, layers of watching. Almost everyone gets a kick out of people looking at people. Just take a look at the documentary film, *Smash His Camera* (Gast, 2010), to be discussed later in Chapter Seven. Every time we see Ron Galella click a camera shot of Jacqueline Kennedy Onassis, we react with anything from a mild thrill to jumping out of our seats. As one film critic (Scott, 2007) has written, "More and more it seems we go to the movies to watch people watching people. Voyeurism is hot again" as exemplified in images that are carefully constructed to draw attention to "the gaze." The films make us, at the very least, into voyeurs. We sit in the dark, watching other people's lives.

Rear Window*: an immobilized photographer voyeuristically stalks his neighbors*

Alfred Hitchcock's (1954) iconic masterpiece of suspense, *Rear Window* is the very first film on the subject of what I am calling voyeuristic sexual stalking. The film's leading character, magazine photographer L. B., or Jeff, Jeffries (James Stewart), is immobilized in his New York apartment, convalescing from a broken leg. He spends most of his time looking through his binoculars at his neighbors, whose intimate lives unfold before his very eyes. The apartment windows he peeps into all look out on the same courtyard that his does. Binoculars appear in this film and others, as the logo, along with the camera, and with the open eye, for voyeuristic sexual stalking. Passively immobile, keenly observant, and obsessed with spying on the private lives of his neighbors as they play out across the courtyard, Jeff, a magazine photographer, is confined to a wheelchair, leg in a cast. Covetous of his own privacy, freedom, and personal space, his physical immobility triggers claustrophobia that he compensates for by using his own time and thoughts to invade the privacy of others via voyeuristic visual stalking. Although he cannot walk, he can and does watch and wait.

Jeff is obviously more involved in his voyeuristic spying on the neighbors than he is in his beautiful socialite girlfriend, Lisa (Grace Kelly), who has a nearly impossible time trying divert Jeff's attention to her and away from his window. He is particularly involved in zeroing in on the apartment just across the way, where a married man and his invalid wife engage his interest by behaving quite suspiciously. Try as Lisa may to make inroads into Jeff's voyeuristic preoccupations that divert his attention from the prospect of marriage to her, he seems to prefer watching others over committed action to her. Director Hitchcock and protagonist Stewart as Jeff have something in common. Dunn (2014), in the only psychoanalytic reference to *Rear Window* that I could find on the PEP CD ROM, believes Hitchcock's own disturbed experiences that stem from his voyeuristic tendencies, which he documents, markedly influenced his making of a film on the subject of voyeurism. Dunn takes a pathographic approach, or one that looks for meanings of a work of art by making inferences about psychological abnormalities in the life story of its creator, as opposed to a purely thematic approach (see Spitz, 1989), as I am attempting throughout this book. Dunn thinks Hitchcock projects onto his protagonist as his double his own anxieties about some day not being able to get out and photograph as he wishes.

This macabre thriller, arguably Hitchcock's greatest masterpiece, was made in one confined set, an apartment, and its courtyard, where Hitchcock's camera shoots scenes of the courtyard through the protagonist's window and through the windows of adjacent apartments and those across the way. We are witness to a whole variety of private lives that will occupy all of Jeff's waking hour thoughts. Hitchcock and his photographers enable us, as audience, to eavesdrop along with his voyeuristic protagonist, Jeff. When I refer to the director's camera, I mean the cinematography staff's camera as well. What one can see of the neighbors through their windows in adjoining apartments sets the mood for Jeff's feelings of immobilization and confinement—castration, if you will—that motivate his voyeurism. We, as film viewers, see the inhabitants in the other apartments almost entirely from Jeff's point of view and, thereby, share in his voyeuristic surveillance of other peoples' lives, notably, their sex-related lives. This prototype of primal scene viewing through *doubling* of two visual points of view, that of director Hitchcock's camera and that of Jeff's eyes, aided by binoculars, will be the theme in the analysis of this and other films about voyeuristic sexual stalking, particularly *Peeping Tom*, to be discussed later in this chapter. The doubling or parallels between Hitchcock's camera and Jeff's eyes is but one layer of doubling. Another resides between Hitchcock's camera and the audience, and yet another can be found between Jeff's eyes and those of the film viewers. Hitchcock has piqued our voyeurism by making us, the audience, be peeping Toms in close concert with his camera and with Stewart's character, Jeff. The film focuses on the layers of parallel subjective psychological points of view of filmer, camera, characters, and audience alike.

I now present a summary version in which I select and do my best to sort out the outstanding narrative thematic elements of the script that could enlighten our psychoanalytic understanding of voyeuristic sexual stalking. Most of these themes contain elements of primal scene curiosity, guilt, and castration anxiety. As the film opens, dawn breaks and Hitchcock's camera focuses on the window of Jeff's apartment through which Jeff will be trying to figure out, by looking out, just what is going on among the people who inhabit the places he gazes at through his binoculars. Hitchcock's initial shot heralds a classic instance of doubling in film. Jeff focuses on what is out there and we are prompted by Hitchcock to focus along with him. We all become a cohort of voyeurs as we watch these often salacious dramas unfolding. You look, you see what the protagonist sees, and then you see how he reacts. This doubling technique lies at the heart of Hitchcock's filmmaking.

As Jeff, the temporary invalid, languishes in the heat, we get to see just what he sees during his voyeuristic stalking ventures and adventures: sexy women, sexual overtures, and suspicious sexual intrigue. After the first fadeout, we see him half-heartedly talking to a friend on the phone while his attention is mostly directed toward what he sees outside of his window. First, we follow his gaze hard upon a ballerina getting dressed and practicing, then on two women sunbathing on a terrace, then up to a helicopter flying above, in which the pilot is obviously getting a better look than Jeff can get. Hitchcock's camera moves from Jeff's eyes to the various scenes between which Jeff shifts his glances back and forth. As Jeff's roving eyes go from window to window, we, as viewing audience, join him in his voyeuristic feast.

Jeff tells his telephone caller that with his broken leg in the cast he has nothing to do but look out the windows at his neighbors. "Then I'll get married and I'll never be able to go anywhere," hinting that marriage is a fate even worse than the broken leg that has rendered him immobilized and consumed by claustrophobic castration anxiety that he drowns out with his voyeurism. Stella (Thelma Ritter), his visiting nurse, walks in, nods at his binoculars, and remarks, "First you smash your leg, then you get to looking at the window, see things you shouldn't see." She delivers her funniest, psychoanalytically relevant, line:

> The New York sentence for a peeping Tom is six months in the workhouse. They got no windows in the workhouse. You know in the old days, they used to poke your eyes out with a red-hot poker. Are any of those bikini bombshells you're watchin' worth a red hot poker?

Hitchcock, here, has Stella set the scene to develop the theme of castration, or certainly its equivalent, as punishment for voyeurism. Her humorous warning is unabashedly evocative of Oedipus's fate of blindness for murdering his father and marrying his mother. Yet, Jeff looks on and on. Stella leaves as he watches, bare-eyed without his binocular prop, an adulterous couple working up toward more and more passionate lovemaking. The couple pull their shade down when they notice he is looking at them. Hitchcock means to convey that, in order to avoid looking inward at his own problems, Jeff looks outward through his rear window into his neighbors' windows at all the anxious-making, but exciting, primal scenes in lives and relationships developing around him.

As night falls, Lisa arrives. She parades a host of temptations and possibilities for real gratifications before Jeff: her beauty, her stunning gown, glamour, the banquet dinner she has ordered in from The Twenty-One Club, and hints of sexual promises to be kept. Greedily opening the bottle of wine and referring to his immobilizing cast, he unappreciatively complains, "I want to get this thing off and get moving." Literal immobility and the fantasized immobility of marriage condense to terrify him. Lisa's offers of real sexuality pale in comparison with the scenes which have been gratifying his desires and assuaging his anxiety through the window. Lisa urges him to choose photography assignments for the future that keep him at home and are not so peripatetic, as she sets her marital sights on him, but to no avail. Then he gazes out his window at a woman setting up a table for an imaginary companion with whom she chats away as she romantically pours the wine and then toasts. He is clearly more drawn to the solo fantasy across the courtyard than to the coupled reality that Lisa provides as she continues wining and dining him seductively. Indifferent to her, he is thoroughly absorbed with peering at the romantic wining, dining, and entertaining going on in apartment after apartment as he looks out of his window and into others.

In a battle of the sexes, Lisa and Jeff bicker about the merits of settling down *vs.* endlessly traveling to new places. He is trying to convince her that she is not meant for his ambulatory photographer's life of wanderlust, as she argues for a more sedentary "wonderlust." She continues, stalemated, "So that's it. You won't stay here and I can't go with you." She summarily leaves the apartment. He scans the windows again, framing familiar scenes through his binocular lens. It looks to me as though he were panning a dozen cinema or television screens of live or reality TV shows at once, and truly getting a kick out of it. Jeff watches other people's lives to try to avoid living out his own. His motives to cover other people's lives by stalking them with audio-visual paraphernalia are very different from those of Gerd Wiesler, the Stasi surveillance stalker portrayed in *The Lives of Others,* to be covered in Chapter Six. The night goes on as he dozes on and off, sitting in his wheelchair. He seems particularly taken with one of the scenes in which neighbor Lars Thorwald (Raymond Burr), the salesman with the invalid wife, carries a suitcase around. When Jeff finally nods off, we follow the suitcase scene through Hitchcock's camera action, and our suspicions about some foul hacking are roused even before the sleeping Jeff's are.

Day breaks on the same old courtyard scene and we pick up further on Jeff's voyeuristic activities that serve both to excite him and also to lessen his anxious boredom that his confinement to one spot inflicts upon him. It will be yet another week before his cast comes off. Stella returns again to massage him, activating his muscles as he lies passively looking at what is out there. He wonders aloud to her what salesman Thorwald might have been carrying in his suitcase at three in the morning. It does not take much for us to assume it is the hacked up body of the invalid wife he murdered. Jeff's tension mounts as he sees Lars alone in his apartment. He tells Stella to move back from the window, hoping Lars will not spot them spying. He looks at the salesman, whom we see is looking furtively out of his own window, and begins to worry that his cover might be blown as his idle pastime morphs into a potentially dangerous situation.

JEFF: What do you see? Get back, He'll see you.

STELLA: I'm not shy. [*Looking at Jeff*] I've been looked at before. [*The scene shifts to the salesman*]

JEFF: That's no ordinary look. It 's the kind of look a man gives when he's afraid somebody might be watching him.

Hitchcock's camera focuses on Jeff moving his wheelchair towards his rear window, then it pans across the salesman's quarters, and then it draws our attention to a dog sniffing at something in an outdoor flowerbed. Along with Jeff, we look back into Thorwald's window and see him washing out his suitcase. We kind of "get with" Jeff's voyeurism and figure out as well the scenario that he is putting together in his ever-curious mind. Jeff asks Stella to bring his binoculars to him as she is leaving for the day. Phase two of Jeff's voyeuristic stalking begins, as we watch through Hitchcock's camera the mystery story that Hitchcock has written and the character Jeff the photographer watches through his binoculars as our audience eyes are riveted on Jeff looking through his binoculars that Hitchcock photographs with his film camera. This parallel viewpoint of both audience and protagonist is yet another quintessential example of doubling in filming. Apparently, mere binoculars do not do the trick, as Jeff reaches for a great big telescope and, after fiddling around with it a bit, he moves his wheelchair nearer to the window as Hitchcock's camera focuses on the lens of Jeff's telescope in which we see reflected the neighboring apartments. Jeff spots the salesman wielding a knife and wrapping something in newspaper. His eyes appear glued to the scene.

Night falls once again and Lisa returns and sexily kisses Jeff, who asks, "Why would a man leave in the middle of the night three times with a suitcase and come back three times." Lisa, undeterred by Jeff's voyeurism, tries to draw his attention back to kissing. Jeff continues, "Why hasn't he been in his wife's bedroom all day? Just how would you start to cut up a human body?" Finally, Lisa's unrelenting desire and determination to seduce Jeff into giving her a tumble give way to her own voyeuristic concentration. Lisa grabs Jeff's binoculars away from him and ties them up so that he cannot get to them. Yet, we can see she is beginning to be interested in solving the mystery that occupies Jeff's mind and is Hitchcock's mission to develop in this film. Lisa, now totally absorbed, tells him to tell her everything he saw and what he thinks it means. She is hooked! From now on, we observe the power of the female gaze, which, in this instance, contrasts in spades to this man's more impotent voyeurism.

Day breaks; Stella returns and gets more voyeuristically involved, herself. Jeff muses with a police friend, Doyle (Wendell Corey), whom he calls in on this gripping case of the disappearance and presumed dismemberment of the salesman's invalid wife. He now verbalizes, and brings the law in to help out with, his suspicion that Lars has gotten rid of her by murder and has then cut up her body, put the pieces in a suitcase, which he has hired some men to cart off while everyone from fifty nearby windows could have seen the whole scene. Jeff actually has put it all together aided by his camera, binoculars, telescope, voyeurism, and curious imagination. No longer distracted by the ongoing scenes and sagas that he has been following as they unfold behind all the many windows, Jeff now single-mindedly focuses his binoculars on Thorwald's, who seems about to leave. Jeff is ready to solve the mystery. Lisa returns, having planned to seduce him away from his "perversion" into normal lovemaking, and to spend the night with him. At the same time, she is totally absorbed and continues to be as much interested in the mystery unfolding before their very eyes. Doyle comes in on the scene and shows increased interest in pursuing the mystery that Hitchcock has created and conveys here with many shots of Jeff's eyes as they look around at all the courtyard-facing windows and then focus on Thorwald's. I could not help but notice that Jimmy Stewart's eyes were big, beautiful, and blue, and that Hitchcock took every opportunity to show them off to advantage.

Doyle leaves, and Jeff wonders to Lisa if watching private lives through binoculars is ethical. He finally questions his incursions into the lives of others, which foreshadow the privacy invasions of internet hacking, a variety of stalking to appear on the global scene decades later. Lisa lowers the blinds and says, "Show's over for tonight," actively trying to draw Jeff's attention exclusively to the two of them and their lovemaking. His big blue eyes finally rest on her as she appears in a revealing nightgown. But she raises the blinds, even more curious than Jeff, as somebody screams and all the neighbors open their windows to look at the dog that appears to have been killed smelling the roses in the flowerbed where the presumably axed Mrs. Thorwald is assumed to have been buried. Lisa is distracted from her coupling with Jeff and turns once again to watch voyeuristically the multiple primal couple scenes in the neighboring apartments that Jeff has been following out of his window. Jeff exclaims, "Look, in the whole courtyard only one person didn't come to the window. Look." He is referring to Lars Thorwald. That evening, Stella, Lisa, and Jeff watch as Thorwald washes down the bathroom where his wife's blood must have splattered a lot. The suspense thickens along with the gore as the game turns into serious sleuthing and Jeff sends Lisa over to Thorwald's apartment with a note asking what happened to his wife, to call his bluff. We as audience wonder when Thorwald will figure out who is watching him. Lisa ignores Jeff's instructions and carries through her own plan of action. Meanwhile, Jeff gets Thorwald out by a ruse, and then looks out the rear window to find Stella and Lisa digging up the rose bed. Lisa then climbs into Thorwald's apartment where she continues jumping around like the spritely sleuth she thinks she is. This is no joke any more. As audience, we have stopped laughing at the clever quips, wisecracks, and fun-gazing at the neighbors' quirky lives that have dominated the conversations up to now. It was film genius Hitchcock's intent to have us look at the lives behind the windows through a lens that provided much humor to mask and to offer relief from the more squalid and tragic possibilities (see Sabbadini, 2014). Thorwald returns at the moment Jeff and Stella discover that this and all the other funny scenes they have been watching behind other people's windows around the courtyard are deadly serious, suicidal, or homicidal. Turning humor into horror is Hitchcock's forte and the genius behind this masterpiece of a film.

The peeping Tom game is over for Jeff and Lisa as they enter into the realm of terror. Jeff desperately calls Doyle and the local police squad as he witnesses Thorwald assault Lisa. She stops playing at sleuthing and screams Jeff's name out of Thorwald's window as she looks up at his, bravely letting the murderer know his enemy. The police enter Thorwald's apartment as Jeff impotently looks on. They arrest Lisa, intending to haul her off to jail. Jeff panics and says to Stella, "Turn off the light—he sees us." It looks as if the gig is up for him, putting an end to his obsessional, yet highly pleasurable, peeping Tomism or voyeuristic stalking. We look at Jeff's terrified eyes as we hear Thorwald's menacing steps in his stairwell and then see him enter Jeff's apartment. Jeff attempts to blind Thorwald with his flashbulbs as Thorwald approaches him. The flash of his camera, the symbol of his means of livelihood, is not powerful enough to stop his quarry, so Jeff fights impotently on. Hand-to-hand combat ensues as the neighbors, the police, Doyle, and Lisa rush in on the chaotic scene. Lars knocks Jeff out of the window. Jeff crashes to the ground, breaks his other leg, and then smiles and tells Lisa he's proud of her. The film ends as Hitchcock's camera pans the courtyard, revealing the happy endings in each apartment in turn, ending at Jeff's. No longer looking around, Jeff is blissfully sleeping in his wheelchair in two leg casts while Lisa peacefully reads an adventure book, *Beyond the High Himalayas*. When she notices that he has fallen asleep, she shifts to a magazine of her own preference, *Harper's Bazaar*, and a shade rolls down the rear window as the credits roll. The incompatibility between the sexes has been resolved, at least temporarily, and voyeuristic stalking drops out of the picture as so-called mature genital sexuality takes over.

Peeping Tom*: a photographer becomes a voyeuristic serial stalker killer*

Peeping Tom, a psycho-thriller directed by Michael Powell, was filmed in 1960. The main character, Mark Lewis (Carl Boehm), like Jeff Jeffries in *Rear Window*, is a photographer. Unlike Jeff, photographer Mark is a serial killer employed by a film studio that specializes in soft-core pornography. Both are voyeuristic stalkers. These two horror films home in on male sexual stalking from the point of view that feminists have called "male chauvinistic phallocentrism" and are permeated with that perverse variety of eroticism known as "scoptophilia" or voyeurism. Film critics initially panned *Peeping Tom* as too grossly offensive and horrid, so it failed. But they reconsidered after the hugely successful Hitchcock era, likened the film to that director's successful *Psycho* (1960), and came to view *Peeping Tom* as a landmark cult film for two important reasons. First, it is an archetypal study of the sadistic voyeurism inherent in much male sexual stalking, and second, it is, like *Rear Window*, a prime example of the voyeurism inherent in the very processes of filmmaking and film viewing.

There's never been a psycho thriller as insidiously skin-crawling as Michael Powell's portrait of a would-be director as a serial killer. Carl Boehm, as Mark Lewis, is a focus-puller at a London movie studio who moonlights as a pornographic photographer and spends his spare time shooting a documentary about murder, starring his victims. Boehm's father, played by Powell, was a celebrated biologist who wanted to chart every stage of human development, and specialized in fear and the nervous system. While using a 16-mm. camera to document his son's growth, he went to fantastic extremes, even scaring him awake with a lizard so he could study the boy's hysterical reaction. Boehm, as Mark Lewis, extends this line of research: he turns the third leg of his tripod into a bayonet, and films his female targets as they die in a state of excruciating fright. *Peeping Tom* is an obsessive-compulsive nightmare, and an eroticized combination of horror and hatred.

The first image and recurring logo of the movie is an opening eye, which recurs as a backdrop in nearly every stalking scene. In the foreground, Mark Lewis reveals his *modus operandi* for stalking and killing his female prey, here a prostitute. He carries a 16 mm camera, similar to the one his scoptophilic father used to photograph him, but with a bayonet attached to its tripod, all hidden under Mark's duffle coat. His *modus operandi* is to follow his female prey, either a prostitute or her equivalent, such as a bland, passive, exhibitionistic "poupee" as though pursuing her sexually, in order to photograph and stab her with the inseparable and indispensible fetishistic instrument of his perversion. Right before the kill, Mark places the lens of his camera, which contains a mirror, right up against his victim's face, so that she sees herself imperiled by the projectile bayonet.

Manninem (2000), in one of very few psychoanalytic studies of voyeurism and scoptophilia as perversion since Fenichel's (1946) paper on the subject, presents a careful analysis of the film and the filming of *Peeping Tom*. She refers to this instrument as a "sadistic phallus," adding that all perversions, and I would include stalking as one, are sadistic. The film begins with a night view of a dark, deserted street. In the forefront of our view, a male figure begins to move in a secretive, predatory stalking way toward a prostitute standing at the end of the street, waiting for a client. In a close-up, we see the man simultaneously getting ready to shoot with a camera he carries on a shoulder strap, as though part of his body. Then the lens of that camera is turned on and points toward the viewer, and seems to take us into itself. As we feel the camera image approach, we watch the man's stalking movements toward his prey. Our view of the big screen is exactly the view Mark sees through the crosshairs of his own camera that is filming within the film. That is, the eye of the viewer is aligned with the protagonist's view through the eye of his camera. These merged views promote the audience's near total empathy with the stalker's sadistic, voyeuristic perversion by connecting us with our own sadomasochistic impulses. Along with stalker Mark, we next follow the woman into her room and watch her undress.

> Suddenly, the camera swings down, but not to shoot anything. At that moment, something is lifted in front of it. The viewfinder then returns to the woman who is looking straight at the camera, first looking surprised but then with her face becoming contorted with ever increasing horror. A scream cuts the picture. (Manninem, 2000, p. 201)

We avidly watch Mark avidly gratify his main desire: to terrorize his victim by forcing her to watch him capture on his film the image of her intense fear, as his father forced him as a child. The prostitute, like all of his victims to follow, literally sees her fearfulness in the mirror attached to his camera-bayonet and grasps all that is happening. It suddenly and shockingly dawns on her in every way possible that she is about to be killed by her sexual stalker. He has set her up to gratify exhibitionistically his intensely pleasurable voyeuristic killer compulsive urge, and, at the same time, to triumph over the trauma he experienced as his father's passive, "feminized" victim. Instinctual pleasure and mastery of trauma do not rule one another out: they are juxtaposed. After the kill, we repeatedly watch him gratify himself further as he watches, again and again, these films of his victim who is terrified by watching herself being killed.

In watching the same films that Mark is watching, we, as the cinematic audience of *Peeping Tom*, witness the pornography photographer

Mark's gaze as he directs his camera's crosshairs to focus on his sexual prey. The film cinematographer uses *his* camera so that the image we see of *Peeping Tom* is out of focus, yet subordinated to the logo camera eye. *We, the film audience, view the superimposition of the real-life camera operator's image and the fictionalized stalker–photographer's image simultaneously*. The logo "eye" image and the crosshairs of the camera that fill the screen are meant to convey the levels of voyeurism contained in filmmaking, itself, as akin to a voyeuristic sexual perversion. The audience–spectator's gaze is not erotically involved initially, like Mark's, but is insistently riveted on Mark's camera's tracking movements, which function, like the eye logo, as our collective eye as he stalks his prey with his lethally equipped camera that continues inexorably on its way. When our look as film spectators is aligned for so long with the stalker Mark's camera shot, things begin to change and our potential voyeuristic tendencies are then released. Film buffs, along with psychoanalytic film scholars, have been particularly influenced by the idea of designating the "male gaze" as a metaphor for filmmaking, itself.

The *Peeping Tom* story depicts a severe perversion located within the psyche, but it also reflects outward to the cinema world's intrinsic fascination with looking and the ease with which it can make Peeping Tom stalkers of all of us, both male and female, wherever we fall on the normative–pathological spectrum of voyeurism. The cinematography of *Peeping Tom*, borrowing from Hitchcock's *Rear Window* (1954) and *Psycho* (1960), epitomizes the multiple layering of voyeurism, essentially the doubling process that I referred to earlier, that is depicted technically, photographically, and psychologically in films about male sexual stalking. Our viewing orientation, in the case of *Peeping Tom*, subtly and almost imperceptibly shifts back and forth between the *Peeping Tom* protagonist Mark Lewis's camera and director Michael Powell's camera. These parallel processes in film content, filming, and film viewing constitute a classical and compelling example of how the pleasures of looking feature in the very culture of the cinema.

The film *Peeping Tom* captures what retrospectively resembles a caricature of male patriarchal gender fantasies that recall the Freud's (1915c) phallocentric, patriarchal view of active, male, dominant, voyeuristic, sadistic sexuality. Freud's early view would imply that shooting, like voyeurism, is male because it is presumably active, whereas posing as model, a form of exhibitionism, is female, because it is presumably passive. That active male–passive female binary (see Gediman, 2005) is the subject of Chapter Five. Freud, however, also knew very well that both voyeurism and its counterpart, exhibitionism, one of his famous "pairs of opposites," are contained in heavily charged motivating fantasies of both men and women. These fantasies are realized in the intrapsychic representations and in the interpersonal behavioral activity of both stalker and stalkee. In *Peeping Tom*, as in other films with similar subject matter, voyeurism–exhibitionism almost imperceptibly blends in with its close psychosexual instinctual counterpart, sadism–masochism. As the camera bears down in its active look on its passive object, the space created by looking is suffused by fear and sadomasochistic excitement. The prostitute, Dora, experiences no small measure of this horrible arousal, as her eyes, like those of all the other female stalking victims in this film, freeze with terror. The pervasive *confluence of terrorism and voyeurism* in male stalking scenarios is not at all coincidental or accidental.

Moira Shearer, the ballet dancer, portrays Mark's next serial murder victim, the actress, Viv. Mark tells Viv that he has to film her in a situation where she would be frightened to death simply for professional reasons related to the documentary he is producing. Viv then dances for Mark to the music on her own tape recorder to "get into the mood" and is excited by her own exhibitionism which she steps up the more she believes that that her dancing before Mark and his camera will advance her own career. Then he approaches her with his bayoneted camera and puts the blade to her throat for her to see with horror in the camera's mirror lens. I will be discussing the sex and gender issues of the stalker–stalkee couple, Mark and Viv, in Chapter Five.

Additional gender issues surface as the early developmental roots of Mark's voyeuristic killer stalking emerge. Mark's neighbor, Helen (Anna Massey) empathically grasps the essence of the young Mark's tortured psyche as she screens, in Mark's presence, the home movies Mark's voyeuristic father took of him as little boy. Director Powell's camera focuses in on the adult Mark's eyes as he, along with us and Helen, watches himself as a child in a film-within-a-film being watched, tormented, and photographed by his obsessionally voyeuristic, coldly sadistic father. We learn from a psychiatrist, late in the film, that Mark's father filmed Mark's entire childhood for his professional interests in the study of fear. It is no accident that Mark becomes a maker of documentary films that feature women whose fear is featured in the film shots of their killing. Mark's father's home movies contextualize and document primal scene oedipal drama and castration in Mark's childhood. Those home movie scenes also suggest that Mark's serial killings serve to repudiate the feminine tendencies that lie within himself. By getting rid of the external real female object, he gets rid of his inner threats to his masculinity.

Mark's horribly traumatic history (Sabbadini, 2000; Sklarew & Akhtar, 2015) of being a childhood victim of soul murder continued shortly after Mark's mother's funeral, when Mark's father became obsessed with other women that he brought home. At that time, he liked to flaunt his sexual relationships and to photograph his young son watching primal scenes. In the home movies, Helen sees Mark as a small boy secretly watching a couple lying on the ground in a park and kissing. The father's scoptophilic obsession with primal scenes primed the adult Mark to turn his own photographic skills into a pornography perversion. He has an uncontrollable urge to photograph a kissing couple as he walks through the neighborhood with Helen and makes an automatic move for his camera, which he had left at home this time. Helen asks, "What was your father trying to do . . . Photographing you at night? . . . What is this?" Mark, reflecting on his mother's death, explains, "I am saying goodbye to my mother." Then we see, coming out of some water, a woman in a bikini whom his father married six weeks after his mother's funeral. Helen intuitively grasps the oedipal primal scene roots of Mark's obsessions to look at films of his father's invasive filming behavior. Mark further confides, "He wanted a record of a growing child complete in every detail . . . by training a camera on me . . . at all times. I never knew in the whole of my childhood one moment's privacy." Privacy invasions into their early lives seem to be important precursors to the invasions that stalkers enact, as adults, with their stalkees. In this case, Mark's most extremely invasive, lethal, voyeuristic stalking repeats, in an identification with the aggressor father and with a subject–object role reversal, the trauma inflicted on him by his father's fearsome home movie-taking. Marks's obsession turns out to be incredibly reminiscent of his father's. In one of these home movie scenes, Helen sees Mark's father give Mark a gift of a camera to encourage him to follow in his footsteps. This total identification with the aggressor determines

Mark's choice of becoming a professional photographer and shooter of pornographic documentaries of his own creation. It also determines his obsessions as a voyeuristic serial killer-stalker.

Helen, visibly troubled, watches films of Mark's father setting up his camera to shoot the fear he induces in his son in the home horror movies. As she looks, Mark wants to photograph her expressions. He waits, as his father did with him, to see on her face what his father saw on his face. In an effort to master the trauma inflicted on him, Mark tries, but now ambivalently, to repeat the fear-inducing voyeurism with Helen that he habitually succeeds in with his victims. He is unsuccessful because she does not cooperate. Mesmerized, she gazes, *actively and compassionately feminine,* at scenes of Mark-the-child being tortured. Helen's feminine sensibilities, quite to the contrary of the man's fantasy, which also involves a repudiation of his view of femininity within himself, translate into her adamant refusal to be watched because she senses a terrible outcome in Mark's need to repeat passively experienced trauma by becoming an active voyeuristic photographer turned murderous terrorizing stalker. She rebels against Mark's gaze by shutting off his projector, refusing his invitation for her to be complicit in his horror scenarios, and, consciously and deliberately, while in full possession of her liberated feminine powers, thwarts Mark's efforts at perverse, fetishistic gratification at her expense. Mark persists in trying, but now ambivalently and in vain, to repeat the fear-inducing voyeurism with Helen that he habitually does with his victims, by showing her films of his stalking murders, but she refuses to show fear. Just as he fails in this final attempt to repeat his pattern, he commits suicide with his *modus operandi* just before the police can apprehend him. Helen has saved her life at the expense of his.

Helen's driven *desire to look* at the visual evidence of Mark's traumatization by his sadistically victimizing father is overtaken by her *desire to understand,* to decipher the psychological implications of the images forced upon her. We, too, as film spectators, especially if we are a psychoanalytic audience, *desire to know via empathy and insightful understanding* about the suffering protagonist's motivations. Helen, along with you and me as audience, are watching films within a film about watching films. We all might be thought of as countering the "masculinized" gender stereotype of the male voyeuristic perversion with another: the "feminized" gender stereotype of the sublimated need to know, to help, and to nurture.

I conclude with some additional ideas about doubling and layering in real life and in the film, *Peeping Tom*. I am struck by a parallel between, on the one hand, the sexual stalker's voyeurism, and, on the other hand, that of the reporters and recorders of these activities. The latter could be construed as the stalker's counterparts. Arguably, filmmakers, cinematographers, and editors and writers like me voyeuristically watch and take pleasure as their creative products take shape.

CHAPTER FIVE

Gender and sexual stalking

Picking up from my reference to male and female stalkers that ended my last chapter, I turn here to a more thorough look at gender issues in stalking. I would consider both male and female stalking to be motivated by one or another perverse scenario, usually sadomasochistic. The erotomanic woman heterosexual stalker, then, like Evelyn in *Misty* and Alex in *Fatal Attraction,* would lower herself, masochistically, to a state of abject humiliation, despair, and panic. After that, she can be resurrected to a state of sexual ecstasy while seeking revenge, sadistically, on the phallic man by whom she feels victimized because he thwarts her sense of entitlement for her ideal vision of romantic love to be requited. In another scenario, found in the typical troubadour ballad, the male lover masochistically and abjectly adores the unattainable and scornful *femme fatale.* In Josef von Sternberg's film, *The Blue Angel* (1930) Professor Rath (Emil Jannings) subjects himself to utter humiliation and degradation by the seductress, Lola (Marlene Dietrich). The film appears to follow the *Horigkeit* script that Kaplan (1991) elaborates of extreme sadomasochistically perverse submissiveness accompanied by sexual ecstasy. *Horigkeit* scenarios often underlie the fantasies of those who cyberstalk the internet's pornographic websites in one-way, extreme sexual bondage to the idealized man or woman who is, in fact, a complete stranger or "part object."

I refer in my book, *Fantasies of Love and Death in Life and Art* (1995), to the fatal attractions in the "*Liebestod* fantasies" of Tristan and Iseult, Petrarch and Laura, Dante and Beatrice, who all romanticized the idea of dying together. In these works, derivative of the troubadour ballad, a smitten male adores and stalks the unattainable *femme fatale*. These songs, myths, and legends are all about men, not women, who clearly can also be beset by fantasies of a certain kind of unrequited love. So, *Liebestod* fantasies may be enacted with similar variants in either men or women whose childhood histories very often include disorganized attachments to, and a wish to refind, a beloved mother. Extreme bondage and submission, then, are perversions of romantic love, either in the acts themselves or in the fantasies that motivate them, and are key factors in the stalking of and by either gender.

A typical scenario of women who stalk in both life and art involves unrequited love that sets off intense feelings, ranging from average expectable vulnerability to rejection, abandonment, and humiliation, up to pathological erotomania and vengefulness, accompanied by murderous rage. Terror, dread, and any other negatively valenced excitement may accompany both stalking and being stalked. Charity, whose case vignette appears in Chapter Two of this book, made perversely enthralling, self-endangering repetitive attempts to maintain maximal sexual excitement via seeking out stalking and by being stalked. As we learned, her pathology is a variant of what Ernest Jones (1927, 1929) called "aphanisis," or the fear of total and permanent extinction of the capacity and opportunity for sexual pleasure and excitement. In men, according to Jones, aphanisis takes the specific form of castration anxiety that ensues from loss of arousal or desire. In women, it consists of separation anxiety and oedipal anxieties about loss of sexual feeling.

By and large, female protagonists in films about sexual stalking are erotomanic and vengeful, whereas male protagonists are voyeuristic and often cruel (see Gediman, 2009b). So, what can we say about gender from these four films that I have explored so far: *Play Misty for Me, Fatal Attraction, Rear Window,* and *Peeping Tom*? Films about female sexual stalking do not seem to correspond with facts: most sexual stalkers are men, not murderous women, no matter how common it is for women off the silver screen to feel vengeful toward their supposed lovers who do not support their erotomania—a quasi-delusional belief that their love is romantically returned. In an era predating the second-wave feminism of the 1970s, most stalking narratives in life and art depicted males preying on females. The story lines circulating then conformed to what gender theorists call a patriarchal–phallocentric cultural stereotype: active male overpowers passive female victim. Film scenarios followed naturally from men's fantasies that influenced psychoanalytic ideas about sex and gender circulating during the time warp of the pre-feminist era. Stereotypical views held that stalking almost always involves a voyeuristic, sexually exploitative man who subjugates and terrorizes a helpless woman. If a woman stalkee wanted to pursue her case legally, the most she could expect was an order of restraint against her stalker that was difficult to enforce. Even women associated with powerful men were limited in what they could do to protect themselves. Jacqueline Kennedy Onassis, as we shall see in Chapter Seven on celebrity stalking, could hardly restrain Ron Galella, her paparazzo celebrity stalker, from following her whenever he wanted to get a good, marketable photograph of her. Today's real life and fictional tales frequently involve a woman who often vengefully stalks a man for whom she has felt strong but unrequited romantic yearnings: that is, she imagines he reciprocates her desires, while, in fact, he does not.

When we speak of gender differences between male and female stalkers and stalkees, we are inevitably influenced by the cultural revolution that has occurred since the 1970s, although those differences certainly do not hold invariably across the board, especially when we visit issues of celebrity stalking. Since then, many psychoanalytically relevant ideas on sex and gender have been developed. Particularly relevant are those concerning real-life situations of unrequited love and stalking, and those directed to the *femme fatale* in the literature of passionate love and romanticism (Gediman, 1995; Person, 1988). Newer views of perversion, such as voyeurism, question both enduring and obsolete patriarchal values and the feminist-grounded opposition to them.

Orit Kamir, in her 2000 book, *The Maintenance of Cultural Myths: The Case of Stalking*, notes striking contrasts between fears generated by *female* stalking and those generated by *male* stalking. People perceive female stalking, she says, as subverting patriarchal sexual norms; and people see male stalking as serving the patriarchal social order. What she has to say seems to embody some newer psychoanalytic interests. Power and vulnerability, as well as sex and aggression, and sex and gender, determine the pecking order within any social structure. Accordingly, female stalking invokes a sense of danger and social instability, because men who are stalked are scared. Scared and vulnerable men, by definition, cannot be regarded as the most powerful members in society. Eastwood's *Play Misty for Me* and Lyne's *Fatal Attraction* portray active, dominant erotomanic female stalkers. Evelyn and Alex may be caricatures, albeit caricatures of mentally disturbed women who have a scripted mission that is consistent with the emergent feminist views of their time. These views purport to partly undo many older patriarchal illusions and assumptions of male chauvinism and supremacy and to deconstruct the male-active, female-passive gender binary that dominated the theories of sexuality of early Freud and later Lacan (2006 [1970]). Gabbard and Gabbard (1993), in their work on phallic women in the contemporary cinema, note that if the old formula for terror in films was an innocent woman pursued by a berserk man, the new formula is a harmless man terrorized by a crazed woman. Although Alex, in *Fatal Attraction,* is an empowered career woman, her persona hardly conforms to the image of the downtrodden female of patriarchal norms. Nonetheless, she feels utterly degraded and victimized as she regresses to abject despair, humiliation, and psychotic erotomania. She manages to project an image that evokes in her audience the contemporary feminist gender-related fears that fit Kamir's classification. Ironically, the female stalker, Alex, is as much a victim, albeit of her own psychotic terrors, as Dan, her male stalkee. Men who cheat on their partners are shaken by this film because of their terror of the psychosis unleashed in this woman.

I do not believe director Lyne was particularly interested in the psychodynamics of infidelity, but his *Fatal Attraction* uses the conventions of the horror film to emphasize the anxieties about sex and gender that jealous and unfaithful partners split off and project. Kales (2003) considers the film to be part of a genre that developed in the postfeminist era, called "backlash" films, that "depict women who either through sexual seduction or professional power seek to dominate and destroy a male protagonist by their drive to possess, devour or annihilate him" (p. 1631). Traditional psychoanalysis holds that a predatory woman stalking a helpless male arouses male anxiety about castration and loss of potency. Alex manifests stereotypically male-identified traits of aggression, anger, and violence that Kales believes portray her as a monster and out of control. Cinematic conventions of the time had Dan Gallagher relating to the two women in his life according to the Madonna–whore split female binary. Dan's wife, Beth, represents the Madonna, or domesticated "good" woman, an elusive object of male sexual desire who represents the immaculate maternal aspect of the feminine split off from the sexual. Alex, in Dan's split object representation, is the "wicked woman," a siren who would lure the innocent husband from his happy home while continuing to stalk that man and his family. Continuing her psychoanalytically based exposition, Kales contends that Alex forces Dan to face his own sexual animalism and aggression as she displays her own. Dan, indeed, begins to lose it when he struggles with Alex for a knife in the kitchen where she had been the sexual aggressor. "His face contorts with brutal fury as he grips her neck and smashes her head against the bathroom tile while the sounds of breaking glass and furniture are amplified in the best horror-genre tradition" (p. 1633). The film continues, to end as a nightmare vision of a disruption in the social order that renders Dan a passive victim conquered by the sexual power and dominance of unrestrained female energy. Kales has captured the essence, psychoanalytically speaking, of erotomanic revenge in sexual stalking. *Peeping Tom,* in contrast, richly provides film scholars with material for a commentary on older psychoanalytic patriarchal views of macho male stalking. Whether it is men stalking women, women stalking men, or same-sex stalking, most cases of stalking constitute a form of terrorism in which this same sort of power imbalance is paramount.

In Freud's (1915c) early phallocentric patriarchal view (see Gediman, 2005) of an active male–passive female binary, camera shooting, deriving from voyeurism, would be considered male because it is presumably active. Posing as a model, because it derives from exhibitionism, would be considered female, because it is presumably passive. However, Freud also knew very well that both voyeurism and its counterpart, exhibitionism, one of his famous "pairs of opposite" instincts, are each contained in heavily charged motivating fantasies of both men and women. These fantasies are realized in an individual's intrapsychic representations, or internalized images of people from the past, and also in the interpersonal here and now behavioral activity of both stalker and stalkee. In *Peeping Tom*, as in other films with similar subject matter, voyeurism–exhibitionism almost imperceptibly blends with its close psychosexual counterpart, sadism–masochism. As the camera, and, of course, the man or woman who is operating it, bears down in its active gaze on its passive object, the space created by looking and being looked at is suffused by fear and sadomasochistic excitement. The prostitute, Dora, experiences this excitement as horrible arousal, as her eyes, like those of all the other female stalking victims in *Peeping Tom*, freeze with terror as soon as the mirrored lens and the bayoneted tripod trigger her awareness that she is about to be killed by her sexually perverted cameraman. The pervasive confluence of terrorism and voyeurism in this male stalking scenario is not at all coincidental or accidental.

Fifteen years after *Peeping Tom*'s initial distribution and box-office failure, film scholar Laura Mulvey (1975) offered a classical Freudian explication of voyeurism as a specifically and exclusively male perversion, because it involves active looking, that she says is uniquely related to stalking. Mulvey says that the opening image of the male–female stalking encounter in *Peeping Tom*, Mark's pursuit of the prostitute, Dora, which I covered in Chapter Four, captures male voyeurism and brings out the male voyeurism in both male and female audience members. Harris and Sklar (1998) dispute Mulvey's claim that there is a perfect fit between psychoanalysis and cinema exclusively afforded by the parallel activity of the male gaze and the literal activity of filming. That is, they do not believe that doubling is a function of the male gaze at the female object of desire. These authors do think there is a parallel between the technology of camera action and of the action inherent in human vision. Those who watch the camera action watch in a way similar to the way the camera watches, and not because they identify with the male gaze. They believe film watching is multiply gendered. They also believe that the feminist film theorists of the 1970s had a rather limited view of the contributions of psychoanalysis to an understanding of film that was restricted to very narrow Lacanian lines, which were, in their minds, all too similar to Freud's early phallocentric view. The exclusive, Lacanian monolithic focus on the male gaze, they say, "permits a woman to enter only as an object of desire, neither the gazing/desiring spectator nor the agent within the narrative and spectacle of the film" (p. 227). Harris and Sklar go on to question the films Mulvey cites to augment her feminist psychoanalytic views. Among them are *Gilda* (Vidor, 1946), about the ultimate *femme fatale,* and *Vertigo* (Hitchcock, 1958). Both promoted the cult of the female star. Mulvey regarded these films as iconic of the obsessional male gaze at the female as sex object, and as meant to enhance the pleasure of control and mastery of possession of the idealized, unattainable woman. Harris and Sklar had a different psychoanalytic take on the films: "Fetishistic scoptophilia or the sadism nested in voyeurism become the intense mechanisms for visual pleasure and control for the male spectator" (p. 229). In keeping with postmodernist feminist ideas about multi-gendered features of film viewing, they conclude that feminist theory of the 1970s, the years of so-called "second-wave", or cultural, feminism, never properly contested the oppositional category system, or binary, of male–female. That questioning came with "third wave", or post-modern, feminism. Their view jibes with my own that holds that women do actively stalk and look, just as men have been looked at as stalkees. Harris and Sklar cite the opening sequence of *Peeping Tom* as the most powerful example of sadism embedded in scoptophilia "in which the camera point of view is that of the serial killer, who himself carries a camera filming his own murderous act" (p. 232).

To my surprise, I found a feminist-compatible image of stalking in Leonor Fini's 1939 surrealistic oil painting, "Two Women." This incredible, and, I believe, only image on record of a female peeping Tom stands quite in contrast to the film images that Mulvey considers consistent with psychoanalytic ideas about the male gaze. The painting is essentially an image of a female peeping Tom who is peeping through a keyhole in a free-standing door at a very exhibitionistic-appearing other woman striding on a floor surface behind the door. The peeper is most definitely gazing—this is no male gaze by any stretch of the imagination. She is what only men had been thought to be: a desiring spectator and the agent of narrative within the frame of the painting. Perhaps some would credit Fini's bisexuality for creating this tradition-breaking image of voyeuristic sexual stalking, but it is, nonetheless, a female, not a male, gaze that we look at. Her paintings were considered erotic and frightening, and this is no exception. They expand on power dynamics between men and women. Fini repeatedly overturned surrealist patriarchal conventions by painting women in positions of power and men as passive, sometimes androgynous, figures. Clearly, the meaning of the gaze in the act of stalking can be multiply gendered, as Fini's image of a woman peeping Tom shows. In 1939, and, I would add, up through 2016, "peeping Tomism" had been regarded as a singularly male perversion. Fini, a major mid-century woman painter known more in European than American circles, explored female sexuality and identity through her unique surrealistic lens. Identifying herself as a feminist as early as the 1920s, Fini celebrated strong, beautiful women, dreamlike elements, provocative relationships, femininity and masculinity, ambiguity, role reversal, and shared dominance of the sexes. She depicted female sexuality from a woman's perspective. Her work is a bold proclamation of feminist art theory and creativity.

The film, *Peeping Tom*, contains quite a bit to question. Even the women in the film audience are absorbed in aspects of this male as well as female identification, whether or not their ideology is consistent with a patriarchal take. If we put aside, for the moment, Freud's male–female binary, or other similar dichotomous views, it is not too difficult to deconstruct these active male–passive female gender stereotypes, even within Powell's film, itself. This is not hard to do once we imagine gazing as having passive as well as active elements, when, for example it is "gaping," or filled with wide-eyed wonder, or visually drinking in the world. Likewise, we can understand a woman's exhibitionism to be actively motivated behavior, as when it actively solicits attention and she is not simply the passive recipient of the male gaze. Viv, the actress who dances for Mark in *Peeping Tom*, stereotypically and mindlessly exhibits herself in the hopes of calling her director's attention to her terpsichordic talents. Viv acts—note I say "acts", to imply an active as well as a passive dimension—to benefit Mark's piercingly lethal camera-eyes, which, she believes, will promote her professional ambitions. Moira Shearer, the ballet dancer, portrays Viv. Shearer also, by the way, appeared in a film version of Offenbach's opera, *Tales of Hoffman*, which was also directed by Michael Powell. In both films, the dancer's exhibitionistic acts program her for her own destruction at the hands of men stalkers.

The clinical and theoretical advance that recognizes male and female voyeurism and exhibitionism as each having admixtures of active as well as passive elements is well illustrated when Viv tries to photograph Mark photographing her. Ultimately, however, his camera dominates her and, once again, the woman fails to assert control over the camera as symbolic protrusive, invasive phallus. Film critics have commented on the juxtaposition of the phallic image of Mark's bayoneted tripod and the empty box that eventually serves as Viv's coffin, the latter image suggesting the phallocentrically based symbolic metaphoric representation of female genitalia as empty box. This phallocentric interpretation is precisely what Harris and Sklar mean by "wild analysis." Such classical, but now obsolete, "Freudian" interpretations of voyeurism as an exclusively male activity now rings particularly archaic when counterposed with certain postmodern and other contemporary views of gender multiplicity as replacement for active–passive gender stereotypes. The older views build on the image of woman displayed as spectacle—passive exhibitionism—that is molded and fashioned to delight the active, voyeuristic male gaze. These images convey stereotypes and do not always evoke real women, but, as Riviere (1929) put it, women masquerading as the type of woman they think men want to see. Viv certainly had it in mind to show off to her director and producer when she danced for her photographer, Mark. Such gender stereotypic images that "working" women like Viv—the prostitute, the pin-up girl, the "poupee"—provide often collude with and feed a certain male fantasy of subjugating and subordinating women. Scenarios based on these fantasies are aimed at male circulation and consumption. Such is the stalker–stalkee couplehood of Mark and Viv.

Unlike second-wave feminists, the third-wave feminists, influenced by postmodernism, have criticized this polarizing iconography of voyeurism and exhibitionism along active–passive gendered lines and have rejected these most questionable and generally abandoned views of Freud. In a more contemporary reading of Freud, the conversion of the sexual component instincts into their opposites could be present in any individual psyche, male or female, but in our older psychoanalytic culture, instinctual aims tended to be personified according to gender stereotypes: male is active and victimizing and female passive and victimized. We question this gender-related assumption that voyeurism is male–active and exhibitionism female–passive even further when we realize that there is a genetic origin of the "gaze" (see Beebe & Sloate, 1982) in both male and female infants in the parent–infant dyad. In early psychoanalysis, the gaze was considered male and active. In present-day psychoanalysis, the gaze is multi-gendered, and, while sometimes an expression of phallic sexuality, it always has its origin in mother–infant merger.

Stalker–stalkee couplehood derives, then, from the earliest stages of life as well as from later ones.

I go back to the film *Peeping Tom* to summarize its gender messages. Mark is enacting a repetition of primal scene trauma by identifying with his aggressor father in a subject–object role reversal of turning passive into active: He aims to inflict on the women victims of his perverse photographic legacy what his father inflicted upon him when he was a little boy. The women he photographs and kills are the objects of Mark's sadistic–murderous voyeurism, just as he, as a child, was the object of his father's sadistic gaze that he adopted professionally. Director Powell said there is nothing more frightening than a camera as objective visual observer watching you. Mark's pornographic documentary filming activity is a lifelong repetitive enactment of the early traumatic interactions with his scoptophilic father that contextualized the son's sadistic voyeurism. We sense the inevitable interplay between the defensive operations that feed his sense of compensatory male power when, as director, he controls via "looking" at the female star, whom he casts, obsessively, as abused object of the look. By projecting his sadistic fantasies onto images of the woman's body, he literally induces and creates in adult women the very wound he experienced when his father symbolically castrated him via the humiliating and terrorizing way he photographed him as helpless boy beset by unrelenting torments of fearfulness. Aided and abetted by the camera's mirror-lens and the tripod's attached bayonet that he points at the woman's throat, he photographs and then wipes out her surface masquerade as vacuous exhibitionist. Mark the adult, then, reverses the threatening image of being the subjugated young boy who feels castrated and feminized by his father who inflicts his piercingly castrating gaze on his son. The adult Mark, in his role reversal, forcefully subjugates the woman by making her look at her own reflection in the mirrored lens at the very moment she knows she is about to be murdered. In his stalking activities as a professional photographer, he thus achieves the simultaneous enhancement and destruction of that which he abhors in himself: his self-image as a feminized castrated male. That he commits suicide with himself as victim of his own favored method of operation would confirm this theory of castration turned against the self.

In the film *Thelma and Louise* (1991), the audience visually experiences a transition that has been occurring in many images of real and fictional women that have appeared since the consolidation of second-wave feminism. No longer are women doll-like pretty, neat, and clean, adorning themselves with delicate makeup, denim, and lace. Rather, they are looking very real as when Thelma (Geena Davis) feels her own power and takes charge of her actions authoritatively. She finds a solution to a money problem by robbing a convenience store, and her aggressive behavior is documented on a police surveillance camera. The male police authority figures who stalk her via their surveillance actually witness her transformation from a victimized woman to one who will determine her own fate no matter what the law authorities intend for her. This film, so clearly about gender, also portrays government-sanctioned surveillance stalking via ordinary video cameras such as we see in department stores, airport security checkpoints, and even in some elevators in the high-rise buildings we live in. In my building, surveillance cameras are "hidden" in the overhead lighting in the exercise room under which women and men do their mat work. These incidents are now so common as to have started today's investigations into rampant Fourth Amendment violations of warranted search. With this transition, I move from "sexual stalking" to my next section on "surveillance stalking."

PART III
SURVEILLANCE STALKING

CHAPTER SIX

Film portrayals of surveillance stalking

Turning from sexual stalking to surveillance stalking, I have chosen four films on my topic. All involve invasions of privacy, a topic that I will focus on more centrally in Part IV of this book.

Francis Ford Coppola's 1974 film, *The Conversation,* is the brilliant forerunner of films in the surveillance-stalking genre that portray professionals who are paid to stalk. The film is a masterpiece about a schizoid private investigator whose personality deteriorates under work-related personal guilt that breaks through his characteristic defenses. In *The Lives of Others* (1984), director Florian Henckel von Donnesmarck juxtaposes perverse sexual stalking and state-sanctioned surveillance stalking. He provides a magnificent account of an East German Stasi investigator whose operations during the "cold war" years produce heart-wrenching conflict. The Stasi operative's audio-visual stalking of a high profile theater couple disrupts his personal equilibrium and turns his political allegiances upside down and inside out. *Caché* (2005), Michael Haneke's highly original French film, centers on the actions of a mysterious, unidentified stalker who disrupts the life of a domestic Parisian couple by surveying their comings and goings to and from the house they live in. The stalker disrupts their lives by hounding them with videotapes as revenge for some earlier activities that he believes ruined his family's life. In the final film I have chosen for this section, *Red Road* (2007), directed by Andrea Arnold, Jackie, who works for the city surveillance police in Glasgow, bugs the life of the man she eventually sex-stalks. *Red Road* condenses themes of both sexual and surveillance stalking as the heroine steps down from her job to stalk a man whom she believes to be guilty of serious wrongdoing toward her late husband and child. All four films poignantly portray the loneliness of the long distance stalker and enable *us* to look, as parallel but essentially excluded voyeurs, at some version of a "primal scene."

The Conversation*: eavesdropping and emotional breakdown in a private investigator*

Many filmgoers have judged Francis Ford Coppola's 1974 renowned masterpiece as one of the best films of all time. The film deals with the work and tormented inner life of a professional private eye wiretapping, eavesdropper, or, in the vernacular, "bugger." In *The Conversation*, Gene Hackman portrays Harry Caul, an audio-visual stalking private investigator considered to be unrivaled in his trade. With his metaphorical sounding name (C-A-U-L) Harry, isolated and schizoid—living as though in a caul—tries to maintain emotional distance and to remain personally disassociated from his clients' personal lives. He has been hired by a client to bug a scheming, adulterous couple's conversation and he then tries to make sense of it throughout the film. Thinking he is simply doing his job impeccably well, Caul is gradually overcome by pangs of guilt, related to a deadly outcome in earlier but similar private eye work, that return to undo him in the film's final scene as his dissociative defenses decompensate into hallucinatory madness.

The film provides us with the richest, most in-depth character portrayal of a professional surveillance stalker that I know of and lends itself to a psychoanalytically relevant study. This major classic among psychological thrillers foreshadows *The Lives of Others* in many ways, particularly with its emphasis on the technological and personal preoccupations of its protagonist. *The Conversation* is a study of electronic surveillance methods and the threat of burgeoning new competitive technologies as they impact on the life of the protagonist, a lonely, detached, expert "bugger," the "best in the business." The *Conversation*, with its prophetic focus on the dangerous technological invasions of privacy intrinsic to governmentally backed worldwide surveillance operations, also foretells *Enemy of the State*, a film to be discussed in Chapter Nine of this book.

Coppola wrote, directed, produced, and released *The Conversation* during the Watergate era. That was a time, like today's internet or cyberspace era, of heightened concern over issues of governmental responsibility for violations of personal and civil liberties in the interests of, at best, personal and national security, and, at worst, unprincipled corporate power and invasion of privacy through eavesdropping. "Eavesdropping" is now a euphemism, I believe, for the taping, wiretapping, bugging, and other surveillance activities conducted by governmental surveillance operatives and by those who work in the private sector, such as the character and protagonist Harry Caul. The Snowden affair, the subject of the documentary film *Citizenfour* (Poitras, 2014), to be covered in Chapter Nine, also epitomizes the real-life actualization of some of the messages found in Coppola's profoundly far-sighted 1974 film. What I think is unique to *The Conversation* is the spot-on portrayal of one private surveillance stalker's personal, highly conflicted, guilt-ridden reaction to his ever-growing awareness that he painfully feels the consequences of his eavesdropping on the private lives of the people that his clients have paid him to investigate.

I have come across only one published psychoanalytic study of *The Conversation*. Zusman (1998), a psychoanalyst and film critic, has emphasized the close connection between cinema and voyeurism. Zusman, like Sabbadini (2000), also finds that the voyeurism of the screen character, Caul, is paralleled by the voyeurism of the filmer, Coppola. Both of those sources of voyeurism trigger the voyeurism of the viewing audience. In his psychoanalytically based character study of the leading protagonist, Zusman finds Harry Caul to be beset perennially with difficulties in distinguishing between the so-called material reality of events that have really occurred and the psychic reality of his inner world that his work influences. For example, Caul attributes literal reality to a dream he has had about the couple he has been paid to investigate. When he returns, after the dream to the hotel that he has visited within the dream, he is clearly confused between what he actually discovered there while awake, and what he dreamed about prior to his working hours professional visit. Additionally, Zusman thinks Caul is cut off, dissociatively, from his longings for warm human contact, as well as seriously schizoid, and prone to paranoid reactions when he thinks he is being followed—stalked, we can now safely say—or when his privacy is invaded: that is, when he believes people get physically and personally too close to him. Even an ordinary friendly personal question about his life can set him off into personally obsessional and paranoidal suspicious ruminations.

Zusman's lone and limited psychoanalytic exposition has left me free to develop my own ideas without being too influenced by those that preceded mine. I start with the plot. Harry has been hired to spy on an adulterous couple. As the film rolls on, we are never sure whether his client represents the couple, Mark and Ann, or Ann's husband, known as "The Director." Director Coppola's deliberate ambiguity keeps protagonist Harry Caul and the film audience on edge throughout.

The film begins with an aerial shot, which we view simultaneously with the opening rolling credits, of Union Square in San Francisco during lunch hour. Many talkative people are walking around amid much motion and loud sounds coming from street musicians and other entertainers. In the very first scene, we, as the viewing audience, see Hackman as Harry Caul in the crowd, which appears to be walking in circles around the square. He keeps his eyes on a couple, a man and a woman named Mark and Ann, engaged in a conversation, hence the title of the film. We learn some minutes into the film that Harry believes his client represents the woman's husband, a corporate tycoon called The Director. The client has hired Harry as a private detective and surveillance expert, but has not explained his reasons for the assignment. We, like Harry Caul, are in the dark from the start, beset by ambiguities and uncertainties about what is really going on throughout this most absorbing and riveting film. Nonetheless, rightly or wrongly, Harry initially assumes that his client represents the wronged husband and not the adulterous couple.

Caul's mission as professional bugger—that is, one who invasively plants high-tech devices that reveal aspects of the personal lives of those upon whom he eavesdrops and spies—is simply to capture the couple's conversation on tape, which he is then to deliver to his client. That is to say, Caul is to tape the talk while they walk the walk around

Union Square. Meanwhile, he becomes completely preoccupied with deciphering the meanings and implications of what they say to each other in their conversation. Because their conversation is blotted out by an unusual amount of background noise, Caul's technical task of getting as clear an auditory rendition as possible from the videotapes of the couple's conversational interchange is long, repetitive, and tedious as it occupies almost the entire time span of the film. In that opening taped surveillance scene, Coppola's camera focuses on Caul's team of cameramen, when they are positioned strategically in three locations around the square, and when they return to their headquarters, an easily identifiable white van equipped to the gills with the newest in technological equipment. The technical surveillance cameramen are shot filming from atop a billboard, from an upper story window, and at ground level among the milling crowd, where they zero in visually and by foot on their prey.

One particular opening image in Coppola's *Conversation* is uncannily similar to the opening of Powell's *Peeping Tom*, discussed in Chapter Four. As Caul focuses his surveillance on the couple, the audience looks simultaneously at the superimposition of director Coppola's crosshairs with his protagonist Caul's surveillance camera crosshairs. To repeat, this kind of superimposition is a cardinal example of doubling in films that occurs so often in voyeuristic sexual and surveillance stalking films as to appear iconic to me in cinematic stalking imagery. We, as audience, notice this doubling exactly at the moment that Ann, the woman of the stalked couple, realizes that the two of them are being stalked. She then makes sure their conversation is innocent except in places where she is certain that very loud street noises will blot out what they are saying. We realize that she knows they are under surveillance each time we see the two sets of crosshairs, Coppola's and Caul's, zoom in upon Ann and Mark. Caul alternates between stalking and returning to his white van that houses part of his surveillance team, to check, personally, on their work. A facsimile or replica of that van is to appear twenty-four years later in *Enemy of the State*, when a surveillance team, headed again by a character portrayed by Gene Hackman, is involved in uncannily similar surveillance stalking operations.

After his day's work in the field, Harry repairs to his office in an attempt to decipher the garbled-sounding conversation on the tape by doing what he can to filter out the Union Square noise. As Harry plays and replays his taped surveillance operation, we hear Mark plotting with Ann. "Later in the week, Sunday maybe," as Ann responds, "Sunday definitely." That part of the conversation comes to haunt us throughout the film. Harry Caul and his assistant, Stan, talk to each other, both watching the tapes for clues to help them understand the implications of what they have recorded.

CAUL: We'd get much better traction if you paid more attention to the recording than to what they were talking about.

STAN: I don't see why a couple of questions about what the hell's going on can get you so out of joint.

CAUL: Because I can't sit here and explain the personal problems of my clients.

The audio output shifts to Mark and Ann's dialogue, on the tape. "The Jack Tar Hotel. Three o'clock, room 773." We become equally haunted by the ambiguous implications of these words as *The Conversation* rolls on.

STAN: If you filled me in every once in a while, don't you ever think of that?

CAUL: [*increasingly, impatiently angry*] It has nothing to do with me, and even less to do with you.

STAN: It's curiosity! Did you ever hear of that? Just Goddamn human nature.

CAUL: [*Beginning to stumble over what he is saying*] Listen, if there's one sure fire rule that I have learned in this business is that I don't know anything about human nature. I don't know anything about curiosity. That's not part of what I what I do. What I—this is my business. And when I'm—

Stan gets up and leaves as Harry continues to wind and play, as he frantically and repeatedly tries to get a clearer rendering of the conversation between Mark and Ann in Union Square. The couple apparently succeeded in their attempt to limit their significant talk to areas where noise would mask on tape anything they were saying.

ANN: [*in an attempt to cast suspicion on her husband*] I think he's been recording my telephone calls.
MARK: We're spending too much time together here.
ANN: No, just a little longer . . . I love you.

Then Mark says something Harry Caul cannot hear. Caul alternates between rewinding and fast-forwarding when he hears Ann say, "I think he's been recording my telephone calls." He pretends to himself that he is simply technically and not personally involved with his eavesdropping into what he is hearing and seeing as the result of his professional bugging activity. When Caul cannot decipher just what the couple is saying, he applies his techniques more meticulously and decisively. Although we are not privy to the fine points of his technology, it is evident that he is painstakingly performing some very intricate operations. He is clearly more absorbed here with his technical work than with the content of the conversation. Finally, he makes what seems to us to be a minor but highly delicate adjustment to his equipment and we hear Mark clearly enunciate what is to become the key line of the entire film: "He'd kill us if he got the chance." Harry sits quietly, thrilled that he has eliminated all of the interfering static, apparently oblivious to any implications of what was said. He nods in great satisfaction, proud of a job well done, and shuts off his equipment as the scene fades.

After numerous viewings of this highly ambiguous film in segments and in its entirety, I decided to see what else I could learn about the film. On his Netflix DVD commentary, director Coppola says he was shocked to learn that the film utilized the very same surveillance and wire-tapping equipment that members of the Nixon administration used to spy on political opponents prior to the Watergate scandal. Although the filming of *The Conversation* was completed before the Nixon administration came to power, the spying equipment used in the film was apparently selected based on knowledge of the technology available prior to the Watergate era. I could only think of the similarities between the technologies available equally at that time to government surveillance operatives, private investigators, and eavesdroppers of all kinds, including those like myself who have become quite taken in their researches by the technological world we live in. Viewed now, *The Conversation* is a profoundly prescient film, raising issues about electronic surveillance that almost nobody was thinking about in the early 1970s, when Coppola finished the script. During filming, news stories began to appear about the break-in to Democratic headquarters to install bugging devices approved by President Richard Nixon.

From the start of *The Conversation*, we are offered important insights into Harry Caul's personality. As we have seen, Harry responds flatly and apparently self-deceptively; he is not curious and does not care anything about the personal lives of his clients who pay him to do his best. On the other hand, we learn early on that certain past work of his led to the murder of an entire family. We can see that this fatal outcome of his past eavesdropping haunts Harry and leaves us skeptical of his professed indifference from the very beginning. The balance of the film, however, develops to the point of crescendo in a nightmare about his intensely obsessional interest in the people he observes during every private investigation he directs. In fact, he has expended enormous psychic energy to avoid bearing guilt or responsibility, or accountability, for any mild or monumental mishaps in the lives of those he bugs and those who pay him to bug. Surveillance stalking can indeed be quite a dangerous occupation. Nothing makes that clearer than Caul's personal disintegration that we witness in *The Conversation*. Harry, quite unlike the celebrity stalker, Ron Galella (see Chapter Seven), is not a sociopath.

When the scene shifts from the Union Square surveillance territory to Harry's apartment, we become witnesses to the personally intimate details of Harry's life. We feel as though we are invading his privacy just as his team of eavesdropping private detectives has invaded that of the couple Ann and Mark. In the apartment, especially, but outside as well, Coppola's camera acts as a surveillance device to facilitate his audience's private investigation of his protagonist, Harry Caul. It does not always track him down immediately but later pans and then locates him. This brilliantly conceived usage of a "doubling" technique suggests that we, as audience, are stalking Caul and gives us a good sense of what it feels to be in his position, perennially ducking the eyes of the spectator in a real or imagined audience. In one iconic scene in this film, we see outside Harry's apartment window a construction crew demolishing a building and Harry playing a saxophone solo, albeit to recorded accompaniment. He bows his head and closes his eyes, as though looking and hearing only inward.

Intensely private, withdrawn, and suspicious, Harry maintains multiple locks on his door and we note the extent of his persecution anxieties as he suspiciously picks up a bottle of wine that his landlady has left inside his apartment to celebrate his birthday. Harry demands that she discard her keys. From then on in the film, we sense from his life style and body language that he is an anxiously paranoid man determined to protect his privacy by isolating himself from most people. His telephone is unlisted, he refuses to answer any question about his personal life, even from his mistress, whom he keeps sequestered in an apartment that he visits at his pleasure. Every time Caul walks anywhere—from his apartment to his office or from his office to his client's headquarters, or to use a public telephone for reasons of secrecy—he moves like a stalker and at the same time glances furtively around to see if anyone is following or stalking him.

Our sense of Harry Caul as a meticulous, dissociated personality becomes even more evident in his work at deciphering the conversation. His office is located in an isolated section of an abandoned warehouse with vast empty areas, and his personal workspace is enclosed in protective mesh wiring. Harry continues methodically sorting through his tapes of the couple, Ann and Mark. In one scene, he threads and synchronizes three tape recorders with the tapes from the three Union Square locales from which his eavesdropping surveillance team stalked the couple. By playing all three recorders at the same time and varying their volumes on a mixer, Harry is able to construct, synthesize, and splice together a fourth and clearer recording onto yet another tape-recording machine. Painstakingly, he rewinds and replays fragments of dialogue, slowly piecing together Ann and Mark's audible conversation that he has sifted out from the noises that the surveyed couple hoped would disguise the giveaway aspects of their forthcoming plans.

At this point, I would like to comment on an experience that I take to be a doubling or parallel process. As I worked at creating my own film clips for forthcoming oral presentations of surveillance stalking, using *The Conversation* as a prime illustrative example, I imagined I knew exactly what Caul was feeling as he kept playing and replaying his clips. I learned more and more via this way of winding and rewinding, as I tried to get my clips timed fastidiously and exactly right. The scene gripped me personally not only because of the ominous content of the conversation, but because it suggested yet another parallel between Caul's work and my own in researching the topic of stalking using film clips. Caul's repetitive winding reminded me of exactly what I had been doing in front of my television screen with my DVD remote control: clicking the forward, backward, and stop buttons to obtain my film clips of protagonist Caul doing his work, which struck me as a parallel doubling of my work, or *vice versa*. I was riveted on him, winding and rewinding just as I was doing while viewing the film and trying to obtain film clips for future oral presentations that would demonstrate Caul's work on bugging as a fascinating illustration of surveillance stalking. Actually, Caul's technology is quite unlike mine, which was just determined and repetitive pressing of the buttons on my remote control DVD device. Caul's devotion to his recorders was a professional technological breakthrough that was touted at a forthcoming eavesdroppers' or wire tappers' convention, while mine was restricted to new illustrations prepared for presentations at psychoanalytic meetings. Most important, Caul sees on his video that Ann knows that she is being walk-stalked and audio-video tape-bugged. Hackman, as Caul, never knew I was doing the same to him. At those times, Ann modifies the conversation with Mark accordingly to discussing something trivial: Mark watches Ann glancing around at Caul and the other members of his team who follow them, a guide for reserving the meaningful nub of the conversation, "He'd kill us if he could," for times when ambient noise was at its height. As a stalkee, Ann adapts her behavior to be maximally self-preservative. Little did she know that Caul would create a technological breakthrough that would preserve every word and nuance of her plans.

Caul's work, once again, is to obtain a clear taping of the conversation by eliminating the background noise, and he goes about it in a cool, professional manner, suggesting that his absorption with technology is holding together, however flimsily, a schizoid personality that functions as a container for his paranoid anxieties. When he finally hears the conversation *in toto* after his technological triumph of eliminating all competing static, it takes the form: "Sunday, 3:25, Jack Tar Hotel. If he had the chance, he would *kill* us." As we will come to know, he finally hears the last part as, "If he had the chance he would kill *us*." This last and entirely different emphasis on the word, "us," rather than on the word "kill," is critical to Caul's eventual comprehension of who was thinking of killing whom and who was paying his client. That reversal of emphasis reflects Coppola's genius in keeping protagonist and audience in a chronic state of ambiguity, so crucial to his creativity in making the film the masterpiece that it is.

Director Coppola leaves it very ambiguous for the viewing audience to know whether the events are truly occurring in objective reality or simply in the psychic and possibly hallucinatory mind of the protagonist. Certain theme music appears to indicate Caul's hallucinatory persecutory preoccupations, and when that music begins, we frequently see the lonely Caul looking over his shoulder to see whether or not he is being followed, or stalked. Just as stalking characterizes his major occupation, it also appears to be a major persecutory preoccupation. When he attends a convention of government and private security wire tappers, Caul's colleagues actually have bugged him, their most formidable rival, by dropping a pen in his jacket pocket in a "spy on the spy game." The practical joke or prank, when he finally notices it, loosens his defenses and instead of joining in the competitive fun, he feels and acts more persecuted as his personality decompensation increases. But Coppola always leaves it to us to guess whether Caul's persecutory reactions are hallucinatory or reality-based.

Caul thinks "The Director", Ann's husband, is behind his client's payments to bug, because he wants Ann and Mark, her lover, killed. Within a dream that Caul dreams prior to closing in on The Director's victims at the Jack Tar Hotel, Caul tells Ann that when he was five, his arm and leg were paralyzed for six months, and he could not walk. Once he punched his father's friend so hard that he died. This dream material within the film represents Coppola's attempt to provide us with the traumatic background for Harry's increasing guilt about the consequences of his paid work and his increasing obsessional concerns about the couple he is hired to wire-tap. After his dream reveals the traumatic underpinning in his own life story, Caul, still within the dream, warns Ann that she will be killed if she takes the chance, repeating more or less the same words of the conversation that he recorded. In the last part of the dream, Caul goes to the Jack Tar Hotel, opens the door of room 773, and sees The Director killing his wife, Ann. Then he sees someone coming out of the bathroom, which is bloodstained. When he wakes up, he realizes that the hooker he had picked up and had spent the night with at the convention had stolen the tapes. Apparently, she had been paid to dupe him, still part of the rival eavesdroppers' idea of a practical joke, by his major east coast professional rival, in a version with terrifying consequences for the "spy on the spy" game.

When Sunday finally rolls around, Caul tries to carry out in his real, waking life what he dreamed he did at the Jack Tar Hotel. For the remainder of the film, he appears to be stalked by his own persecutory ideas. Because the real-life scene mimics the dream content so accurately, some interpreters assume that this dreamed event also really happened later, while others consider this replay to be pure hallucination, marking Caul's psychotic breakdown. Yet, director Coppola himself, in the Netflix DVD interview, says things like "maybe this," "maybe that." It is crystal clear that Coppola's intention throughout his masterpiece is to leave the viewing audience with an overwhelming sense of uncertainty about what is real, what is unreal, what he intended, and what the audience thinks he intended. That is, one of his major missions is to induce a sense of uncertainty and ambiguity about what is objective and what is subjective.

In the meantime, it is important to note Harry Caul's totally undignified position as he goes to work in the same room he has dreamed about, crouched under the sink and taping the toilet in the room adjacent to 773 in the Jack Tar Hotel, where he is convinced he overhears The Director, Ann's husband, killing his wife and her lover. As viewing audience, we see only the overflowing toilet with blood and toilet paper spilling out, a dreamer's or waking person's nightmare if there ever was one. The image is very suggestive that no one has been thrown down the toilet but that Harry is hallucinating. Yet, to repeat, ambiguity is never absent even in this take on reality. The crowning uncertainty comes after Caul leaves the hotel and spots the supposedly murdered wife, Ann, sitting in a Mercedes and then, shortly after, he reads in the newspaper of The Director's death in an automobile accident. Still ambiguous, the accident could have been a frame or staged cover-up for his murder, or it could have really happened. By now, we see that Caul might have gotten it all wrong. We are never sure, and neither is Harry Caul, who had been paid to stalk the couple.

In the last scene, Harry realizes that once again he had become inadvertently involved with a killing in the course of his work because he could not dissociate himself personally and completely from his clients. Back in his apartment, playing his saxophone, he hears and rehears Mark's words on the tape differently from the way he had been hearing the conversation all along. Instead of "He'd *kill* us if he had the chance," he hears the conversation as "He'd kill *us* if he had the chance." Whether he hallucinated the critical difference in emphasis, or whether it was real within the confines of the film, his guilt plagues him for two reasons: first, he feels responsible for a murder and, second, his meticulous technological proficiency cannot guarantee against mistakes in judgment. The slight shift of emphasis in what he hears puts the focus on the couple, Ann and Mark, as the ones contemplating murder. Caul's guilt is as profound here for his assumed responsibility for The Director's death as it was when he thought he might be responsible for the couple's impending death. We see and hear him playing his saxophone, solo, to a background of recorded music, when his telephone rings. Harry picks up and there is no answer, although someone clearly remains on the line. Looking troubled, Harry returns to his chair and resumes his solo sax against the recorded background. A few minutes later, the phone rings again, and the *dénouement* begins. Harry, worn down by these intrusions weakly but anxiously mutters, "Hello", and we hear the sound of a rewinding tape coming through the speaker. Then a voice threatens: "We know that you know, Mr. Caul. For your own sake, don't get involved any further. We'll be listening to you." Through the speaker, he hears the background recording of the music he has been listening to while he plays. That is, Harry hears what he has just been playing on his saxophone played back over the phone. The best wire-tapper of all times has been given a warning that he is now the one being bugged.

We, the audience, wonder if Caul is hallucinating this whole thing or if he has been bugged as a practical joke by his professional rivals, just as they had bugged his fountain pen at the eavesdroppers' or private eyes' convention in a previous scene. It could be either, or other things as well; thus, the uncertainty on our, the audience's, part. Caul never finds the device. As we now know, Coppola meant to keep levels of Caul's reality testing ambiguous. In the Netflix DVD interview Coppola says, "Maybe there was no bug at all, maybe the bug was in the saxophone, the only place Harry did not look. Who knows?"

Some viewers assume that the call has come from Harry Caul's client, who seems in the end to be protecting the young adulterous couple, and not The Director, as Harry originally assumed. Others believe the call might have come from the jokers at the convention who were Harry's rivals and who had bugged him earlier as a practical joke. Still others, like Zusman, maintain that Harry has hallucinated the call, as well as the idea that his apartment has been bugged. Whatever the case, the torment Caul feels is, first and foremost, his own self-imposed retribution for his guilt and shame at being more personally involved than he ever would have admitted to. This theory suggests that he is having a serious emotional breakdown as his entire defensive system that propelled him to the top of his profession has cracked. Whoever made that final call, whoever telephone-stalked Caul in this way, whoever eavesdropped on Caul by placing bugging devices in his sanctified apartment, Coppola meant for many of the specifics of the case to be ambiguous. As the film ends, Harry turns his apartment upside down, searching for the bug, but to no avail. We watch him on hands and knees combing every inch of his floor for electronic bugs. His expertise in planting such electronic bugs on others' territory has prepared him to search and rip apart almost every inch of his own apartment. The background music plays on as he slowly and deliberately unscrews every fitting and upturns every corner that he himself would have put a device in had he been the orchestrating culprit rather than the bewildered victim. Once Caul has vandalized his entire living space, at first slowly and deliberately, then moving on to frenzied violent destruction of his property and possessions, he sits down with his saxophone and plaintively plays on in the midst of the war zone he has created.

The final mocking, voyeuristic, observational shot pans left, right, and left again, across the disintegrated rubble of Harry Caul's apartment. He sits amid the devastation playing a solo blues number on his saxophone, assuaging himself with its sound. He has not found the bug that Coppola has elsewhere hinted might be in his saxophone, and he who had been perpetrator is now the ultimate victim of both his own conscience and of today's miraculous electronic surveillance, stripped of all personal privacy. So, this film shows transformations in the sanity of a surveillance stalker, a man who initially averred no guilt, to a man obsessed with guilt to the point of possible psychotic disorganization. Harry Caul, the professional eavesdropping private eye, is now the quintessential Stalker, Hacker, Voyeur, and Spy, in this morality fable of our time.

The Lives of Others: *remorse in a state-sanctioned Stasi stalker*

I move now from surveillance stalking in a private professional life, as told in *The Conversation*, to a film about surveillance stalking in professional political life. *The Lives of Others* portrays one particular Stasi surveillance stalker's politically sanctioned spying in the East German state in the year 1984—yes, *1984*—five years before the fall of the Berlin wall. The Stasi were the secret police of East Germany, the official state security service of the German Democratic Republic (GDR). The group has been regarded as the most effective and repressive intelligence and secret police agencies to have ever existed. The Stasi was also one of the most hated and feared institutions of the East German government. In this film, directed by Florian Henckel von Donnesmarck, the late, great German film star, Ulrich Muhe, plays Gerd Wiesler, the chief Stasi operative who is assigned to videotape the lives of an artistic couple, an actress and her playwright, who is also her lover. At first, Wiesler seems politically motivated to perform his sleazy job, but later becomes poignantly attached to the loving or "primal scene" couple, Christa-Maria Sieland (Martina Gedeck), the actress, and Georg Dreyman (Sebastian Koch), the playwright. Minister Hempf, the nefarious leader of the GDR in East Berlin, has political motives to destroy the free-thinking writer, Dreyman. He also has erotic designs on Christa-Maria and orders Wiesler to personally monitor the couple under direct audio-visual surveillance so that he, Hempf, can get any evidence he can against his sexual and political rival, Georg's possible defection to West Berlin, in order to get rid of him. Wiesler, the Stasi operative, stakes out his targets and meticulously bugs their apartment by setting up his audio-video equipment on the floor above.

Once again, as in *The Conversation*, we witness the workings of the surveillance technology of our times in its most destructive and invasive capability. From his prime spot on his victim's premises, he spies into their lives by personally monitoring and recording all that he sees and hears, quite absorbed with the intimacy that the couple display during their close and loving personal and sexual contacts. As he witnesses their sexual scenes, we, in the audience, in yet another instance of doubling in the film, are also witness to these primal scenes. That is, director von Donnesmarck focuses on protagonist Stasi operative Wiesler's video equipment as it focuses on the primal scene between protagonists Georg and Christa-Maria. Additionally, we witness a scene in which Wiesler's boss, Hempf, who is giving all of these orders in the first place, regularly, each week, gropes and rapes the heroine, Christa-Maria, forcing her to submit to his sexual advances. Our privacy is, in a sense, invaded, even though we are willing and usually eager witnesses of this brilliant film. Such is the "normative" voyeurism of filmgoing and film loving.

In the first scene in which the surveillance operation is being set up, Wiesler observes Christa-Maria returning to the home she shares with Georg. He looks pensively at her stepping out of Hempf's car after one of her regularly scheduled tryst meetings with the boss. She believes she must continue the reprehensible sex *rendezvous* as blackmail victim to protect her beloved Georg's art, the book he is currently writing. Most importantly, she believes she has no choice but to submit to sexual assault in order to save their lives from ruination by the reprehensible GDR. Wiesler then sees Georg leave, the signal for him to knock on the Stasi surveillance van for them to set up shop in their stalking perch. The Stasi team of surveillance stalking eavesdroppers then leaves their home-base van to the accompaniment of stealthy sounding background music, approaches the front door of the Dreyman house, and, with highly professional looking equipment, open the lock on the front door. The van is reminiscent of Harry Caul's base of operations in *The Conversation* and of the one that appears later as its double in *Enemy of the State*. This scene then repeats and creates logos for similar ones in other films about breaking and entering by private, professional, and government sponsored surveillance operatives who spy on others for their livelihood. The details here are psychologically chilling, as compared with, say, *Enemy of the State*, to be discussed in Chapter Nine, in which they are thrilling in the mode of the classic film car-stalking chase. The penetrative action of drilling the keyhole in *Lives* is a premonition of the sexual activities the Stasi are preparing to spy on and record. In the next scene, Wiesler has the surveillance camera upstairs focus on George and Christa-Maria who are tenderly kissing prior to more passionate foreplay. As their explicitly sexual behavior commences, the camera filming *The Lives of Others* shifts from downstairs to upstairs so that we get a good look at Wiesler, who has been looking at their love-making through his surveillance camera, and recording via typing down upstairs everything they are doing intimately downstairs. He baldly writes, "Then they presumably have intercourse." Once again, we are participants in an instance of doubling technique, this time of the film director von Donnersmarck's camera and the Stasi protagonist's camera, just as we were in watching *Rear Window, Peeping Tom,* and *The Conversation.* Once again, we see how this film technique has been tailored to convey primal scene stalking in film representations, adapted here to the context of state sanctioned government surveillance. Wiesler's relief operative takes his Stasi buddy's place at the home-installed technological viewing stand and he remarks lewdly as he tries to engage Wiesler in some fun at their government job: "They're already at it! Unbelievable! These artists! They're always at it! That's why I prefer monitoring artists to priests or peace activists." Wiesler does not find the remark funny, hangs his head, sadly, and leaves, clearly questioning what he has been asked to do in this professional assignment of invading the most intimate privacy of others. By now we are immersed in a political surveillance stalking culture that does not hesitate to stalk the sexual lives of others, although with varying degrees of emotional distance.

In a subsequent scene, we get a good look at the *modus operandi* of Minister Hempf as he reaps the rewards of the Stasi stalking operation he assigned to Wiesler. He follows Christa-Maria in his chauffeured car, and reprimands her for missing their last scheduled Thursday meeting. "Come on, get in," he says. She accedes as he forcefully says, "You don't know what's good for you." We are forced to witness and listen to his mounting sexual excitement as he fondles her against her will. Hempf taunts, "Tell me you don't need it too. Just tell me and I'll let you go." He increases his assault on his victim, Christa-Maria, as we watch. In films of explicit sexuality, the film audience, as well as the protagonists who are sexually assaulted, is assaulted in a scene that arouses unwanted sexual involvement. Hempf's sexuality is perverse because through it he makes use of the actress as a sex object to gratify his sexual and political ambitions. Christa-Maria submits to this callously powerful representative of the GDR patriarchal state in an unfortunately self-sacrificial attempt to save her beloved's life and art, at the expense of her own. In this post feminist era, we are shocked to see a powerless, sexually submissive woman who becomes the targeted rape victim of the male sexual stalker who has gained the support of an infamously patriarchal political culture.

The film proceeds as Wiesler, at his surveillance post in Georg Dreyman's home, hears Hempf's car as it arrives to drop off Christa-Maria once again. In a slowly developing but definitive change of character, Wiesler has just noted to himself, "Time for some bitter truths." He decides to tip off Georg about Hempf's presumptuous blackmailing of Christa-Maria and anonymously rings him up to prompt him to go to his front door and to look out and figure out what has been going on between his beloved Christa-Maria and Hempf. Wiesler surveys the scene he has set in motion through the same surveillance technological equipment that served his wrongdoing as a voyeuristic stalker. In this instance, his allegiance to the GDR has shifted to a well-intentioned good deed to convey the terrible truth to Georg. Georg overhears Hempf saying to Christa-Maria as she alights, "Next Thursday at the Metropol." Von Donnersmarck's camera switches to Wiesler, who now focuses his camera on the shower and he watches Christa-Maria wash off the remnants of her bodily submission to Hempf that she has once again detested and revoltingly endured for the presumed sake of her lover and their art.

Having interceded truthfully with Georg, Wiesler now turns to helping Christa-Maria. When his Stasi relief operator comes in to continue the surveillance watch of the couple, Wiesler stalks off, reprimanding his collaborator: "What are you staring at?" In an incredibly heart-breaking scene, he goes to the nearby bar where he knows Christa-Maria repairs regularly, in a compelling sympathetic attempt to turn his malevolent spying into a benevolently truthful stalking cause. After his second double vodka, Christa-Maria walks in, orders a cognac, and sits at the table in front of him, her back to his seriously glancing eyes and face. He approaches her table.

WIESLER: Madam?

C-M: Go away, I want to be alone.

WIESLER: Ms. Sieland,

C-M: Do we know each other?

WIESLER: You don't know me but I know you. Many people love you for who you are.

C-M: [*Clearly indicating that she can trust this man, if only with pessimistic and fatalistic reserve*] Actors are never who they are.

WIESLER: [*revealing he knows what has been going on between her and Hempf and trying to indicate not only that he does not judge her poorly but that she is not obliged to be doing what she is doing for survival reasons*] You are. [*He sits down now, facing her eye to eye in a mutually gazing loving connection.*] I've seen you on stage. You were more who you are than you are now.

C-M: So you know what I'm like.

WIESLER: I'm your audience [*a double entendre referring to the theater in which she performs and what he has surveillance-stalked from his Stasi perch*].

C-M: I have to go. [*She stands up but does not shift her gaze from him*]

WIESLER: Where to?

C-M: I'm meeting an old classmate. I . . .

WIESLER: [*aware that he has just heard the same cover-up that she has used with Georg*] You see? Just now you weren't being yourself.

C-M: No?

WIESLER: No.

C-M: [*slowly sitting down, with pathos and still not shifting her gaze*] So you know her well, this Christa-Maria Sieland . . . What do you think? Would she hurt someone who loves her above all else? Would she sell herself for art?

WIESLER: For art? You already have art. That'd be a deal. You are a great artist. Don't you know that?

C-M: And you are a good man.

The scene ends with her leaving the bar and him looking sad as he is overcome with a prophetic feeling that this is not going to end well.

When I attended a dinner party hosted by the German Psychoanalytical Association at the 2007 meeting of the International Psychoanalytical Association in Berlin, some German psychoanalysts at my table started a discussion of the film, *The Lives of Others*. They seemed unanimous in their understanding of what caused Wiesler's change from ruthless Stasi investigator to humane champion of the loving couple: curiosity about the primal scene. These psychoanalysts had all lived through the struggles and dangers during the cold war periods when East and West Berlin were separated by the wall, and some had lived through the Second World War Nazi era as well. Yet, they believed, largely, that the single theme of this film is "primal scene" fantasies of a voyeur-stalker who values art above politics. From their point of view, the surveillance stalker's guilt about inserting himself voyeuristically into the intimate lives of the lovers was the one factor that ultimately motivates him to the selfless heroism that dominates the latter part of the film. They seemed to be unaware of the centrality of the political surveillance motif. The non-German attendees appeared better able to grasp the confluence of primal scene voyeurism and political surveillance stalking that grew out of GDR ordinances. Visitors argued that as the film develops touchingly toward its *dénouement,* the operative, Wiesler, forfeits any and all political ambition and opportunity in his final and deliberate decision not to deliver the videotapes to his boss, Hempf. Instead, he takes the moral high ground as he decides to use his privileged and prestigious position to free and save the couple whose intimate sanctity the state had ordered him to violate. The non-German dinner guests, those who had not lived in Berlin during the cold war, believed that symbolic "primal scene" material was indisputably a motivating force, but was secondary to filmmaker von Donnersmarck's intentions to convey the psychological nuances of human rights violations inherent in the surveillance stalking sanctioned by the GDR. As focused as they were on primal scene elements, they were chiefly interested in Wiesler's positive humanistic personality development. The Stasi operative started out as cold, depersonalized, dehumanized, and robotic, and threw his weight around by spying on the lives of others. Later, however, in a mesmerizing transformation of character, he becomes immersed, enmeshed, and very sympathetic to the free, fulfilling, and rich lives of the artist couple, lives, unlike his own, that flout Nazi–Stalinist totalitarianism. Perhaps the non-German visiting psychoanalysts were more able to distance themselves because they had not been subject to the political immersion that still influenced their German colleagues.

Wiesler's personality as a Stasi stalker, then, morphs into the *reverse* of the more usual portrayal of the surveillance stalker, as we saw in *The Conversation,* as a calculating, socially alienated user of people to gratify personal and narcissistically driven desires that include power and money. He changes from an isolated investigator for the totalitarian state, who had used people to satisfy state interests, into a more or less complete and connected human being. He sees, in the couple he stalks, a passionate commitment to art and to each other. He experiences their fulfillment as a principled rebuke that becomes a transformational incentive to change his own limited and manipulative life. This loner, this solitary state-sanctioned clandestine predator, develops a large measure of sympathy and love for his "quarry," with some similarities to Harry Caul's caring about his victims in *The Conversation*. The big difference between the two is that Wiesler develops and applies to life an admirable moral compass, while Caul falls apart at the seams.

Wiesler tips off Georg about being under Stasi state surveillance, but, in his commitment to trust and truth, his personality metamorphosis fails to save Christa-Maria. Her guilt and shame about succumbing sexually to Hempf overcomes her wish to survive: she throws herself suicidally into the path of an onrushing car that kills her. Despite the primal scene elements and voyeurism that guide his video surveillance, Wiesler's love is not perverse. He is instinctively drawn to the quarry he has captured on videotape because of the loving humanity of the artistic couple he longs to be with and to be like. Although he is still beholden to the thuggish political minister, Hempf, who commands and masterminds his voyeuristic occupation, Wiesler's new unbidden perception frees a heart-rending potential for love that truly transforms him. After the fall of the Berlin wall in 1989, the playwright, Georg Dreyman, researches his case that is stored in the post cold war East German Archives. He learns that his former stalker, Wiesler, had become his savior and he is overcome with gratitude. Dreyman discovers that Wiesler has been demoted from his prestigious Stasi job and now earns his living as a postal delivery worker. We now witness a dramatic surveillance role reversal. The film ends as Georg benevolently follows Wiesler in his car, looking at him as he proceeds along his mail route delivering letters. Then Georg car-stalks his erstwhile surveillance stalker. Their stalker–stalkee roles are reversed. Our eyes, and von Donnersmarck's camera, are now focused on Wiesler, following his every move, whereas, until this point, the film's camera was focused on Wiesler following Georg's every move. In one move near the end of the film, Georg asks his driver to stop, gets out of his car, and follows postman Wiesler on foot, stops, returns to his car, and orders his driver to take him home. In the next shot, we, in the film audience, are the only stalkers left, as we follow Wiesler with our eyes and find him stopped in front of a bookstore. We then follow him into the bookstore where we watch him buy the book that Georg Dreyman wrote in Wiesler's honor, *Die Sonate vom Guten Menschen,* translated into the English language as *Sonata for A Good Man.* Georg fully credits Wiesler in his front page dedication: "In gratitude to HGW XX17," Wiesler's Stasi identification number that Georg Dreyman had found in the post 1989 Berlin archives. All breathe more easily after this surveillance-stalking tale ends well, ultimately directed to the best in humankind. The uplifting finale could not contrast more with the devastation of surveillance stalker Harry Caul in *The Conversation,* and erotomanic sexual stalkers Evelyn in *Play Misty for Me,* Alex in *Fatal Attraction,* and voyeuristic killer–stalker Mark in *Peeping Tom.*

Caché*: political terrorism inside and outside a stalkee's mind*

Director Michael Haneke illustrates the inner workings of the minds of terrorized stalkees every bit as much, if not more than, any other filmmaker noted in this book. Extremist socio-political events loom at the forefront of the plot and provide reasons for surveillance stalkers to terrorize their prey by various and ingenious methods. In this case, the stalker's motives, while indisputably personal, are embedded in a terroristic political context. The major theme of this surveillance-stalking film is guilt. The major characters, like those in *The Conversation* and *The Lives of Others,* are plagued with guilt for something they have either done or felt at an earlier time in their lives.

The film *Caché,* translated as "Hidden," was directed by Michael Haneke and stars Daniel Auteuil as Georges Laurent and Juliette Binoche as Anne Laurent, a Parisian couple with a teenaged son, Pierrot (Lester Makedonsky). An anonymous videotaper whose precise identity we do not know at any time during the film, proper, stalks them but those "in the know" do identify the individual as the final credits roll. The stalker, from the beginning, deposits anonymous videotapes on the Laurents' front doorstep. The tapes show their house under surveillance, presumably by a hidden camera located across the street. Their everyday comings and goings in and out have been recorded for them to see. One learns as the film progresses that the videos are the anonymous stalker's terrorizing attempts at revenge for some alleged past involvement in political terrorism as a consequence of the 1961 Algerian War and the Parisian massacre of Algerians. Someone, whom we notice only in the images accompanying the final rolling credit lines of *Caché* has been identified by film buffs as the culprit, at least by those sharp-eyed viewers and critics who notice what goes on "out of the box" or the usual boundaries of a film's beginning and end. The Laurent couple views each of their stalker's videotapes, the visual context of which often simply doubles the images of the house and its surrounds that have been captured by Haneke's camera, and that we, as viewing audience, have just looked at for many minutes as very long and quiet scenes.

Anne, early on in the film, shows one of the tapes to her dinner guests after telling them when the doorbell rings, "I think it's our stalker." Georges adds, "It's presumably to show we're under surveillance." And are they scared! Anne believes they are being stalked in connection with an adulterous affair she is involved in with a man named Pierre. Georges has other ideas. He believes an Algerian man, Majid (Maurice Benichou), now living in Paris, but who, as a child, lived with Georges and his family of origin, might be the stalking mastermind behind the planted cassettes. Georges's parents had promised to adopt Majid when he was six years old, about the same age Georges was then. Instead, Georges's parents reneged and sent Majid to an orphanage after his parents had been dismissed from their employ during the 1961 war. Majid's parents were killed during the 1961 Algerian riots and massacre of Algerians living in Paris. Georges, bearing transgenerational guilt, is convinced that Majid is terrorizing them and attributes to the murdered Algerians' son the motive of revenge toward him personally for a lie about Majid that Georges told his parents at the age of six that led to Majid's underprivileged, underclass life, while Georges, in contrast, was treated as a little king. The entire film develops the theme of these origins of the guilt of the stalkees to be, although the plot elements of Anne's guilt are subordinate to those of Georges.

I select the film for two important illustrative purposes. For one, it gets to the heart of the frequently seen psychological and socio-political interface of surveillance stalking. For another, it provides a fascinating, often one-on-one, juxtaposition of the camera work directed by Haneke and the camera work of the surveillance stalker who terrorizes the couple with home videos. It is, to my mind, the best example we have of the doubling and parallel processes that are so ubiquitous in films about voyeuristic sexual and surveillance stalking. It is sometimes, but not always, possible to distinguish who filmed which scenario we see, Haneke's film-making camera or the terrorizing film tapes generated by the surveillance cameras that constitute a major part of Haneke's narrative. This ambiguity in the origin of the images we gaze at is paralleled by ambiguities in the narrative plot throughout this masterpiece of a film. We are not tipped off by literal crosshairs such as those in *Peeping Tom*. We are, therefore, often left to guess whose camera has taken the shot we see before our eyes: Haneke's or that of the fictional videotaper who surveillance-stalks the Laurents.

The film opens with the introductory credits accompanied by a background scene of the Laurents' house that has been bugged. We do not know it, but Haneke's camera work is signaling us to keep our eyes open during the opening and closing credits to help us detect and identify the surveillance stalker. As we watch line after line of the opening credits, our eyes are glued to Haneke's image of the house at which the stalker leaves the videotapes that feature the very images we are watching. All is silent and we do not even know that the film has begun behind the credit display until we see a man walking and a few more scenes of real-time life. Then the two cameras zoom in on the house, at which time we, as film spectators, see the same scene of the house that the stalked couple is watching on their television screen on which they view the deposited videotape for a clue to make sense of their creepy sensation of being stalked *in vivo* as well as on video. We become aware of this uncanny doubling from the very start: Haneke's camera and stalker protagonist's camera do more than alternate their images of the very same shot of the house. To repeat: they superimpose them without the clue of crosshairs that customarily characterize doubling. A full five minutes later, the scene shifts from the exterior to the interior of the house we have seen in the two superimposed viewings. The couple who lives inside, Anne and Georges Laurent, are trying to figure out what could be going on with regard to the videotape left on their doorstep. Georges concludes, "Some idiot playing games." Then they realize their son, Pierrot, is missing, and they discuss the tape further. Director Haneke very subtly attempts to draw our suspicions toward the boy as somehow involved in the video stalking. Pierrot returns and joins them at the dinner table. He is vague about where he has been. Haneke fans, and those like me who have watched this film numerous times in order to figure out its subtleties, would know by now that Pierrot's vagueness and slow conversation provide significant clues as to who the stalker might be, and that the stalker might be working in cahoots with Pierrot. This film indeed requires multiple viewings and prolonged study if it is to be understood at all.

The scene shifts to the swimming pool at Pierrot's school, another clue to the possibility that Pierrot and his coach might be stalkers working in tandem. At this point, however, we have no idea why the coach might be involved. He is simply prompting Pierrot on as he swims, and then the scene shifts quickly to another view of the front of the Laurents' house. People and cars pass, doors open and close as in the opening shot of the house front. The eyes of the audience have been glued for a full three minutes to this still shot. Anne, alone at home now and obviously frightened, calls Georges to come home from work to watch the creepy videotaped scene that we, the film audience have just witnessed. The tape left on the stalked Laurents' doorstep is exactly the same as the one we have just spent three minutes looking at as film audience of *Caché*. This is the second time we screen, this time along with the Laurent family protagonists, that long, quiet scene of their house front. We are beginning to get a feel for what the characters in the film are feeling as they are being stalked because we have just seen what they have seen and, as the saying goes, a picture is worth a thousand words. The plot thickens. Along with the tape, the stalker has left a crumpled picture, apparently drawn by a child, of a face with blood pouring out of the mouth. Anne wonders whether to call the police while Georges opts not to. Once again, Pierrot is missing, and Haneke's signature clue is present: that Pierrot must be involved in the videotape deliveries because they arrive only when he is away. The Laurents then receive some troubling hang-up phone calls, another common form of stalking, which they connect in their minds to the stalking tapes.

Next, the Laurents have an altercation in their street with a black man, presumably an Algerian, who is riding his bicycle in the wrong direction. We sense that the racial disparity will be important to this plot. Georges even wonders if he is their stalker. The scene immediately shifts to the steps of Pierrot's school, where Georges picks up Pierrot. This is the very same background scene that will appear at the end of the film behind the rolling credits. Here, we watch Pierrot walk down the steps and get into his father's car. The plot thickens, again, as Pierrot shows his father a postcard that a teacher had given him with the same image that George and Anne have received: that face with blood coming out of its mouth. Is Pierrot being stalked, too? Will we ever understand how these spooky images come together into a cohesive narrative, or will they just continue on associatively, as it were, with no conventional boundaries to guide our comprehension of the narrative? Unless, of course, we figure out that someone inside the school, such as Pierrot's swimming coach, is a culprit. The very next scene is of a dinner party at the Laurents' home. In the middle of animated conversation, the doorbell rings, and another videotape is delivered. Georges opens the door, picks it up, and stares down the street. We see a figure moving here and another moving there but have no idea who they are. Fear in the viewing audience mounts suspensefully. Georges challenges the stalker to show his face, but the stalker, if around, is hiding in the dark. George removes the tape from its familiar white bag along with yet another drawing, this time of what looks like a bird with blood spurting out if its neck. When he returns to his dinner party, Anne tells the guests that she is on edge because in the last few days, when the doorbell rings, tapes have been left. A guest asks Georges, in front of the other guests, if he has gone to the police. Georges prepares to show the tape to the guests and tries to explain it away by saying that someone appears to be interested in Anne's comings and goings, diverting us away from the political and toward personal marital suspicions. But this tape turns out to be different from its predecessors. It is of a rural scene of Georges's childhood home.

Next we see Georges paying a visit to that home, where his mother now is dying. He tells her a dream he just had about Majid, the boy, now a man living in Paris, who had expected Georges's parents to adopt him at the time of the Algerian crisis. In this shift of locale to his childhood home, Georges also introduces to us, the film audience, the name of Majid, the man that he now suspects is his stalker. His mother claims not to remember anything about the name that appears to be plaguing Georges in this way. He spends the night at his childhood country home, and either dreams or imagines the next image, an axe cutting off a chicken's head, spattering blood all over a child's face and torso. It looks as though the child Georges had killed the bird and blamed the child Majid for his deed, perhaps the basis for Georges's parents sending Majid to an orphanage, perhaps not. But the incident was surely the basis for Georges's fear and guilt and of the entire later stalking scenario. Then we see an image of Georges as a child watching that chicken die in apparent torture. We immediately know this scene corresponds to the image of the crumpled notes that accompany the stalker's planted videotapes of the Laurents' Paris home. In Georges's dream, the child Majid approaches him with the axe as though to kill him, and Georges wakes up from his nightmare, terrified and short of breath. We apprehend the deadly terror that these real and fantasied images of stalking can induce in a guilt-ridden man.

The scene shifts back to Paris, where Georges is driving through an Algerian neighborhood that is clearly downscaled in comparison with the gentrified one he and his family inhabit. The lifestyles of the people who live in this strange place must, like the servants in the childhood home he has just visited, be in startling contrast to the lavish cocktail and dinner party circuit to which Georges and his unoppressed peers have become accustomed. Georges has been driving to a particular low-rent apartment located in this Algerian neighborhood by following directions presented on a tape that had landed on his doorstep. We are led to believe, falsely as it turns out, that Georges's stalker is the adult, Majid, who has left explicit instructions for Georges to visit him. If by now the reader is a bit confused by the sequence of events I am recounting, that is because I am trying to follow Haneke's sequence, which deliberately attempts to convey the time non-linearly. Nonetheless, I shall try to convey the images of this film as director Haneke intends for us to see them. Anne now becomes convinced that Majid has been terrorizing them, and Georges sets out on his own to confront the presumed stalker-terrorist. The adult Majid opens the door, and recognizes Georges, whom he has not seen since childhood when Georges axed the chicken and Majid got the blame. On first viewing the film, I was sure it was Majid who had been sending the tapes. On further viewings, the ambiguity that Haneke intended to convey as to the stalker's identity became quite evident. Majid is a least likely candidate, except for those who are xenophobic about French Algerians. Georges, nonetheless, is completely taken up with his guilt-ridden fantasy and assumes that Majid has been blackmailing him with the videotapes. He asks him if he wants money and Majid seems surprised. Georges shows him one of the crumpled pictures, but nothing about it seems to register with Majid. Georges thinks Majid is playing a game, but we are beginning to know better, and realize that Georges, via his own projected guilt, has constructed a false narrative. The picture does ring a bell in Majid's mind, but he is obviously taken by surprise. Haneke has given us even more reason now to suspect that it is not Majid but someone else who has been stalking the Laurent couple. Nonetheless, he has Georges persist with his theory and his guilt-based fantasies, and has him accuse Majid directly. Majid believes Georges is replaying the unequal relationship dating from their childhood, during which Georges would often accuse Majid unjustly. Georges counters that Majid was the older and stronger child, and that does not give him license to threaten George's family now. In a counter terroristic attempt at self-defense, Georges admits that he is threatening Majid in the here and now, leaves, and apparently reports the French-Algerian to the police in a request for an order of restraint. The stalkee has become the bully, but, as it turns out, of the wrong man.

The scene changes immediately to Pierrot swimming in his school pool, as his coach walks back and forth at the side of the pool while the swimmers swim their laps once again. All of director Haneke's hidden elements—the literal translation of the term *caché* is "hidden"—once again add up to Pierrot's involvement in this bizarre stalking scenario within a weirdly off-beat film about stalking. Pierre wins the race as his parents cheer him on from the poolside, and they hug him. Suddenly, in Haneke's typically non-linear and bafflingly boundary-shifting style, the scene goes back to Majid, still sitting where we last saw him, in the kitchen of his apartment, thinking of the confrontation with Georges and the tragic childhood reminiscences it has evoked. He begins to weep and then sobs as he looks at the crumpled picture of the child with a bloodied face. It turns out that this very scene of Haneke's has also, within the film plot, been videotaped and delivered, and we wonder if Majid did not do it, then who did? Once again, we watch the Laurents viewing a recently delivered copy. It seems, now, as though someone other than Majid is doing the filming. Could it be his son? Is there a connection between Majid's son and their son, Pierrot? Who knows? *Caché* is a film about the psychic reality of men who feel terrifying guilt about past wrongs. Haneke is not concerned with objective or material reality. In the DVD interview with Haneke, the director says that throughout the film he has constructed images capable of multiple interpretations, so reminiscent of Coppola's. "I want to keep *The Conversation* uncertain and its interpretative possibilities ambiguous."

Georges, however, holds on to his version of objective familial and political reality. He lets on to Anne that he has suspected Majid. He explains that, in 1961, following the Parisian massacre of Algerians, all remaining French Algerians were asked to leave Paris. Majid's parents left, but Georges's parents promised their son, who remained, a better life, such as the Laurent couple now live with their son, Pierrot. They did not keep their promise. Short-changed by Georges's parents, who apparently believed their son's lie about who killed the chicken, Majid also survived his parents and the tens of thousands of his people who were murdered. Presumably, he was left with a burden of guilt of his own. Georges admits to Anne that he threatened Majid when they were boys and they agree that Majid then might have wanted revenge, which the couple think he must now be carrying out toward their family. Georges learns from the television studio where he is a producer that a tape of his recent visit to Majid's Parisian apartment has been sent to his studio, but has been destroyed. We now realize that someone other than Majid must definitely have been filming and depositing the tapes. Georges returns to Majid's apartment and rings the bell, but no one answers. The scene shifts to Anne and Pierre, the man she has been having an affair with. She returns home to find Georges watching a television broadcast about a new Algerian crisis. Once again, they notice that their son Pierrot is missing, as he always seems to be whenever a tape has been left on his parents' doorstep. They cannot find him and call the police with a charge of kidnapping. Georges returns with the police to Majid's apartment. A young Algerian man, who turns out to be Majid's son opens the door. His appearance allows for the interpretation that he may have taken the pictures and stalked the Laurents with his terrorizing videotapes. Is Majid's son Pierrot's swimming coach? Will we ever really know when Haneke's reality seems so different from Georges's? The police, who explain to Majid's son they are investigating a kidnapping, ask about the child, Pierrot, and the young Algerian asks, what child? Majid and his son are taken to jail and we get a good look at Majid's son's face in the police wagon. Both father and son are released because the tapes hold no evidence that they are the culprits.

The mother of a friend he was visiting returns Pierrot home. Director Haneke's camera shows once again the front of the house scene that appears in most of the stalking videotapes. These familiar superimposed camera views suggest once again a connection between Pierrot and the stalker. Pierrot lets his mother know that he never called about where he is staying because he is angry with her for having an affair with Pierre. So she feels guilty for her own reasons just as Georges feels guilty for his. She defensively explains to her son, but he remains sullen. In this way, the oedipal narrative enters the picture and prepares us for the interpretation that Majid's son, the swimming coach, and Georges's son, Pierrot, share common motives for stalking Georges. Once again the scene shifts to Pierrot's school, where his parents accompany him to the swimming pool. That recurrent scene is not as incidental as we once might have thought and the pool is beginning to look more related to the stalking than it did in its first appearance. Georges returns to Majid's apartment at Majid's invitation. We are about to witness some gruesome sadomasochistic violence. Majid gently bids Georges to enter, and tells him he had no idea about the tapes. He then says, "I wanted you to be present," takes a knife, and slits his own throat in a way shocking to the character Georges and the viewing audience. Majid's blood splatters the wall in a scene undeniably representing the blood of the chicken in the sketches that accompany the planted videotapes of Georges's home. Georges returns home, overcome with horror, sorrow, and confusion. Most important, both he and his wife Anne also appear overcome with their personal guilt, Georges for his family's ostracism of the Algerian, Majid, and Anne for her marital infidelity, with which this terrible act seems to resonate. We, the audience are formulating even more possible motives for the stalkees not getting more serious help in tracking down their stalker. Their stalkee psychology is made quite clear, made up of many different and not always clearly related reasons. Grievously, slowly, and deliberately, they discuss an alibi for Georges's absence from home at the time of Majid's violent suicide in the event that the police become suspicious of their past and present connections.

To complicate matters even more, Georges goes to work and waits with Anne's lover, Pierre, for the elevator. The Algerian boy whom we saw in Majid's apartment, his son (Walid Afkir) and Pierre's swimming coach, as far as we can tell, and believe me, it is not so easy, is also there. Majid's son tells Georges he wants to have a word with him. In this scene, Haneke clearly, that is, by association and contiguity of scenes, wants us to know that the young Algerian is somehow involved. He gets in the elevator with Georges, we get a good look at his face, and he descends to Georges's floor, stalking him into his office in a new way. Majid's son asks, "Why are you so scared, sir?" clearly aiming at his stalkee's inner related guilt. At the same time, he seems to want to avenge his father's death by making Georges feel more and more guilty for the crimes against humanity of his family before him, those committed by Georges's parents when they reneged on their promise of adoption by committing Majid to the orphanage that impacted so enormously on the Algerian Majid, his parents, and his son. Georges offers his sympathy and then turns on him when he will not leave the office and accuses him of being the stalker who planted the tapes, and tells the young man that he feels the guilty pain of the stalkee as the police corroborated his statement. He transfers his sense of guilt into accusing the young Algerian of the criminality. Georges says he will call the police to have Majid's son, the young Algerian swimming coach, ejected. He feels stalked again as the swimming coach son refuses to leave. Georges angrily confronts Majid's son: "You terrorize my family and me. Your father wasn't capable of that." The son counters that the orphanage Georges' family sent his father to, in a betrayal of their promise to adopt him, breeds hatred. They go at each other, each feeling guilty for his own reason. Georges accuses Majid's son of an obsession, now believing him to be the stalker. The mystery still remains. Does Georges suspect that his own son, Pierrot is the stalking accomplice of Majid's son? Could the sons of different fathers be conspiring to terrorize one father, the more fortunate of the two, yet both standing for the iconic oedipal object?

In the final scene, Haneke's camera dwells on the Laurent house façade for a long time just as it did in the first. We see Georges entering the front door. He takes some pills, calls Anne to reassure her everything is all right, and repairs to bed for the night. He dreams, once again, of his childhood home, replete with images of chickens walking around in front. He and Anne visit, then drag a reluctant boy, presumably Majid's son, their stalker, to their car, and drive away as we hear the boy say "Non, non." The scene quickly shifts to Pierrot's school, and to the same scene that was shown behind the introductory credits of the steps where parents are waiting to pick up their children who are leaving at the end of the school day. We see Pierrot leave, and talk to a man, whose identity remains ambiguous, presumably the swimming coach, who appears now to be Majid's son. The closing credits roll. When credits roll, we ordinarily do not pay much attention to background images, but Haneke's creative genius, or as some have said, wish to pull our leg, lies in his assumption that solving the mystery he created requires crossing boundaries. If we simply pay attention to the rolling credits as rolling credits, as we are accustomed to do, we would never pay attention to the background images that might solve the mystery not so much for the protagonists as for us, the audience, that Haneke has set us up for through an entire film. But if we, too, think out of the box, we will see Pierrot meet up with a man whom we may assume is his swimming coach. Haneke does not make it that definite even with his final *tour de force* and we fully expect to see Majid's son, who, yes indeed, is the swimming coach. Our eyes remain glued as though we were the voyeuristic stalkers, especially if we are film buffs and know what Haneke has been up to to tip us off as to who the stalkers are. But Haneke has deliberately kept their identity ambiguous and allows room for multiple interpretations, and seems to get a kick out of the idea that for people like us who are used to definitive endings, the idea of multiple possibilities in the unraveling of a mystery in horror films is very disturbing. Among those possible was that Pierrot and Majid's son were complicit in the stalking of Pierrot's father, two sons with oedipal motivations for vengeance against one of their fathers, Georges. Like Coppola discussing *The Conversation* and suggesting perhaps the unfindable bug was left in Harry Caul's saxophone, Haneke also wants to leave us hanging when it comes to the absolute truth. Is this ambiguity in interpreting the thematic meanings in these two films about surveillance stalking meant to convey the ambiguities and uncertainties that torment the mind of a person who is being stalked? Will Coppola and Haneke ever give us the answers?

In this film, more than any other on our topic, our preconceived beliefs probably predetermine what we see. If we view the film only once, will we interpret Majid's stalking revenge to be activated by childhood hurts and the political wrongdoing of the Parisian Algerian massacre? For example, some viewers see Pierrot and Majid's Algerian son together in the final scene at the bottom of the screen just before the credits come on. Others do not. Seeing them together fosters the interpretation that the sons together were the perpetrators of the surveillance stalking, and suggests the possibility that the youngsters have been in on it together from the beginning. The film is now clearly about the sins of the fathers being visited upon the next generation, promoting an oedipal revenge motive for the stalking, or even a child's interpretation of the primal scene. After all, the tapes are delivered accompanied by sketches on paper with a child's primitive drawing of a face spurting blood that either foretell Majid's suicide, or repeat the trauma of killing chickens during his childhood relationship with Georges after his parents' disappearance during the Parisian massacre of Algerians. Not seeing them together, except in scenes of impersonal coach and swimmer, promotes other interpretations as to the identity of the stalkers, or leaves their identity ambiguous, or even unsolved and unknowable. Such is the ambiguous terror of stalking and being stalked.

Red Road*: a police surveillance monitor sexually stalks her quarry*

I end my section on surveillance stalking with *Red Road*, a little known Scottish film directed by Andrea Arnold that illustrates the convergence of sexual and surveillance stalking. In it, a police surveillance worker, Jackie (Kate Dickie), discovers a man from her past, Clyde (Tony Curran), on her monitor and literally leaves her post to sexually stalk him. Clyde had significantly changed her former personal life before she began her governmental surveillance job. In this example, revenge, voyeurism, and, eventually, erotomania are critical to the theme of the movie. Jackie is a lonely, withdrawn Glaswegian CCTV police surveillance operator who, from headquarters, monitors some 300 cameras strategically rigged around a particular neighborhood in one of Glasgow's high crime areas. In the film's first image, Jackie quietly sits in front of, and intently looks at, an entire floor-to-ceiling wall of monitoring screens, and operates some surveillance equipment that allows her to zoom in on anything that looks suspicious to her or that simply arouses her curiosity. Early in the film, we see a shot of her eye, not unlike the artistic rendering of the eye logo in *Peeping Tom*, and like the classic eye logo in nearly all films about voyeuristic looking. Jackie enters on her keyboard a written description of something she sees on her computer screen, and then moves the lever on her computer, described best by the slang term "joy stick," to further home in on a man behind a glass window, somewhere in the precinct,

Red Road, that she is monitoring. He does not, of course, know that he is being surveyed. In a subsequent scene, we see her gazing at a monitor that displays her major prey, Clyde, from the rear, as he copulates, fully dressed, with an unidentifiable woman. Jackie's hand caresses the "joy stick" as the scene fades out. One could easily imagine that she is simply a voyeur, well suited to her job as a surveillance operator, but these images of her mode of surveillance stalking set the scene for a very complicated and elaborate plot about how personal sexual arousal can infuse surveillance stalking. Jackie moves on from her paid job of professional surveillance monitoring through voyeuristic video stalking into real, actualized perverse sexual stalking of her target, Clyde.

Clyde, some years ago, had, while stoned on drugs, accidentally killed Jackie's husband and child in a car crash. Her facility in tracking his trysts on her monitors makes it quite easy for Jackie to develop a plan to nail him in a sting operation, which she plans, step-by-step. Her idea is to sexually stalk and then seduce him into initiating sex with her in such a way that she can accuse him of rape and have him put behind bars. Only then, she imagines, will she achieve satisfaction for the losses that his manslaughter has caused her to suffer. Jackie finally emerges from behind the legitimate position of monitoring her screens to stalk him, vengefully, in the flesh. From this moment on, according to Desson Thomson, Jackie's dramatic evolution from a quiet, demure employee to a creature of *dark and predatory purpose* becomes the real story. As soon as Jackie catches a glimpse of her quarry, she transforms from a passive, lonely official eye to an obsessed techno-stalker. She follows her quarry from surveillance camera to surveillance camera, and then on foot from street to street. *Red Road* has been described as "unsavory surveillance". Like Jackie, who both surveys and stalks, we feel as though we are prowling the wilds of the actual Red Road in one of Glasgow's high crime neighborhoods. One commentator notes that this film's action often takes the form of a doubled surveillance: the film reviewer studies Jackie's profile, while she herself studies Clyde's moves across multiple screens. *New York Times* reviewer, A. O. Scott (2007), says that in *Red Road,* the director's "style of shooting and editing is like a more artful, more expressive adaptation of the surveillance cameras." That is, the film's cinematographers mimic the surveillance operators whose work they are filming. In yet another remarkable example of this kind of "doubling," we, the audience, visually stalk the voyeuristic stalker who is the protagonist of this film as she walks slowly along a street in her quarry's territory, eyeing everything that we viewers eye as well. The film director's camera alternates between shots of what Jackie is looking at, and of her eyes, looking. As audience, we are fascinated with both perspectives.

In the scene in which Jackie finally stalks Clyde in the flesh, we see one of the best available film images of a walk-stalk as she follows him to the café that he habituates. In this preparatory scene, she follows him on foot to the café, and then watches him trying to make out with his sexy female server. Knowing Clyde's routines and sexual preferences, Jackie sets off to stalk him in the flesh as she initiates her sexual sting plan. As she rides in a bus toward Red Road, where his apartment is located, we view her profile as she stares out of the bus window. As she gets off, Arnold's camera is focused on her back so that we get a new view of her walk-stalking. On and on she walks towards Clyde's Red Road apartment building, passes by his locksmith van that we have already seen through her surveillance viewing lens, and see her, now in profile view once again, staring up at his window, as though she were calculating the sting scene to come later in the film. She watches him exit his building, and she hides behind a pillar as he approaches and then walks past her. Jackie then follows Clyde down the road as the director's camera has us looking at her back while she looks at Clyde's back, never taking her eyes off him as he walks down the road ahead of her. She stops only to pick up the sharp stone that she intends to use to mutilate herself in the later sting scene that she will choreograph to justify rape charges against him. Then she continues her walk-stalk, following him first up a hill, and then to his favorite café, where she looks at him through the window and then enters.

She sits down behind him, gazing at his back as the flirtatious woman server approaches him. Clyde turns his gaze toward Jackie gazing at him. This is a moment neither forgets, and changes the course of the plot and their feelings for one another. As she sits at the table behind Clyde, she is at liberty to gaze to her heart's content at a very sexualized, or primal scene, encounter between Clyde and the server. The camera focuses for a long time on Jackie's eye in profile gazing at them both. The viewing film audience inevitably will note the power of Clyde's gaze, the quintessentially iconic image used by filmmakers who aim to convey sexually voyeuristic looking. If you cannot get what it might feel like viscerally to be a literal stalker from this scene, there is little chance you can get it anywhere else. Clyde lustily eats and savors his food while Jackie looks on, primly. At one point, he draws on his cigarette, turns, spots her, and their eyes meet in a mutual gaze that is held for several long seconds. As viewing audience, we know at this point that he has visually taken her in and would remember her in any future encounter. Still gazing, Jackie sees the server return and Clyde slip his hand up the back of her thigh. Clyde looks at his seductive server and licks his plate in an unmistakable suggestion of cunnilingus. His server responds, "Ah, you're a fuckin' animal." As he licks away, Jackie gets up and stalks out the door, as if she now knows what she set out to know, and can continue on with her plans for the rape-sting.

Back in the police surveillance headquarters, director Arnold's camera once again focuses on Jackie's profile, particularly on her eye, a shot we come to know well, as she stares at her screen and completes her day's work. Jackie now programs her camera to search out Clyde, as we watch her stare intently at wherever she can find him. Contrary to gender stereotypes of the day, she is obviously gratifying the voyeurism that this film indubitably identifies as intrinsic to female and not just to male surveillance stalking. Additionally, she is working to inform herself of his current life and his habits in preparation for stalking him in the flesh in her pre-planned rape-sting. Both sets of motives, fantasies, and gratifications are enabled by her privileged position as legal spy, paid well enough by her local city government.

In preparation for the final sting, Jackie gains entrance into Clyde's apartment building and somehow convinces the concierge to let her up. She has begun to invade his private space, an activity, sometimes explicitly motivated, of nearly all stalking activity of any kind. She learns the lie of the land and who his roommate and their friends are, and how to navigate her way around his apartment. In a prelude to the sting scene, she and Clyde finally meet up and have the following exchange, which sounds like an unbelievably intimate dialogue, considering her nefarious aim, all the while with sensual music playing loudly in the background, to which guests at Clyde's party are dancing:

CLYDE: Have we met?
JACKIE: I saw you in the café.
CLYDE: Aye. The café, I remember.

Clyde takes her hands, gazes into her eyes, and gently pulls her to him to dance. They gaze and then he strokes the back of her thigh and buttocks. The chemistry between them as they dance is startling. Suddenly, Jackie bolts and leaves, nauseated. Then she throws up as the scene fades out. At this point she cannot carry out her plan to arrange rape charges against him, both immensely attracted and revolted at the same time. The plan will have to wait.

In a subsequent scene, she returns to Clyde's Red Road apartment. In the film's most dramatic moments, we, the viewing audience, are trapped as we are made to watch, voyeuristically, the vivid on-screen depiction of Jackie's vengefully obsessed intensely lustful sexual encounter with Clyde, her prey. We are forced to look at her high level of sexual arousal and erotic pleasure. During her explicitly depicted hot and heavy oral sex and then intercourse with Clyde, she is able to mutilate her face and genitals to carry out the sting. She collects graphic evidence to bring to the police and to set up a rape charge against him to avenge her husband's and daughter's deaths.

According to her carefully planned strategy to exact revenge for his causing the automobile accident that has left her bereft of family love, Jackie, as sexual predator–stalker, had seduced Clyde at a party held in his apartment. Once Jackie has nabbed her surveillance stalkee, it appears she has fallen for him and feels inclined to forget about the rape charges that she has so carefully set up. Apparently, Jackie has worked through her determination to seek revenge. After the rape set-up sting, she has become enamored of her prey, and once again sets off to stalk him, but, this time, more in the erotomanic style that we have become familiar with in the films *Play Misty for Me* and *Fatal Attraction*. Once again she goes to his neighborhood, gets off the bus, and Andrea Arnold's camera focuses on the back of her head as she walks along in search of Clyde. We see him walking toward her, her face bruised following the self-mutilation she effects to prove the rape charges against him. He turns and walks away from her as she moves toward him in a friendly attempt to engage him positively.

JACKIE: Hi. [*Then, walking toward him, we are reminded of the rebuffed Alex in* Fatal Attraction *righteously declaring, "I'm not going to be ignored, Dan."*] Don't you ignore me!

Jackie runs, catches up with Clyde, and presumptuously throws her arms around his waist to turn him around.

CLYDE: What the fuck are you trying to do?

JACKIE: You're gonna knock me over, are you? You killed my family.

CLYDE: [*Backing off as Jackie flails out physically at him*] Oh, it wasn't my fault.

JACKIE: [*Baring her teeth vengefully yet, at the same time, obviously enthralled in trying to win him*] You got drunk and off your head on crack. I want you to tell me about it.

CLYDE: I can't believe I've even known you.

He runs off as she continues trying to review their past as though to settle it and move on with him romantically. He boards a bus, sits down, and she desperately knocks on the bus door, shouting and then weeping: "Please, please." As the bus pulls off, we cannot help being reminded of the unrequited love scenes in *Play Misty for Me* and *Fatal Attraction*. She now stalks him for reasons of unrequited love in a way similar to the erotomania of the other female stalker cases I have reviewed earlier in this book, while he spurns her efforts. As he dodges her less malign efforts to pursue him, she plaintively begs him, repeating, with the very words Alex used with Dan in *Fatal Attraction*, "Don't you ignore me." She had been the vengeful surveillance stalker who stalked the sexual stalker, and then transformed into vengeful sexual stalker, smitten by love that is unrequited by the man whom she wrongly accused of rape. Like *The Lives of Others*, *Red Road* deals with state sponsored socially sanctioned surveillance, but this film depicts sexual stalking as well. Both films provide a window for watching the voyeurism endemic in electronic surveillance stalking. And in both films, the stalker falls for the stalkee in one way or another. Director Andrea Arnold masterfully juxtaposes sanctioned surveillance stalking with the obsessional sexual stalking that set in after Jackie's rape setup by having us as audience visually homing in on voyeuristic surveyor Jackie as she manipulates a joystick that enables her to track and zoom in on the movements of the visually targeted objects of her searches. The stick appears to function as a symbolic erotic enhancer of both her visual surveillance stalking and our own voyeuristic leanings as film viewers. After assuming her primary identity as the terrorized victim whom Clyde forced into premature widowhood, Jackie transforms into the hunter in her single-minded pursuit of a sexual stalking encounter with her persecutor. The director has endowed a tale of female rage and then of unrequited love following intense erotic attachment with a disquieting resonance for feminists. In *Red Road,* the female stalker, empowered by the state, is in charge of the destiny of her stalkees, until the end, after she has climaxed sexually with her stalkee. Successful state-sanctioned revenge transforms into lust, and then lust into love. *The Lives of Others* has a different twist on the readjustment of a moral compass. It deals with patriarchal cultural themes of submission to the powerful male stalker who determines the destiny of his stalkees, and who thus transforms his state-sanctioned revenge into personally gratifying benevolence.

Red Road, in addition to being a film about surveillance stalking, utilizes all the film techniques of doubling that convey the shared voyeuristic leanings of the protagonist and the audience viewing the voyeuristic surveillance stalking. In addition to doubling, the film recreates the sexual stalking of other films that portray erotomanic *leitmotifs* and the shame and predatory vengefulness attendant upon being ignored. This little known film is really quite remarkable. Even though Jackie's fully expressed female sexuality is not in itself perverse, her use of Clyde as a sexual object for perverse purposes is the reason I consider her behavior exemplifies vengeful, eroticized, predatory stalking. Jackie is both turned on and simmering with hate. That is, until the final stalking scene, when Jackie has a true change of heart for Clyde, which remains unreciprocated. Clyde, furious with her for the trumped-up rape charge against him, evades her amorous pursuits as she seeks him out as her sex object without her former vengefulness. And we watch it all.

As you might well imagine, once again I caught myself up short when I realized that by zooming in on my television screen to view the DVDs to get my surveillance and stalking film clips of the film I am reporting on here, I was doubling the stalking characters' and their cinematographer's actions. That is, I was a voyeur, myself, as I was using my remote control to wind, rewind, start, and stop the film as I selected and recorded for my DVD the scenes that I presented directly to my audiences for them to look at.

I will not show even the briefest film clip with images of Jackie's intense sexual experience that, like all such images, are inherently bound to the voyeurism shared in common by protagonist, cinematographer, and audience. I want to protect my audience from being forcibly trapped, as I often felt when looking at explicit sexual film material, into being the unwitting voyeuristic witness of the highly eroticized and potentially disturbing visual material that the director and her crew have set you up to be. Arnold has endowed a tale of female rage with disquieting social resonance, I cannot ever recall having seen a more vivid example of the ways in which filmmaker, protagonist, and film audience are implicated in more or less sublimated, yet nonetheless vicarious, obsessional, voyeuristic sexual stalking and surveillance.

In closing, and on moving on to the next section of my book, which covers real-life invasions of privacy, I want to emphasize that stalking found in real life, fantasies, case studies, and film is an aberration, possibly a perversion, and may be understood, psychoanalytically, from many points of view. Stalking today is also a cultural, social, and political phenomenon that is more prominent in our cyber-age when the interface of stalking with state-sanctioned surveillance is omnipresent. What was once regarded as just psychological pathology is clearly on its way toward becoming a political–social–legal inevitability, if not horror.

PART IV

STALKING AND HACKING IN THE WORLD WE LIVE IN: THE PLANET EARTH AND CYBERSPACE

Introduction

In this last part of the book, I move on from case histories and film portrayals to events in which real people stalk and hack other real people on earth and in cyberspace. Mass media has made possible invasions of privacy in today's new world that otherwise might never have been imagined. Starting off with celebrity stalking, I then proceed to global surveillance issues that have frequently been front page news of developments in a major conflict of our times: privacy and civil liberties *vs.* security against terrorism. That conflict is central to the fictional film, *Enemy of the State*, and the documentary, *Citizenfour*. As diligently as I try to make the distinction between life and art, I have not completely succeeded in my mission. These days, it is often impossible to distinguish public from private lives and factual from fictional accounts of the developing and expanding world that we all inhabit and that we try to comprehend. When, at the time of this writing, terrorist activities stepped up with the ISIS attacks in Paris, the conflict between privacy and security reached a pinnacle in private minds and public media. In fact, an article by Wesley Morris and A. O. Scott (2015) about the film *Caché*, discussed in Chapter Six, appeared in

The New York Times the very day I was working on Chapter Seven in this Part IV. The film was thought to be particularly relevant to our tasks of moving on after the Paris attacks. The writers note Haneke's great final closing-credit sequence that I emphasized in my account, in which two sons, one from a developed nation and one from an underdeveloped nation, are seen to be accomplices in terroristic stalking of the father of one of them. Morris and Scott believe the image at the end of *Caché* points to the importance of a future generation that is reckoning with a past generation's failure to move past complacency in reckoning with terrorism and violations of human rights.

CHAPTER SEVEN

Celebrity stalking

Much, if not most, of the celebrity stalking that becomes prominent in the media speaks to our fascination with erotomania, as I shall highlight in the case of Nell Theobold, the woman who stalked Birgit Nilsson. Many others like her have also gone in enthralled pursuit of operatic divas. We can, however, detect many other reasons for chasing celebrities. In Ron Galella's photographic and litigious pursuit of Jacqueline Kennedy Onassis, and in Monica Lewinsky's crush on, and adoration of, her president, William Jefferson Clinton, friends of the media and enemies of the president alike were eager to spread the stalking news beyond its usual tabloid coverage. Erotomania may have driven Ron Galella's camera stalking of Jacqueline Onassis, but his motive to profit as a photographic superstar figured more importantly. Monica Lewinsky, unlike Jacqueline, was happy to have her privacy invaded by the media when the intimate details of her life spread not only through tabloids, but also through the more respectable media. News is news and attention grabbers get their coverage for all it is worth, for better or worse.

Most erotomanic celebrity stalkers have the delusion that someone of higher status, usually famous, loves or is in love with them. If love does not enter the picture for the celebrity stalkees, beliefs that they are coveted and desired for something they have got that is irresistible certainly do. In most cases, celebrity stalkees barely know their stalkers. They might have had minimal passing interaction with them, but never on the scale the stalker imagines. In that regard, they are similar to erotic stalkers and to patients who have erotic transferences toward their analysts, whether or not they have actually stalked them. Despite the disparity in highly personal involvement, stalker and stalkee are a "couple." In the few psychoanalytic accounts that are available on the topic, more attention is paid to the motivations of the stalker than of the stalkee. The stalkee is generally thought of simply as the victim of some sort of perverse enactment of a wish: perhaps erotomanic, perhaps voyeuristic, perhaps sadistic, to terrorize in one degree or another. Usually, stalkees rely on stalkers to keep alive a certain degree of sexual and aggressive excitement to avoid what Ernest Jones called "aphanisis," or the dread of losing the capacity to feel one's own sexual excitement.

Celebrity-worshipping stalkers often genuinely believe that their stalkees are in love with them, or, if not quite that, they have some other entwined destiny. Like all stalkers, those who pursue celebrities feel a persistent obsessional need, hardly distinguishable from an addiction, to stalk their *inamorata*. They often become genuinely dangerous to the stalkees whose lives they invade. Episodes of stalking may take over the erotomanic celebrity stalker's entire psychic life. Such stalkers may remain convinced for their lifetime that there is a reciprocal feeling on the part of the stalkee, when most often there is not. Painfully for the stalkers, celebrity stalkees regard them as but a nuisance. Stalkers, in contrast, interpret, over-interpret, or misinterpret every little gesture that could, only by a long stretch of the imagination, be regarded as a deep connection. The media, however, exploits as many interpretations as it can come up with, satisfying both itself and its feeder systems. Trespassing into the lives of the rich and famous may be a major invasion of privacy. It may be aggressive, and it may be lethal, as was the case in Mark David Chapman's murder of John Lennon, and for Jodie Foster's stalker, John Hinckley Jr., who attempted to assassinate President Ronald Reagan in 1981 in an insane attempt to get Foster's attention.

Although common belief holds that sexual stalkers are overwhelmingly male, Dowd (2005) insists that that notion is based on stereotype, not fact. In her wry reference to Monica Lewinsky's 1950s-style seduction measures to bag Bill Clinton, her president, Dowd distinguished the fine line between trapping and stalking. "In old movies," she says, "girls would have to do shoe-leather investigating if they wanted to be romantic gumshoes." Monica, familiar with the ways of romantic pursuits, to say nothing of presidential schedules,

> stationed herself in flashy dresses and her trademark black beret, on rope lines and in the path of the presidential motorcade. She studied her prey's preferences and bought them for him, enticing him further in her premeditated stalking safari. (p. 23)

Lewinsky undoubtedly perceived the president as omnipotent and seductive, yet withholding (see Ainslee, 2006), qualities of a celebrity stalkee that egg a stalker on. According to Dowd, Monica was designated by quite a few in high positions as a stalker. Among them, Sidney Blumenthal, a Hillary Clinton confidante, discredited "slimy Monica Lewinsky" as an unbalanced stalker (p. 291). In Blumenthal's testimony to the grand jury in the Bill Clinton impeachment hearing, he swore that the president had told him that Monica had confided: "They call me the stalker . . . If I can say we had an affair, then they won't call me that" (p. 322). Dowd accuses some present-day [Hillary] "Clintonite feminists," who have characterized Lewinsky as a slutty stalker, as having committed a human rights violation by blaming the victim. She contrasts those "sexists" with earlier second-wave feminists who spent decades fighting the double standards climate that designated as a stalker a woman who was raped or sexually harassed because "she flirted, wore short skirts and liked sex" (p. 292). To her credit, Dowd's point is that complex feelings enter the picture in cases of celebrity stalking when the stalkee is rich and has a high and famous position. Such stalkers can be quite fragile, and that fragility, along with their grandiosity and delusional or even quasi-delusional ideas and fantasies, sets them off in their obsessional pursuit so that celebrity stalkees often take out orders of restraint against them. Such was the case with Jacqueline Kennedy Onassis, who took well-publicized measures against her paparazzi stalker, Ron Galella. Birgit Nilsson took no such legal action. The differences in these two celebrity-stalking cases should be as illuminating as their similarities.

Nell Theobold and Birgit Nilsson: the erotomanic stalker and the diva

I present here a case that might be more dramatic, perhaps, than other cases of celebrity stalking. Nell Theobold's pursuit of Birgit Nilsson, the grand opera singer, from 1968 to 1977, tells a tale of what could stand in for many similar scenarios. Theobold's tragic adventure tells of a woman's crush on a celebrity performer. Nell Theobold was convinced, as are other erotomanic stalkers, that their love or other life-consuming romantic crush is reciprocated when it is not. This example of thwarted idealized love of one woman for another woman on whom she had an all-consuming crush includes many of the elements I have been discussing as gender issues that usually, but not always, differentiate women from male stalkers. On the other hand, there are certain intricacies and nuances that do distinguish it. Stalkers smitten by unrequited love are not limited to heterosexual women stalking idealized men, but may be admirers of any sexual orientation. In the August 2009 issue of *Opera News*, Kathryn Leigh Scott reports on the real life of actress–model Nell Theobold, a true impostor beset with *Liebestod*, or love–death fantasies (see Binion, 1993; Gediman, 1995), who stalked the opera singer Birgit Nilsson unremittingly for nine years. The tragic story is also reported by Nilsson herself in her autobiography, written in 1995 in Swedish and also available in a 2007 English edition. As in all cases of impostors, real or fictional, it is very difficult to articulate who is who in their real and fictional worlds. I ask my readers to bear with me patiently as I try to differentiate one individual, real and/or fictional, from another.

Theobold had become obsessively hooked on her idol after seeing her perform Isolde in Wagner's opera, *Tristan und Isolde*, which undoubtedly prompted her to enact her own *Liebestod* fantasy. Nell Theobold, as the stalker, took on the imposturous identity of "J. Black," who was based on the fictional American heiress, Elsie de Haven, the stalking heroine of the novel *Of Lena Geyer*, written by Marcia Davenport (1936). Geyer was novelist Davenport's fictional composite of two other opera singers, Alma Gluck and Lilli Lehmann. Davenport was, in fact, Alma Gluck's daughter. In her novel, *Of Lena Geyer*, Davenport used the name Elsie de Haven for the stalker who followed the diva, Lena Geyer, all over the world, in pursuit of her passion for opera.

Nell Theobold, in her worldly strategies as stalking opera buff, tried to pass with the fictional name she gave herself, J. Black. She presented her stalkee, Birgit Nilsson, red roses with mash notes, signed "E. de H," before every performance, the typical stock-in-trade offerings of many stalkers of famous performance artists, paraphernalia that enhance the illusion or delusion of a reciprocated romance. In Davenport's fictional account, the diva, Geyer, as stalkee, behaved as obsessionally as the stalking young heiress, by taking her stalker on as her life-long companion. Those two became an inseparable couple, stalker and stalkee, as it were, until Lena Geyer's death. Obviously, Nell Theobold wished she would fare as well with Nilsson as Elsie de Haven fared with Geyer, but she did not. She hoped, in vain, as a celebrity-stalker, that her love would be requited. The real life enactment between Nell Theobold and Birgit Nilsson had a very different outcome from that of the fictional couplehood Nell tried to emulate. Nell tried, but failed utterly, to have her life repeat fiction in her construction of an idealized, reciprocated celebrity love affair that existed only in her own mind. During her time of passionate and totally unrequited love, Theobold, aka J. Black, bought airplane tickets for seats next to her stalkee, Nilsson; booked adjacent hotel rooms prior to opera performances all over the world; and gained backstage access to Nilsson's performances. The more Theobold clung and went in search, however, the more Nilsson pushed her away, an outcome quite the opposite of her delusional expectations that her life would mirror that of Davenport's fictionalized Elsie de Haven's successful mutual attachment to Lena Geyer. Rather, this interaction between Theobold and Nilsson was yet another version of the common erotomanic sexual stalking scenario of unrequited love and fatal attraction, a variant of the events leading up to the love death scenes in the films *Play Misty for Me* and *Fatal Attraction*. Theobold stole Nilsson's stationery, and wrote love letters to herself, imagining she was Nilsson, and forged Nilsson's signature. Then it was one thing after another, until she finally killed herself in a living out of an archetypal *Tristan und Isolde Liebestod* fantasy: if she could not live with her fantasized beloved, one or both must die. In fact, Theobold wrote a provision in her will that her ashes be scattered on Nilsson's farm in Sweden. According to Scott's *Opera News* account, after hearing her idol perform in *Tristan und Isolde*, Nell returned to her room at the Sachar Hotel in Vienna where both she, as stalker, and Nilsson, as stalkee, were staying and prepared to take her life. In her suicide note to Nilsson, she wrote, "'Seat number twelve in the first row will be empty tomorrow. Isolde's poison means Tod! Tod duns beiden! (Death! Death to us both!)'" (Nilsson, 2007, p. 219). Nell's hope for a double suicide accompanied her to the grave, but not Nilsson to hers. What better example, throughout the history of romanticism in art and life, can one find of the confluence of obsessional stalking, imposture, and the merging of fantasy and reality in the enactment of a *Liebestod* fantasy.

I now contrast this arch-romantic version of a real-life occurrence to a much more prosaic but common form of celebrity stalking, which, nonetheless, was far more thoroughly covered in our mass media: that by Ron Galella, the photojournalist, of Jacqueline Kennedy Onassis.

Ron Galella and Jacqueline Kennedy Onassis: the paparazzo stalker and his stalkee

When *paparazzo* photographer Ron Galella followed Jacqueline Kennedy Onassis around New York City during the years she was married to Greek shipping magnate, Aristotle Onassis, he invaded her privacy, particularly that between her and her children, in order to get a good shot of her. Mrs. Onassis did not hesitate to accuse her intrusive follower of stalking her. Whether or not Ron Galella's stalking motives included some degree of erotomania, voyeurism, and other traits we have come to associate with typically valent psychological motives of sexual and surveillance stalkers, Galella did what he did to earn a living. The better he did it, the more money he made. The more he made, the more he was respected for his professional skills, which were, indeed, considered to be amazingly good. Photojournalist Ron Galella's stalking invasions of the privacy of Jacqueline Kennedy Onassis's personal life became a prominent news item. Each member of the couple had something to gain from the exciting publicity of their stalker–stalkee couplehood. And each came to his or her positions for reasons unique to their own individual personhood. This case is quite different from most cases of celebrity stalking, such as Nell Theobold and Birgit Nilsson. Usually, the celebrity stalker suffers from the erotomania of an overwhelming crush on a famous person that is not reciprocated, although it is often imagined to be. This dissonance in passion leads the vengeful, often suicidal, stalker into troubled waters. While Galella might have suffered some degree of erotomania, his major pathology was closer to sociopathy. As for Jackie, the long legal battles to stem stalking in order to secure privacy had unique meanings for her. Jackie's awareness that she was a woman considered to be one of the most beautiful in the world resonated with Ron's ambition to be the professional artist whose camera work also made her the most photogenic.

The *paparazzi* photographers who stalked Jacqueline Onassis could easily be thought of as voyeurs, or as voyeuristic cameramen who were just conducting their professional business, and not necessarily as erotomanic loners. Ron Galella, however, was considered a ruthlessly ambitious photojournalist and the most notorious *paparazzo* of them all. Although he camera-stalked many famous people, mainly from the entertainment industry, there can be no doubt that Jackie was his favorite quarry. Earlier, Galella had camera-stalked Liz Taylor, Mick Jagger, Elvis Presley, Kate Moss, Richard Burton, who sent hired hands to steal his film, and Marlon Brando, who knocked out five of his teeth. Whether or not he was a voyeuristic stalker, like the cameramen portrayed in *Rear Window* and *Peeping Tom*, Galella was indeed a stalker and also a wonderful portrait photographer of the rich and famous who knew he had been chasing them. His payoff lay more in his doggedly successful pursuit strategies than in his attention to angles, positioning, and other photographic composition skills. Yet, he loved photography as a valued and valuable art form, and his works now hang in many galleries, including New York's Metropolitan Museum and the Museum of Modern Art. His story is one of passion and obsession for his own portrait photography that the best museums would want to buy and show above all others, and for his celebrated subjects who enabled him to realize his dream. We might say that any erotomania on his part was directed toward photography itself. Along with his voyeurism, his erotomania was sublimated into his overwhelming general mania for meticulously collecting, preserving, and storing more and better shots than anyone else in the business. His mania in this case, whether "eroto" or otherwise, was not delusional, but entirely self-promotional and resulted in lasting works that found their niche in the art world. As for his stalking behavior, *paparazzo* literally translates as annoying insect, visible and obnoxious at the same time. For Galella, being a successful *paparazzo* involved nothing subtle or nuanced, but meant simply finding out where your subjects were going, beating them to their destination, and being on the sidewalk or wherever before they got there. Things do not work out quite like that in today's world where photographing of celebrities is done *en masse*: a signal is usually given and everybody shoots at once. Good stalking skills are no longer the guarantee of getting the best, as they were in Galella's heyday.

Galella and Jackie had a most interesting relationship during Jackie's marriage to Aristotle Onassis. Their connection has been characterized variously as co-dependent, as their being an odd couple but certainly a couple, one member obsessed with pursuing the other and the other loving to be pursued. Whatever kind of duo you call them, they were most definitely a very well matched stalker–stalkee couple. He was one of many *paparazzi* who adored her, and, more than most of the others, put her on a pedestal. Because she was always smiling, even if bitterly, like the "Mona Lisa Jackie," Galella believed she loved being pursued by him. Before, during, and after the time they were engaged in their may lawsuits and countersuits, Galella bribed doormen, romanced family servants, jumped into the family's bicycle paths, and invaded the privacy and school performances of her children by her late husband, President John F. Kennedy.

When Galella sued the secret service agents who protected the children for restraint of his trade, he lost his case. The agents countersued, along with the U.S. government, for an order of protection against Galella for interfering with their attempts to keep the children secure. The U.S. government provides this courtesy to both the current president and to all past presidents. When the agents demanded film holding the children's pictures, Galella refused, so they drove him to the 19th precinct on Manhattan's upper east side where he was then arrested. Galella countercharged, claiming false arrest, malicious prosecution, and unlawful interference with his trade. Jackie countersued and took Ron to court twice, charging him with invasion of privacy, assault and battery, intentionally inflicting emotional distress, and engagement in a harassment campaign. Galella's charges against the security agents were dismissed and Jackie won her injunction for a restraining order to prevent further harassment of her and her children (see Galella *v.* Onassis, United States Court of Appeals, Second Circuit 487F.2D 986, 1973). Galella was enjoined from

> harassing, alarming, startling, tormenting, touching the person of the defendant ... or her children ... and from blocking their movements in the public places and thoroughfares, invading their immediate zone of privacy by means of physical movement, gestures, or with photographic equipment, and from performing any act reasonably calculated to place the lives and safety of the defendant ... and her children in jeopardy.

Galella was eventually ordered by the court to stay at a distance of 100 yards from the apartment, 100 yards from the children's schools, seventy-five yards of either child, and fifty yards from the defendant. The court found Galella guilty of harassment, intentional infliction of emotional distress, assault and battery, commercial exploitation of the defendant's personality, and invasion of privacy. Interestingly, the injunction did not include the word, "stalking," but the judgment did officially rule that Galella had "insinuated himself" into the very fabric of Mrs. Onassis' life. We generally think about restraining orders such as these as the usual legal restrictions now in place to combat stalking. We know more about personal struggles that restraining orders provide than we do about the psychoanalytic and other psychological meanings that I aim to elaborate in this book. But, I have no doubt that some good psychoanalytic nuggets are bound to show up in this "textbook case."

Leon Gast (2010), in his documentary film, *Smash His Camera*, profiles the life and career of Ron Galella, clearly portrayed here, at age seventy-eight, as a specific type of stalker. The documentary opens with Galella happily saying, "I'm Ron Galella, *paparazzo* superstar," a self-descriptive expression that he repeats proudly at significant intervals throughout the film, and a signature statement that reveals his character. Gast's bias toward Galella is positive, yet still leaves room for the viewers to judge the photojournalist in keeping with their own positive or negative slants. Gast raises intriguing questions about freedom of the press, the right to privacy, and our celebrity-obsessed culture. Looking at this little known documentary, which appeared long after the *paparazzi* brouhaha occupied the public's attention, we see Galella as some sort of egomaniac, if not erotomanic. He always viewed his stalking of the stars, particularly Mrs. Onassis, whom he claims to have loved, as ego syntonic and totally necessary to the development of his self-proclaimed consummate skill as a great portrait photographer.

Galella considers one particular week in October of 1971 as the best week in his career of shooting Jackie: "One week I got her five times. The 7th was my great day when I got my 'Windblown Jackie,' which I call my Mona Lisa . . . I don't think she knew it was me, that's why she smiled." No qualm whatsoever on his part is detectable. Yet, we, the audience, tend to feel sympathetic toward this man who knew what and how to get just what he needed to fulfill his dreams through his photography that was aided and abetted by stalking quite sociopathically. The "Mona Lisa" photograph shows Jacqueline Kennedy Onassis as beautiful as she has ever been captured on film, and easily makes us wonder if she was an unwitting accomplice in the stalker–stalkee couple. Who would not welcome an historical portrait in which one is arguably the most beautiful woman in the world? Despite his character flaws, our heartfelt thanks go out to Ron Galella for earmarking beauty so unforgettably. Unlike other stalkers we have come to know through the media and otherwise, he does not frighten or terrorize us, and Gast makes sure that he enlists our admiration and even our affection. Sociopaths, we know, can do that with ease.

The documentary, *Smash His Camera,* at one point shows satirical journalist David Frost explaining that in certain primitive tribes the natives have a horror of being photographed. They fear the photographer will steal their very souls. "Actually," he says, "there is a tribe here in America that feels the same way." He shows us footage of Katherine Hepburn, who hides from Galella as we see scenes of him good-naturedly trying to shoot her. As Ron tears away the leaves in Hepburn's hedge to make a hole in which to insert his camera, he endearingly says, "The *paparazzi* need a viewpoint. We have to create it sometimes." Hepburn hides, and then he car-stalks and camera-stalks her to a theater where she is starring in a play. Frost wonders why a photographer would camera-stalk someone who has let it be known that she yearns to stay out of public view. Galella says she is a great superstar and that is why he has to get good pictures of her. I am reminded of Willy Sutton, who, when asked why he robbed banks, replied, "Because that's where all the money is." Ron acknowledges that Hepburn guards her privacy, and that her attempts to shield herself makes her a difficult subject to shoot, but that he needs up-to-date pictures to expand his files. His total self-centeredness and disregard for his subject's personal feelings are known to us by now. We wonder how he can care so much about collecting mounds of finished products from so many people and yet at the same time be so callously indifferent to their needs. And oh, what files they are. Cartons and cartons and cartons, containing over three million images, have been meticulously arranged and labeled on shelves in a room that appears to be the size of the Library of Congress. He is matter-of-fact, yet, from the positive slanting of the documentary, we feel with, and even for, him. He is so matter-of-factly-persuasive that I, for one, feel with him, in a limited kind of way, I hope. I am hooked, despite what I know of the fear and excitement that photojournalists like him who pursue others so relentlessly can induce in their subjects, who are objects to them. Frost asks him if this is a decent way to make a living. Galella responds, "I believe in what I do and I do not have any guilt." At this point, the sociopath does not lack self-knowledge.

Within the documentary, experts offer further opinions of Galella's psychopathology and diagnosis. A series of commentators offer condensed opinions in quick shots that alternate between disdain and warm admiration: "a gentleman;" "a creep;" "soft-spoken;" "money-grubbing;" "scum;" "polite;" "I love Galella. I think he's a national treasure." Then, in all seriousness, psychoanalyst, psychiatrist, and corporate consultant Kerry Sulkowicz comes on screen:

> When Ron offers instructions or tips to young, inspiring photographers, I think it's clear that he gives a bit more, offers a bit more than if you were in photography school and you learn how to use a camera and compose the subject and develop the pictures and so forth. He gives some tips that would probably be classified as tips on how to be sociopathic.

Is Gast intending for Sulkowicz to have the last word on Galella's psychopathology? If so, does Gast also present evidence that Galella's guiltless sociopathy contributes to the personal pleasure of those who cough up what the market will bear to promote art at its best? In *Smash His Camera*, Galella presents the most likeable psychological picture of a stalker that I have ever seen, and it gives me pause to know that I think that. We shall see, soon, that if I am duped, I am not alone.

In the documentary section labeled "On Ron Galella's Rules," the seventy-eight-year-old Galella gives a few tips on how to be the best photojournalist of personal portraits. Among them are sneaking in and crashing events, forging credentials, and shooting fast to elicit a surprised expression on one's subject's face. "And the way I shoot is this way:" He holds his imposing camera away from his face, brings it near, his eye not looking through the camera's lens as he looks, bare-eyed at his subject: "Shoot, shoot, shoot, not look through the lens but at the subject's eyes." He continues that if you shoot fast and the subject does not want to be shot, you already have a few pictures: "You have to be one up on these people. This is the art of *paparazzi*." He shows no concern whatsoever that he is invading privacy, and indicates with insouciant pride that such invasions are his major aims, the secret of his success, and that any good photographers should aim similarly, even though he confidently believes himself to be peerless in the technique.

In a scene of events postdating the Onassis days, director Gast literally follows Galella's stalking trajectory from his Tony Soprano-like home in New Jersey to the ballroom of the Waldorf Astoria Hotel, where Galella plans to shoot Robert Redford. Redford, like certain of us who watch this documentary, seems complacent, even content to have the honor of being shot by this pleasant, likeable, familiar guy. Galella goes on, with special reference to Redford, suggesting that his subjects are objects rather than individual human beings. "In my career it's necessary to sneak in because I'm a freelancer, and you're the last to get invited, because these people, I don't know, they're like Gestapo." The good-natured Redford shakes hands with Galella and we like them both, Galella laughing all along. Is it because he has the last laugh on us or are we taken up and in by his carefree spirit in the work he does? This dilemma about how we feel about Galella permeates the entire documentary. "He is singularly unaware of the impression he gives to people," says commentator Peter Howe (2005). This happy-go-lucky lack of self-awareness must be the trademark trait of stalkers like Galella.

How did Ron Galella get started as a *paparazzo*? By his account, it was simple: his mother was interested in famous film stars. In fact, she named him after Ronald Coleman. But it was the 19th Air Force that gave him his career, as celebrities visited the base newspaper. An unidentified voice says the *paparazzi* are parasites and profiteers with lives full of rejection. Gast then shoots Dick Cavett saying. "The *paparazzi* are defined as pests at best, leeches at worst because the 'papa . . .' comes from the popping of flashing bulbs, I guess?" He had better keep guessing because Ron continues to have the last laugh, not disdainfully, but good-naturedly and comfortably self-satisfied. Ron knows that he is a superstar as a photographer and believes that his fine reputation will follow him forever. Howe says, "The real *paparazzi* are the ones who come up with these amazing creative ways of invading somebody else's privacy." He seems tickled pink, as do many others among the telegenic interviewees in Gast's propagandizing documentary. Galella acknowledges that celebrities want to control their images, but he wants to control them too because "I'm the artist, this is my medium." A celebrity asks him, "Do *you* want to be somebody famous?" Ron laughs, and says, "I am. I am Ron Galella, *paparazzo* superstar."

Chuck Close, photographer and photorealist, says it is easy to be a photographer but damned hard to have recognizable authorship, and maintains that Galella did both. He falls, says Close, in the grand tradition of street photographers—Close's euphemism for stalkers—where there has to be something that is useable, if not great. Obviously, Close is making the distinction between Galella's work as financial success and as art. He goes on to say that if someone says you had made money on it, then you have done your job. Galella could not have cared less about the people. I certainly believe Ron Galella's handling of his photographs of celebrities reveals narcissistic, sociopathic indifference, but could it also express loving regard for his subjects? Perhaps the jury is still out. Perhaps both dispositions figure into the complicated psychology of this particular individual stalker.

Now I turn back to the unusual relation between Ron Galella and Jacqueline Onassis, which this documentary illuminates unusually well. There is often someone photographing Galella photographing Jackie, so his photographic stalking techniques are preserved for the record. Ron muses about Jackie. His first take of her was in 1967, when she was married to Onassis. He had found out that she lived at 1050 Fifth Avenue, and says that from then on it was a marathon. She did not go out often so it was hard to get her unless you waited outside of her house, which, of course, we all know Galella did. In Gast's documentary, gossip columnist Liz Smith says it was unimaginable for Jackie to have married Aristotle Onassis. Smith, carefully chosen as Gast's spokesperson, remains sympathetic with Galella throughout the documentary. Galella tipped the doorman who, in turn, tipped him off to help him initiate his stalks of Jackie and her children. John and Caroline Kennedy were often in Central Park with secret service agents who protected them. Jackie was known to have requested of one agent, Mr. Connelly, "Smash his camera." This remark obviously inspired the title of Gast's documentary.

Psychoanalysts should not be at all surprised at reversals of roles in the lawsuits and countersuits between Galella and Onassis. If Ron and Jackie are a stalker–stalkee couple, their roles are understandably reversed as each alternately imagines and lives out either position in the stalker–stalkee relationship. In *Smash His Camera,* photojournalist Peter Howe says, "This is an alliance between the photographers, the celebrities, the publishers and the readers of the magazines and the viewers of the programs on television. You can't separate any one of those pieces of the alliance." What statement could come closer to expressing the psychoanalytic view of the intimate relation between the two participants in the stalker–stalkee couple that I have been emphasizing throughout this book? The more the fame of the stalkee, the more money the celebrity stalker who gets the pictures is going to make. The more pictures that are displayed, the more fame the celebrity will attain. That simply stated interrelationship is what we mean by co-dependence, a word often used to characterize the relation between the celebrity and the celebrity stalker that binds them into a couple. When Jackie countersued for harassment, claiming Ron was terrifying her and her children by stalking them, Galella claimed he thought she would settle but then concluded she decided to go to court because Ari paid the bills. Ari paid $500,000 "while my lawyers charged me $40,000. It was a bargain!"

The case contained many precedents involving conflicts around rights to privacy and conflicts around the rights of the press and of the photographers serving the press, quite reminiscent of today's conflicts between security surveillance and privacy. The year 2015 recapitulates 1969. Galella's attorneys, Alfred Julien and Stuart Schlesinger, argued the constitutional issue that if you are a public person you might not have completely free rein, but you have certainly got rights that are different from those of a private person. In this case, it came down to how famous Jacqueline Kennedy Onassis was, and the conclusion was that she ranked with Queen Elizabeth. Be that as it may, Galella argued that because his photos of Jackie usually showed a smile on her face, she could not have been terrorized, or even harassed, frightened, or alarmed by him at all. Thomas Hoving, director of the Metropolitan Museum of Art at the time, had a different idea and opened up the subject of the right to privacy. "If you stalk somebody time after time after time, it's depressing, it's demoralizing on the subject, for him to have great art." We had the right of privacy against the government but not against each other. Yet, many felt strongly on Galella's side because he did nothing criminal, he only tried to make a living. Yes, decisions are still pending on the First Amendment on freedom of expression. The controversy centers on what the press person—and, in these days, our government agencies such as the CIA or the NSA—does to get the information.

Neil Leifer, photographer, gets to mention stalking, specifically, as he sums up his opinion of Galella: "His tactics are despicable. I think of him as a stalker. I think there are legal stalkers. You can take the First Amendment to its furthest point, and then you have Ron Galella sitting there protected by it." Floyd Abrams, First Amendment expert responds,

> Well there's certainly a First Amendment issue surrounding what *paparazzi* do. *Paparazzi* play a news gathering function. They're allowed to use the streets, as you and I are, they're allowed to take photographs. The hard questions arise when you ask, well, are they allowed to take a picture inside my home? Are they allowed to go up to my children if I'm a movie star and start talking to them and follow them around? In some of the things that were done to Jackie Kennedy, for example, Ron Galella went so far over the line that there's hardly a judge, however dedicated to the First Amendment, who wouldn't find something he did to violate the law. In a single day, he jumped at her in a restaurant from behind a coat rack; he sneaked into John's school for a Christmas pageant; and at one point, he hired a guy in a Santa Claus suit to stand next to Jackie! She dodged Galella all day.

Galella, knowing Jackie got annoyed, tells Gast, as nonchalantly as anyone could, that he put on disguises, mustaches, and African wigs; that he dated her maid, to get information, mainly, such as when Jackie was going for a facial, or to her hairdresser. Jackie saw Galella making out with her maid and fired her. There is the First Amendment and there is the character of a charming sociopath who gets to folks like you and me.

We are glued to the screen as Galella asks, "Why did I have the obsession with Jackie? I analyzed it." He answers his own question amazingly and outrageously: "Because I had no girlfriend." He was not yet married at the time in the late 1960s that he was musing about. "I wasn't tied down, married, and she was my girlfriend in a way." Howe agrees, saying this was a personal relationship that was conducted through the camera. Liz Smith, gossip columnist, said, referring to the best of Galella's shots, including the Mona Lisa Jackie, "That's Jackie at her most fetching. 'Don't touch me, don't ask me any questions, and just don't follow me.' He really captured something that was very elusive about her." The stalker, I say, knew exactly what he wanted his complementary stalkee to be, and knew how to get it by stalking her. Bonnie Fuller, former editor of *Glamour* stepped out on a limb to say Ron really loved Jackie, so reminiscent of the way many were later to say that Monica Lewinsky loved President Clinton. Fuller appears to have given no thought to the possibility that Galella was putting Jackie and her family in harm's way. Liz Smith then gets to the heart of what I am calling the mutual dependence of stalker and stalkee, or, with a bit of a stretch, calling the back and forth lawsuits between Ron and Jackie a marriage made in heaven. The prevailing sentiment was that Galella, the sociopath, was a monstrous rat and villain. He had attempted to bribe Ari Onassis for money to drop his lawsuit. The judge got annoyed and this time ruled in favor of Mrs. Onassis, getting a permanent injunction against the freelance photographer, ruling he could not get within fifty yards of her or seventy-five yards of her children. Jackie capped his lens, but Ron appealed and got the yardage reduced, in 1975, to twenty-five feet for Jackie. He violated the court order again in 1981, and she brought him back to court while he professed his love. The court threatened six years in jail if he persisted, and he turned to camera-stalk Princess Grace of Monaco.

Consensus has it that Galella's photographs are not wonderful from a photographic standpoint, but are wonderful from a subject standpoint. It is the subject that attracts you, not his photograph of it. Yet, curators want Ron's work for galleries and museums all across the world. People say Galella seemed sad at Jackie's death, "My most iconic subject, dead, you know." Referring to his "Mona Lisa" photo, he said, "I don't think she knew it was me, that's why she smiled a little." Liz Smith thought Jackie was posing for him more than we know, concluding that she must have had more than a little feeling for Ron. That is one way of looking at the affair between this celebrity stalker and his most celebrated stalkee. At seventy-eight, in 2010, he was still at his celebrity stalking, having discovered the profitability of photo-stalking Angelina Jolie and Brad Pitt.

CHAPTER EIGHT

Stalking in cyberspace: hacking and spying

Countless national, international, and global events have dominated the news since I began my initial drafts of this chapter. The mass media has exposed us to a proliferation of news and opinion pieces on conflicts between security and privacy. In fact, one of the debate questions directed to the candidates running in the 2016 Democratic Presidential Primary Elections attempted to distinguish their points of view on where they stood on the privacy *vs.* security issue and the role of Silicon Valley in releasing top-secret encrypted information. Clearly, our interests in stalking have spanned the space between the consulting room, the political arena, and the planet. I begin by presenting three case vignettes that came to my attention simultaneously with the rising media coverage of rampant invasions of privacy by governmental agencies such as the Central Intelligence Agency (CIA) and the National Security Agency (NSA). These three patients had specialized backgrounds and personal predilections for invading the privacy of individuals who had disappointed them via one or another form of rejection. Initially, I did not connect their personal dilemmas to the larger socio-political scene. Now, of course, I do find significant similarities between the individual and the organizational dynamics of stalking. Personal loss and humiliation triggered these patients' vengeful stalking via their use of communication devices to maintain contact that might reach into cyberspace: as a simple example, discovering the rejecting person's locale by applying the latest technological advances of their applications, or "Apps." The corresponding news explosion gathered momentum from the Snowden case and the release of the documentary film *Citizenfour*, about Snowden's leakage of classified information about U.S. government surveillance. This film, along with ubiquitous press coverage, raised public consciousness to take in the ever-present conflicts between maintaining the American people's security against terrorist attacks, and guaranteeing their Fourth Amendment rights to privacy and freedom of expression. I have been living through months of these daily accounts of Fourth Amendment guarantees and infractions with the aim of processing them to include reasonably up-to-date accounts of the nationally scaled conflicts in this section of the book. The fairly limited psychoanalytically based story I had been slowly building over the years about the sporadically covered story of stalking in cyberspace has mushroomed into a far more ambitious attempt to present a review of cataclysmic world events.

Before I go to Snowden and *Citizenfour*, I will comment on the earlier film, *Enemy of the State*, which also bridges stalking and spying in the inner worlds of our minds and the vast outer world we call cyberspace. I aim to convey the prophetic nature of this blockbuster movie as an important linking event in the cosmic world we live in. By way of introduction to these important films, I return to my molecular level of clinical vignette to introduce my topic of social conflicts with some commentary on their individual clinical underpinnings.

The telephone and the internet: some clinical commentary

I introduced some ideas about telephone stalking in my coverage of *Fatal Attraction* in Chapter Three. When Alex Forrest began her campaign to stalk Dan Gallagher, she resorted to the phone primarily for the pleasure of a pyrrhic victory by making hang-up calls to disturb the intimacy between Dan and his wife, Beth. Her desperate calls succeeded in annoying the couple, but did not boost her confidence in being able to force Dan to reciprocate her love. Her vengeful calls to Dan's wife or to the couple, Dan and Beth, in bed served mainly to discharge narcissistically rageful tensions, but did not have the long-lasting effects that the variety of telephone stalking that I am about to discuss often does.

Persistent telephone calling, and leaving many unwanted and intimidating messages on someone's answering machine or voicemail might not immediately strike the reader as a form of stalking, but I believe it qualifies. Orders of restraint have been requested and issued for such harassment, but, more customarily, the victims of this variety of unwanted, unsettling pursuit are legally advised to keep taped records of such insistent threats in the event that any of the telephone stalker's threats might some day materialize into actions with more harmful consequences.

A "Dear John" letter or its equivalent is often just the trigger that provokes telephone and internet stalking responses that point to a significant degree of erotomania on the part of the rejected suitors who receive such dismissive messages. Vengeful feelings transform their sense of powerlessness into one of illusory power that eggs them on to make invasive contact with the one who was once easily accessible. Rejected partners might also persist until they believe they have been "heard" the way they want to be heard. The louder and more frequent their intimidating messages, the higher the hopes of undoing their loss. It is not unusual for rejected partners to stalk via lengthy telephone messages left on voicemail until the tape fills up. Many of us hear such reports from patients; many know of it first hand in our lives.

The term "Dear John letter" was coined during the Second World War to refer to a letter written by a girlfriend of an overseas serviceman to inform him of her decision to end the relationship in his absence. Brooks (2015), in his *New York Times* "Op Ed" piece of March 3, 2015, "Leaving and cleaving," has, I believe, transposed the essence of a Dear John letter into the related realm of telephone stalking by rejected lovers. One might wonder whether Brooks had thoroughly read, and been influenced by, Hermann's (1976) classic paper, "Clinging-going-in-search." His column deals essentially with unrequited lovers who have been abandoned and who then are driven to make internet contact with their former partners who have taken leave of the relationship. Brooks quite explicitly uses the word, "stalking" in connection with behavior that I am referring to in this book as "cyberstalking." He writes,

> We all know men and women who *stalk* ex-lovers online; people who bombard a friend with emails even though that friendship has evidently cooled; mentors who reject their protégés when their emails are no longer instantly returned; people who post faux glam pictures on Instagram so they can "win the breakup" against their ex. (Brooks, 2015, p. A29)

Furthermore, Brooks appropriates a clinician's role as he becomes quite explicit about how he would eliminate the vindictiveness, such as I have highlighted in my case examples and film portrayals of sexual stalking and that I aim at this point to illustrate in telephone and internet stalking. He makes a plea to the potential stalker who has been left out in the cold to desist:

> . . . the person doing the leaving controls the situation, but greater heroism is demanded of the one being left behind. The person left in the vapor trail is hurt and probably craves contact. It's amazing how much pain there is when what was once intimate conversation turns into unnaturally casual banter or just a void . . . the person being left has to swallow the pain and accept the decision. The person being left has to grant the leaver the dignity of his own mind . . . The person being left has to suppress vindictive flashes of resentment and be motivated by a steady wish for the other person's ultimate good . . . That means not calling when you are not wanted. Not pleading for more intimacy or doing the other embarrassing things that wine, late nights and instant communications make possible. (p. A29)

Whether or not one agrees with Brooks' proscription for what the abandoned person should do rather than stalk, one cannot help being impressed with his conclusions, even if dismayed by his failure to credit any specific psychoanalytic source, or even the general psychoanalytic corpus and attitude for the basis of his ideas and his conclusions. The rejected one, as Brooks points out so well, loses power—not just a sense of power, but real power, when desperate attempts to make contact are spurned. Since, in any relationship, the one who can and does walk away has some real power, the one who is walked away from attempts to restore power by stalking the one who has left him. I use the male pronoun to restore balance between the sexes because most of my illustrative examples have located erotomania in women, not men. Men do indeed gain confidence by exploiting superior strength over women and assume that corporal strength alone confers advantages exclusively to the male sex. Fantasies of extending that physical power to psychological power underlie a version of unrequited love, in which men support illusory psychic power by raising the decibel and forcefulness levels in the terrorizing tone in the phone messages or email pleas they leave for their captive female audience. And one must not forget the pleasure accruing from the sadism that real and illusory power brings. Sadistic pleasure has always been one powerful motive for inducing fear and terror in the one being forced to hear or read messages they do not want to hear or read. Tracking the whereabouts of the "lost" object, often aided and abetted by a "Locate the iPhone App," also features formidably in this kind of stalking fantasy. A rejected lover might analyze the relationship to death, hoping to repair old rifts and to restore old connections if he only hangs in there long enough and offers up persistent enticements. Such enticements will fail when the words proclaim love but the tone betrays anger. Endless "I love you" edicts are then bound to be experienced as invasive stalking and reinforce the rejecting stance of the person who issues them. A man who telephone-stalked several of his rejecting serial significant others offered up what he thought would be irresistible: romantic trips to one paradise resort or another with "all expenses paid." Instead of letting go and moving on, as Brooks (2015) suggested was the way to go, he only stepped up his efforts to perpetuate a disorganized, albeit temporary, attachment pattern which reeked not only of invasiveness of his erstwhile partner's time, space, separateness, and privacy, but of personal terrorism. Telephone stalking raises immediately experienced fears because it brings to the recipient of the call startling and sometimes mysterious disruptions that raise all kinds of persecutory and other terrorizing fantasies. The persecutory masochism of the telephone stalker is outstanding and often matches that of the telephone stalkee. It never works except to guarantee that he will get the response he seeks.

A case in point can be found in Shelby's (1997) patient, Mr. G., who was anxiously preoccupied with telephone-stalking his ex. He came in to treatment one day, horribly embarrassed and humiliated about reporting this behavior, which he ended suddenly in order to be able to talk about it at all in treatment and to try to "get over it." He confessed to calling his former partner's answering machine repeatedly, just to hear his voice, but would then hang up without leaving a message. His former lover traced the calls, angrily called the patient, and told him to stop or else he would accuse Mr. G. of stalking him and take out an order of restraint. Mr. G. was greatly relieved when his therapist responded empathically to his longing and emptiness. Mr. G.'s stalking attempts to hear his lover's voice were not criticized or even interpreted as sadistic action, but were understood compassionately by his analyst. He was apparently able to internalize the analyst's response to his way of trying to self-soothe his sense of devastation by creating both self-cohesion and trying to restore the earlier ruptured and lost union. Cases with less favorable outcomes than Shelby's involve telephone stalking that aims to express continuously intense rage at an object who appeared to cause both narcissistic and libidinal loss.

A patient I shall call Golinda reminds me of Nin's (1954) *A Spy in the House of Love*. Golinda, like Nin's Sabina, was a modern day internet hacking spy in the house of love of her family of orientation. Internet hackers, like telephone stalkers, Peeping Toms, and other spies may also be voyeurs and detectives. Unlike Nin's Sabina, whose crime was adultery, Golinda's crime is a Google-stalking variant of spying on her parents' "primal scene." Golinda, like Sabina, is a beautiful woman. She worked with a therapist to try to stop her secretive, if not outright dishonest, ways of hacking into her parents' email accounts. According to Wikipedia, Sabina is a beautiful, lying wife who desires to seduce every attractive man she can. Sabina tells her story to a "lie detector", who is something like a detective, something like a media fact-checker of political candidates' public statements, and something like a psychoanalyst, whose job is to listen to others and separate truth from lies. The lie detector traces Sabina's calls and continues to follow Sabina, revealing in the end the folly of her ways.

Golinda started individual treatment at the age of thirty. She went to a prestigious college and is a business school MBA graduate who had the reputation of being a successful chief executive officer (CEO). Her parents certainly believed that to be the case. Like the celebrity stalker, Nell Theobold, who stalked the diva, Birgit Nilsson, Golinda is an impostor. In fact, she never practiced as a business person. Perhaps the connection between imposture and stalking is not completely coincidental. Secrecy is certainly essential for successful stalking to occur, and should understandably be studied more seriously to look into other commonalities between imposture and stalking. If Golinda had

Googled me before consulting me, and I am quite certain that she did, she would have discovered that I had written several works on imposture (e.g., Gediman 1985; Gediman & Lieberman, 1996). She believed that her father, a businessman, and her mother, an administrative assistant, knew nothing of her unemployed status. In many ways, they appear to have colluded in Golinda's myth of being a successful CEO. Her husband, Henry, however, knew she did not work and quipped that his wife's occupation is to be "a woman stuck on the couch for four years." Golinda describes herself as "inauthentic" and "fraudulent," totally aware of living a lie, which not only embarrasses her, but also has started to spawn a spate of other lies to cover the original one about her employment. The lying–spying had mushroomed out of hand, and became intolerable for her to bear.

Golinda is a real life "spy in the house of love." She intrudes upon the primal scene in a most twenty-first century style and manner. She set up her trusting mother's email account, complete with user name and password, some years ago, and now breaks into that account regularly, in order to keep up with her parents' communications to each other, under circumstances that remain a secret to all except her husband and her analyst. No case better illustrates the connection I am suggesting between sexual stalking, surveillance stalking, and primal scene curiosity. This case has, in addition, all the hallmarks of a daughter's unrequited love and painful feelings of exclusion in a classical oedipal triangle. When father was at his work and mother was apart from him at hers, the two parents emailed each other frequently. That is when Golinda hacked in and noticed a pattern: when she did not receive an email from her father for several days during her parents' separation from each other, her mother and her father had been busy emailing each other with disparaging remarks about her. To Golinda's surprise, they obviously knew she was not working as per her pretense, and centered their intimate communications on their daughter's cover-up. During her stalking, hacking, and spying forays into the internet, she learned that her so-called secret was no secret at all to her parents, who were anxiously concerned about their daughter's imposturous professional life. Golinda's compromised identity can be understood as a projective identification that fuels psychoanalytic speculation. She intrudes into the intimacy of the primal scene parental couple and collects evidence that she is the loser in the oedipal triangle. She amasses proof that her father loves her mother more than he loves her, but she emerges victorious as the hacker-spy. You might find that a poor trade-off, but, clearly, Golinda does not.

As it turned out, Golinda did indeed Google-stalk me before she selected me as her analyst. That routine was not as common then as it is with today's millennial generation. In fact, I believe it was the exception among prospective patients then, yet very much in keeping with Golinda's character. She liked my formal credentials better than those of anyone else she had researched on the web.

Criminality from a sense of guilt (see Freud, 1916d) reinforces the primal scene motives of Golinda's stalking pattern of hacking into her parents' emails. In keeping with Freud's understanding, Golinda got caught in a cycle of committing crimes to "fix" her guilt on something she felt she could control herself, thus protecting herself from the potential accusations of doing things that made her feel guilty but that she could not control. The more she spies, the more she feels guilty. The more she feels guilty, the more she "fixes" the guilt by stepping up spying on her parents. That guilt-ridden spying, in turn, raises the guilt level, which then drives her on to more behavior that increases her guilty feelings. Those feelings prompt her on to more guilt-ridden behavior, which she anchors by fixing the guilt even more in place until the cycle has reached the status of a compulsive addiction. She became addicted to a cycle of guilt-ridden and then self-punitive behaviors and self-degrading commentary about herself in sessions with me. I consistently interpreted her self-degradation as chronic self-punishment for her crimes that she covers up with additional crimes that both fix the guilt and aggravate the self-punitive tendencies. She is not, then, like the true imposter, without conscience. That is, she is not, as Ron Galella is believed to be, a sociopath. One wonders what would happen if she had truthfully let her parents know she is not functioning as a CEO. She might certainly have dreaded their censure of her for falsely misleading them, but, if lucky, she would have gotten the same non-censorious empathic support she aimed to get from me. Living with some guilt generated by invasive behavior could be a very small price to pay for freedom from the compulsive–addictive cyclic behavior of a spy in the house of love.

I turn now to another patient, whom I call Lola, because, like Lola in the song from *Damn Yankees* (Abbott, 1955), "Whatever Lola wants, Lola gets," or she thinks she gets. Lola was a well-paid professional hacker whose territory spanned the globe. Like Evelyn in *Play Misty for Me* and Alex in *Fatal Attraction*, she resembles the erotomanic sexual stalker who believes the man she loves and idealizes reciprocates her feelings when he actually does not. Her professionally powerful skills did not extend to her love life. In fantasy, she is totally empowered to master the internet as a successful professional hacker. Lola, like Golinda, researched me carefully on the internet, undoubtedly more carefully than I can possibly ever know, before choosing me as her therapist because she found out I had written several papers on lying, deceit, and imposture. Like Golinda, she knew of, and was concerned enough about, these qualities in herself to seek help for the trouble they were causing her in several important personal relationships. Beholden to a wealthy mentor who essentially supported her financially, she was emotionally hooked on another man who had spurned her and chosen a woman other than her as his "significant other." Lola hacked in to the correspondence between her ex and his new paramour and learned from her personal spying efforts that she was definitely left out in the cold. As was the case for Golinda, she was an expert at hacking into other people's computers, but, unlike Golinda, she had reached professional heights in jobs for which she had been very well compensated and acknowledged in the world she worked in.

When I started my work with Lola, I did not know what is, by now, fairly common knowledge to many, if not all, of the millennial generation, those born between approximately 1980 and 2000, that hacking into emails and internet records is not only not difficult to learn about and do, but is rampant. There is an extensive literature right on the internet itself, instructing you how to invade other people's space in this way. As we have heard time and again, there is, apparently, no such thing as a private email. At the time I was originally writing my vignettes on these patients, I had not yet gotten wind of the widespread government hacking of telephones and internet accounts that was to achieve such widespread publicity in just a short time, and which will be more fully documented in Chapter Nine. However, I include some of the basics to end this chapter and move into the next.

Interpol is a law enforcement group, the world's largest international police organization, responsible, among other things, for combating cyber threats. The group uses tools and resources supplied by feeder organizations that supply information on the latest threats that have been discovered by agents and operatives working in cyberspace, sometimes referred to as the "cyber landscape." "Trend Micro" is one of these many feeder groups with an easily accessible website that advertises its training program to Interpol staff members and any interested others to allow for improved cybercrime investigations. That promotion enables member countries of Interpol to "fight the global hacker community."

If you Google "hacking instructions," you will be directed to a website <http://ushacker.co/how-to-hack-an-email-account.php #hackermail>. You will then be instructed to enter the email address you wish to hack. The site provides all the instructions you need, providing you reveal the personal information that would enable you to get the information you seek. Could Lola have done something similar when she got into the emails of her former lover and his current partner? Clearly, one need not be a member of a government organization that traces hackers to come by explicit instructions easily.

I am including this information at this juncture primarily to underscore how vulnerable we all are to being hacked. I did not follow the instructions given on the website because they require information, such as the email address I would like to hack, my own email address, and other information that I believe could have left me open to receiving all kinds of information, for example: "Someone tried to use your email account today at 4.45 p.m. If you are unaware of this activity, we thought you would want to know." Too many of these apparently benevolent warnings would undoubtedly slow down my computer use schedule for the day, and time is still precious to me. However, any reader is free to log in to <ushacker.com> and fill out what is asked for.

A front-page article, "Need a little espionage done? Hackers are for hire online" (Goldstein, 2015) documents how commonplace hacking for hire has become. The website, <hackerslist.com> contains an "A" list of hackers and those who want hackers to do jobs for them. Goldstein cites Thomas G. A. Brown, a former chief of the computer and intellectual property crime unit of the United States attorney's office in Manhattan: "Hackers for hire can permit nontechnical individuals to launch cyber attacks with a degree of deniability of lowering the barriers into online crime" (Goldstein, 2015, p. A1). An organization called "Hacker's List" began a website evaluating various hackers online shortly after federal prosecutors and FBI agents in Los Angeles completed a two-year crackdown of the hacker-for-hire industry. According to Goldstein, however, the market for hackers, and for matching hackers with clients' needs, shows no signs of slowing. The FBI named one marketing initiative "Operation Firehacker" and filed crime charges against many people across the country who were involved in either breaking into a person's email account or soliciting a hacker to do the job. "Still, the market for hackers, many of whom comply with the law and act more like online investigators, shows no signs of slowing. Many companies are hiring so-called ethical hackers to look for weaknesses in their networks" (Goldstein, 2015, p. A1). On its website, "Neighborhood Hacker" describes itself as a company of "certified ethical hackers" that works with customers to "secure your data, passwords and children's safety." You might wonder if that is as reassuring as it sounds, or if there may be a downside that they do not report. It seems as though private eyes are now employing hackers for hire to expand their network of clients. The source might easily develop into a secret stalker's delight.

CHAPTER NINE

Privacy *vs.* security in present-day cyber attacks

"I can't in good conscience allow the U.S. government to destroy privacy, Internet freedom and basic liberties for people around the world with this massive surveillance machine they're secretly building."

These are the words of Edward Snowden, who leaked top-secret security information to the press. Ironically, libertarian Senator Rand Paul, the conservative Republican who ran in the presidential primary election, could also have spoken them. Whether from the far left or the far right, we are being swamped with ideas about our new national dilemma: how to maintain the Fourth Amendment privacy rights of all Americans while, at the same time, supporting government efforts to maintain security against terrorist attacks. Dialogues and big conversations have been erupting around mastery of encryption via maximal surveillance selective stalking by hacking into our bulk telephone records and cyber systems. I have set order to the material relevant to Snowden's leakage and our new dilemma by beginning with the prophetic "fictional" film, *Enemy of the State*, (Scott, 1998) and then going on to *Citizenfour* (Poitras, 2013), the documentary film about former National Security Association (NSA) contractor Edward Snowden's whistle-blowing on the NSA. Undoubtedly, the best known events of stalking as privacy invasion of all United States citizens are those surrounding the NSA's unbridled efforts to ensure security for all following the 9/11 World Trade Center bombing catastrophe. Much of the highly classified information that Snowden dispensed during the real-time filming has had effects that are ongoing at this very moment. I wish to keep this ongoing stalking episode in American and world history at the center of these concluding chapters. I shall end by reviewing the varieties of current post-Snowden media coverage that have alerted people the world over to the dangers of too little or too much high-tech surveillance in our efforts to maintain an optimal balance between privacy and security.

Enemy of the State

The amazingly prophetic film, *Enemy of the State* (Scott, 1998) resembles both Coppola's 1974 classic, *The Conversation,* discussed in Chapter Six, as it carries through its ideological and cinematic conclusions, and Poitras's 2014 *Citizenfour,* to which it stands as a stunning prelude. Looking backward to the Coppola–Hackman masterpiece, film buffs will undoubtedly discover intended and unintended similarities, including a lengthy homage to Coppola's great opening surveillance stalking scene. Looking forward to the documentary *Citizenfour,* civil liberties is the issue *du jour*. In *Enemy of the State,* not only is Big Brother watching us, he masterfully bugs our public and private lives. Roger Ebert, in his November 20, 1998 review on his website, notes:

> "Enemy of the State" uses the thriller genre to attack what it calls "the surveillance society," byte by byte, because [of] proof that a congressman was murdered for opposing a bill that would make government snooping easier ... As the Will Smith character dodges around Washington, trying to figure out who's after him and why, the story is told with footage from spy satellites, surveillance cameras, listening devices, bugs, wiretaps, and database searches. The first time I saw a movie where a satellite was able to zoom in on a car license plate, I snickered. Recently I was able to log onto a Web site (www.terraserver.microsoft.com/) and see the roof of my house—or yours. If Microsoft gives that away for free, I believe the National Security Agency can read license plates.

I can only imagine Ebert's shock preceded the present-day taking of GPS technology for granted. This chilling thriller predates by years the present-day Patriot Act congressional disputes and even the 9/11/2001 World Trade Center attack. Its central theme is the conflict between America's security needs *vs.* its obligations to protect privacy down to the level of invasion of the home and even the bodies of the people who live in them. The film revolves around Congressional attempts to pass a bill that would expand the National Security Agency's surveillance powers. Directed by Tony Scott (1998), and set in pre 9/11 Washington, D.C., the film advocates an outright attack on the surveillance operations rampant in America at the time, and, as we all now know, more so ever since. The messages in this film are specifically and pointedly directed at the arguably terroristic governmental operations of the National Security Agency. Gene Hackman—yes, H-a-c-kman once again plays a hacker, or tapper, or eavesdropper, or bugger, named Edward Brill Lyle, though always called simply "Brill." He thrills us once again in a *tour de force* segue, if not deliberately planned yet uncredited sequel, to his portrayal of Harry Caul, the technology-obsessed private-eye investigator in *The Conversation,* covered earlier in Chapter Six on film portrayals of surveillance stalking. Hackman, in both films, is the "stalker, hacker, bugger, spy," personified peerlessly. No other actor can match him at this. He seems to have been born into the role. Hackman makes his first appearance as Brill a full sixty minutes into the film, when he connects with his co-stalkee, Robert Clayton Dean (Will Smith). Dean, an innocent but fugitive lawyer who is accidentally caught up in political high-tech gadgetry, needs the aid of ex-intelligence operative, Brill, after they both get caught by chance in a web of political corruption and are terrorized by a grungy group of computer geeks and nerds. These Silicon Valley-type men, in effect an irresponsible but innocent gang, come on as the counterpoints of the Mafia which, with its corresponding henchmen, also makes an appearance in this fast-paced, comedic, yet serious, film. This geeky gang serves as the support staff for NSA chief, Thomas Reynolds (Jon Voigt), who, from their innocent point of view, requires them to play with techie toys that are, in fact, automated computer systems. "Big Brother is watching you" takes on new and ominous meanings as these anonymous and automated computer systems themselves are the chief culprits that invade the privacy of the very American citizens they are supposed to protect. Although the year is around 1998 as opposed to 1974 of *The Conversation*, or the proverbial 1984 of the *Lives of Others*, also covered in Chapter Six of this book, or 2014 of *Citizenfour*, to be covered later in this chapter, the set-ups in the earlier and later films are amazingly similar.

In this story, congressman Phillip Hammersley (Jason Robards) is murdered for refusing to back a privacy bill. His murder is caught on film by a bird-watcher (Jason Lee), who happens to be on the scene and who is similarly taken out after planting a copy of the murder evidence on attorney Dean. The ultra-secret National Security Agency, which is behind all this, targets the innocent Dean. He gets smeared, loses his job, and is booted out of his home. In order to "get his life back," he enlists the help of the grizzled, former NSA man, Brill. The crack squad of grunge nerds monitors every move the dynamic duo makes. These stalkers use visual display units that resemble those in the white surveillance van featured in the opening Union Square scene in *The Conversation*, and those on display later at the eavesdroppers' convention. In both films, it is hard to distinguish at times whether these men are practical jokers or serious, governmentally employed private eyes. Are they like the prankster eavesdroppers at what is identified in the film as the "Buggers" convention in *The Conversation*, who get off uproariously on what they see, or are they serious private eyes doing their job to protect the security of their private clients and, as is the case for *Enemy*, of the American people as a whole.

Fugitive lawyer Dean's only friend is the shadowy underground figure, Brill, who was an American spy for the NSA until 1980, and since then has lived an invisible life as a hired gun in the outlands of intelligence and communications operations. His headquarters area is a high-tech hideaway in an old warehouse building, where his equipment is fenced in by copper mesh to stop the snoopers. There is more than a mere echo here of Coppola's 1974 film, *The Conversation*, which, to repeat, also starred Hackman as a paranoid high-tech eavesdropper; the workplaces in the two films resemble each other—deliberately, I assume. By now, I am in agreement with Ebert and most other thoughtful reviewers of this film: we must assume that the government can listen to any phone call it wants to and does so much more often than the law suggests it should. This excessively vigilant surveillance has provoked the current national debate about the pros and cons of the Patriot Act and bulk collection of telephone calls. To quote

Ebert once again, on *Enemy*: "In its action and violence it shows us how the movies have changed since 1974 . . . 'The Conversation' is a similar story that depended only on its intelligence and paranoia for appeal." Coppola's film was also prophetic of the Snowden affair and of the documentary film about it that followed, *Citizenfour*, to be covered in the next part of this chapter

Meanwhile, the fictional NSA chief, Reynolds, in *Enemy of the State*, has mounted a technology war to support a bill under consideration in Congress that would advance his career to its zenith. Reynolds, operating in the 1990s, pre 9/11 and before the onset of true governmental counterterrorism, is motivated both by his narcissistic ambitions for self-promotion and by a truly calculating sadistic temperament. His official aim, like many who advocated the later post 9/11 counterterrorism surveillance policies, was to protect the American people from terroristic attacks. He supported the bill that would increase the surveillance activities of the U.S. government using satellites and GPS technology to locate and then direct the up-to-date highly professional technologically guided stalking of its enemies. Adversaries of the surveillance bill believed the forfeiture and downright invasion of privacy rights justified killing the bill. Reynolds then personally supervised the murder of the major opponent of the bill, Congressman Phillip Hammersley. His last words before the murder that opens the film were ". . . I'm not gonna sit in Congress and pass a law that lets the government point a camera and a microphone at anything they damn well please." Hackman and Smith, as Brill and Dean, enter the picture because a photographer of nearby geese at the rural assassination site happened to have taped Reynolds directing Hammersley's murder, while one of Reynolds' men photographs the NSA murderer *in flagrante delicto* and must get rid of the proof of Reynolds' crime. That photographer then drops the tape right into Dean's shopping bag, planting the evidence on Dean and making him the fall guy in full view of the grungy stalking network who then tape this photographer, who was witness to the murder, as he unloads his compromising evidence onto Dean. Dean, of course, is totally unaware that he is being set up in this way to be stalked for the remainder of the film. Secrets abound. While Brill, like the Mafia and like Caul in *The Conversation*, are in the business of making money, Reynolds is in the business of promoting himself politically by prioritizing the protection of security rights above the protection of privacy rights. Furthermore, Brill maintains anonymity, keeping himself and the precise nature of his work a secret from Dean, his client, just as Reynolds, as head of the NSA, jokingly known as "The National Secret Association," keeps his work a secret from his constituency, the American public.

From here on, the film centers on the terroristic, state-directed surveillance stalking of Robert Dean, by satellite. Dean engages Brill as his associate, even though he does not yet know that the murder tape has been planted on his person. The arguably most skilled surveillance stalkers, that is, the nerdy bunch, then stalk Dean and Brill. I say "arguably," because Brill, as a former NSA spy, now engages his new buddy, Dean, to join him and to create their own summit-level techno-stalking counter-terrorizing operation against the NSA. In *The Conversation,* Hackman plays a surveillance stalker whose techno-stalking is directed toward a prey whose identity is unknown and whose motives present a total enigma to him. As the character Brill, in *Enemy,* having been trained by the NSA and having worked for them as a spy, he is well primed to grasp every detail of the technology and the counter-technology of every strategic move his pursuers make and to deliver back in kind with even greater expertise. Dean finds his phones tapped, clothing bugged, and house burgled, among other attempts by the NSA to get him. Brill, the ex-spy, knows how to counter all of these professional bugging techniques. Former real NSA Director, Michael Hayden, was deeply worried about the perception this film created, according to information to be found in James Risen's (2006) book, *State of War: The Secret History of the C.I.A. and the Bush Administration.* Risen hit the news again in 2015 in regard to his *exposé* of the American Psychological Association's support and cooperation in the torture of prisoners occurring around the same time. The information that Risen disclosed has caused a new barrage of outrage by psychoanalytic psychologists of Division 39 (Psychoanalysis) of the American Psychological Association, and other professional mental health organizations as well.

Enemy of the State, in addition to resembling *The Conversation,* is, in some ways, reminiscent of the film, *Peeping Tom,* discussed in Chapter Four of this book. Both films, the latter about voyeurism in male sexual stalking, the former about sadism and terrorism in government-sanctioned surveillance stalking, employ a doubling process to convey the essence of voyeurism in filming, whether originating in a man's mind or in a satellite. Many aspects of *Enemy of the State* deal with doubling in addition to the parallel process of making a film about surveillance stalking and what stalkers of all persuasions actually do, themselves, in the course of their work. In the case of *Peeping Tom,* the director, Powell, and in *Enemy,* director Scott, create images of the crosshairs of a camera focusing on a target. Scott's multiple crosshair images of satellite stalking cameras represent the satellite's viewing apparatus. Those images are incredibly reminiscent of director Powell's camera crosshairs that we see in photographer Mark Lewis's voyeuristic sexual stalking shots in *Peeping Tom.* That is, the crosshairs of the director's camera catch the crosshairs of the photographer protagonist's camera in one film and the satellite images show the same relative positions of crosshairs in the other. In one such scene in *Enemy,* the film audience views a taped conversation between Dean and Rachel (Lisa Bonet), with whom Dean had had an adulterous relationship, and who is the secret go-between for him and private investigator Brill. Dean must keep their connection secret both to protect his marriage and to hide his connection to surveillance stalker Brill from the Mafia. This camera stalking scene in *Enemy,* in which we see the crosshairs of the satellite zooming into Dean's conversation with Rachel, is immediately reminiscent of similar stalking by Hackman playing private eye Harry Caul in *The Conversation.* There, we see Hackman as Caul taping the adulterous relationship he is hired to record. In both films, the sophisticated film viewer will also notice the centrality of that identical-seeming white van that is the headquarters for the surveillance activity. In *The Conversation,* the van contains recording equipment for Hackman-as-Caul's private eye investigation of the adulterous couple, and, in *Enemy,* the NSA geeks' vehicle is equipped to receive images from the satellite that is stalking Dean. The similarity between the adulterous *rendezvous* scene set-ups and plot devices in *Enemy* and *The Conversation* are so striking that I had the eerie feeling that director Scott was deliberately borrowing from the earlier film as an insider joke for film buffs. The images of stalking in both films have scenes so similar that they might be interchangeable.

Themes common to *The Conversation* and *Enemy* would be of interest to psychoanalysts who are also film critics, and to film buffs in general. Most of all, they would fascinate anyone who is stunned, as I am, by the prophetic nature of the films from the 1970s through

1990s on surveillance stalking that I am covering. All augur today's ever-present concern with invasions of privacy. Maslin, in her 1998 review of high-tech surveillance in *Enemy of the State* for *The New York Times,* notes director Scott's allusions to Coppola's premise that privacy is imperiled by runaway electronics. During the week that she published her review, the nation was listening to surreptitiously taped Washington telephone calls. During the year 1998, a prophetic year for foretelling the NSA scandals recently leaked by Snowden, Peter Travers of *Rolling Stone* explicitly mentions stalking and believes that director Scott references Hackman's seminal role as surveillance expert Harry Caul in Francis Ford Coppola's 1974 *The Conversation* when he shows Brill holed up, like Caul, in a warehouse filled with bugging devices. It is, Travers says, a sight that also evokes other potent paranoid thrillers of the Watergate era. The film, *Enemy of the State,* he believes, is, thus, a planned segue, whether conscious and deliberate or not, that moves forward from *The Conversation* by using its magnificent star once again in a mind-blowing *déjà vu* experience for the audience to ponder.

Citizenfour

This extraordinary documentary film that occurs in real time reveals the National Security Association's (NSA) bulk collection program of internet and telephone data from millions of American citizens, a program that Edward Snowden, a contractor to the NSA, discovered was a "meta" program that was meant to be limited to targeting terrorists. Snowden leaked the documents to which he was privy because the NSA was directing its efforts largely toward you and me, and not simply our enemies. As whistle-blower, Snowden used encrypted mail under the alias "Citizenfour" to contact documentarian Laura Poitras and journalist Glenn Greenwald, lawyer and reporter for the *Guardian,* to meet him in Hong Kong. There, he would reveal what he had learned about the NSA's excesses in intercepting emails, phone calls, and web searches of American citizens. He would then leave it to Greenwald to decide when and how the information and accompanying documents would be made public. The entire documentary could be thought of as a planned and choreographed "outing" to the American people of Snowden's disclosures of the massive amount of information that the U.S. government kept secret about its invasions of the privacy of the American people. In its efforts to balance the public's right to know with the government's right to collect intelligence in the fight against global terrorism, this documentary tilts toward transparency over secrecy as a legitimate sociocinematic choice and because that civil libertarian side of the story had been the lesser known since 9/11. The film argues for a need to promote ongoing debate on issues of proper balance between privacy and security.

Laura Poitras's documentary, as far as I can tell, was more instrumental than any other factor in enabling the leak that Glen Greenwald orchestrated for Edward Snowden in his consequential whistle-blowing on the NSA surveillance practices that had gone awry. Her award-winning documentary film, then, is a prime example of art influencing life. In her film about the leak, Poitras precisely outlines the surveillance stalking operations of indiscriminate bulk tracking of mass communications. She had begun to investigate these actions in real time before connecting with Snowden to help her bring this film to life. *Citizenfour* was to win the 2015 Oscar for best documentary of the year 2014. She warned, in her academy award winning film,

> For now, know that every border you cross, every purchase you make, every call you dial, every cell phone tower you pass, friend you keep, article you write, site you visit, subject line you type, and packet you route *is in the hands of a system whose reach is unlimited but whose safeguards are* not. (My emphasis)

From its start, the film records the chronic emotional tensions of many individuals who participated in outing the stalking situation in which the outreaching NSA has placed every one of us. With the opening credits still rolling, we learn from William Binney, former NSA crypto-mathematician expert on mass internet data analysis, that, only a few days after 9/11, before Poitras and Snowden connected for *Citizenfour*, the NSA decided to actively spy on everyone in this country. If I felt shivers of paranoia, albeit justifiable, running through my mind and body, imagine what the people involved in creating, producing, and distributing *Citizenfour* felt when, knowing themselves to be objects of public scrutiny, they enabled Snowden to whistle-blow. Binney, who retired from the NSA after concern about its indiscriminate scope of surveillance practices, testifies that men with guns raided his office at about the time in 2011 that the NSA built the world's largest repository for intercepted communications. Poitras adds that the NSA has never collected more personal information in its entire history than it does now. Binney testified that, despite congressional denial that any such wrongdoing was going on, customers of AT&T knew it was occurring, and filed suit against the NSA for tapping into its San Francisco network. In a shot of a U.S. Senate hearing about linkability of diverse sources of information, we learn about the common practice of linking of locale identification, such as that determined by cellphone or by New York City's Metrocard, with credit or debit card. Such generalized linking comes under the rubric, "metadata" and enables the NSA, when it collects and collates this knowledge, to discover where anyone is located and what they might be purchasing at any given time. Collecting metadata such as this, limited to cellphone linkability of location and purchases, enables you to be targeted, and you can be followed for the rest of your life to see if you committed a crime. This possibility of lifetime pursuit and stalking sent chills through me as well as through an entire court audience filmed in the documentary. If there is truth in what we have been hearing in *Citizenfour* about metadata, then we are all being stalked by a government agency, the NSA, that has no checks on its oversteps. When we realize that this spying is truly going on, we understand that frightening, terrifying, and terrorizing massive repression could follow if this process is allowed to unfold, unchecked. During a congressional hearing, an informed representative denies that NSA ever wittingly targeted any member of the American population for these invasive purposes, clearly indicating he knew it was possible for quite the opposite to occur: any of us could be targeted at any time. His lying was documented very persuasively by his impotent cover-up attempts. This documentary activates memories of Watergate, as do the surveillance films of the 1970s through the 1990s that I have been reviewing and that have taught the lessons from Watergate very well.

Glenn Greenwald, Laura Poitras, and Edward Snowden and, in addition, Ewen MacAskill, also, like Greenwald, of the *Guardian*, finally meet up for an in-person encounter at the Mira Hotel in Hong Kong on June 3, 2013. This sanctuary kept Snowden reasonably safe from immediate attempts to find him personally and allowed him to delay his plan of action until the time was ripe. On August 28, 2015, when I started to write this chapter, I was amazed at how far and fast his leakage had progressed. Poitras sets up her camera and starts filming an encounter that will last for just over eight days. The director enables us to see this eight-day process in real time. That is, the protagonists do not yet know, any more than we in the audience know, of the implications and outcomes of what is going on before our very eyes. We learn of decisions they are about to make just as those preparing the public leakage are in the process of deciding and strategizing. As media representative Greenwald begins his interview that will eventuate in the *exposé* of NSA, Snowden summarizes his investment in the project: "It all comes down to state power against the people's ability to meaningfully oppose that power." He concludes there is no way to oppose that power without the state changing its policies. He explains the gist of some significant examples of what the documents he will hand over to Greenwald to announce to the press contain. He discloses that you can actually watch surveillance activities in real time: for example, you can follow surveillance drone activity for hours and hours by just clicking on which segment you want to see. Snowden goes on to say that because we now have evidence that we are being watched, people have become very careful what they type into search engines.

> I remember what the internet was like before it was being watched and there's never been anything in the history of man that's like it . . . I am more willing to risk imprisonment than I am willing to risk the curtailment of my intellectual freedom.

Citizenfour informs us that the infrastructure that is in place in cyberspace is built with the cooperation of other governments that can intercept all communications and, either now or in the future, can select and use that information in ways that presently have no limits or restrictions. Snowden, himself, as a top level NSA contractor, has access to the highest level of secret information. He has the capacity to reveal anything in the documents but would not like the responsibility of making decisions about what information is to be disclosed. That is one reason he prefers his store of knowledge about how the system works to be released through the press and this documentary than personally. He is essentially putting the responsibility on Greenwald's and, eventually, Poitras's shoulders. The agreement is that Greenwald will start leaking to the networks and the press any day now. We are watching history and personal psychological reactions develop as they occur.

During these critical eight days, Snowden reveals to the documentary makers that the United Kingdom's Government Communications Headquarters' (GCHQ) network intercept program, Tempora, is the most invasive anywhere in the world. Tempora, in advance of the NSA spying network, has had access to highly specific content (e.g., just what is purchased by whom in what place) in addition to metadata (e.g., cellphone and credit card number)—on everything in its system. Snowden becomes increasingly convincing as he gives us solid facts as the documentary goes on. In a humorous interlude, he conveys simultaneously to his group and to us, the documentary viewers, in just what ways he thinks the Mira hotel room where they are meeting is bugged. He lifts the telephone to show us where it most likely has been tapped. Because he suspects visual bugs as well as auditory ones, he places a blanket over his face and hands, laughing all the way as he types a password into his laptop computer. He convinces us that all of the documentary participants holed up in the hotel are being surveillance-stalked at that very moment, and that their surveyors can tap into anything at all that the documentary team does or says. Greenwald laughingly refers to the fact that nothing can shock him now as they are getting used to being bugged and he jokes that he will never leave anything in his room alone again. Here, he is alluding to the "paranoia that happens to all of us," sometimes known, as I have said before, as "justified paranoia," an unpleasant feeling that must inevitably accompany the knowledge that one is truly being stalked. Clearly, that humor can be a very effective defense against the nerve-jangling information that those in the room making the documentary and we, the viewing audience, are probably hearing for the first time ever. We next hear an incredibly cool and, at the same time, mind-boggling explanation from Snowden of how various aspects of the surveillance system work. As a part of this real-time documentary, his explanations, accompanied by his verifying documents, will air on American and British television within the next days. We will learn, for one, that surveillance operators can, at the push of a button on a computer, collect one billion telephone and internet sessions simultaneously, so that twenty sites at the Department of Defense can collect twenty billion sessions at a time. Snowden reinforces the worrying reality of these figures, "It's not science fiction. It's happening right now." Greenwald expresses how just seeing the equipment that Snowden is demonstrating brutally hits in a super-visceral way that is so needed to bring the facts and dangers back home for all to evaluate.

What is not so funny, according to Scott (2014) in his *New York Times* film review, is that although the film is a documentary by form, it is also a spooky horror thriller. Something akin to an ever-present stalker haunts us, the viewers, just as it haunts the protagonists, throughout. "It is everywhere and nowhere, the Leviathan whose belly is our native atmosphere." Mr. Snowden, unplugging the telephone in his room, hiding under a blanket while typing on his laptop, looking mildly panicked when a fire alarm is tested on his floor, can seem paranoid. He can also seem to be practicing a kind of *avant-garde* common sense. It is hard to tell the difference, and thinking about the issues Ms. Poitras raises can induce a kind of epistemological vertigo. What do we know about what is known about us? Who else knows about it? Can we trust them? These questions are terrifying, and so is *Citizenfour*. It is particularly terrifying to watch after the Paris and San Bernardino terrorist attacks in November and December 2015.

Six hours after Snowden's revelations that I have just summarized above, Glenn Greenwald releases his first story and the scene shifts to the television set in the hotel room, on which we see Wolf Blitzer on CNN broadcasting the breaking news, that "your privacy is being invaded to protect America's security." He notes that a court order gives NSA blanket access to millions of Verizon customers' records on a daily basis. The network shows reporter Glenn Greenwald being publicly congratulated on his scoop. Greenwald explains that this intrusion into the lives of Verizon customers was sanctioned by the U.S. Patriot act of 2011, which allowed the government very broad powers to get records with a lot of information about people based on just a low level of suspicion and without standards for probable cause. Greenwald continues that this act does not require that a person has to be suspected of terrorism to be surveyed, but allows bulk invasion and collection of anyone's records, including yours or mine. The government program is indiscriminate and sweeping because it can collect information about people even if those who administer it have no reason to think that their targets have done anything wrong. Hence, *Citizenfour* breaks wide open the heart of the issue between privacy and security, between civil liberties and protection from terrorists, that calls for meaningful and productive debate from this point forward in our history as a nation.

Glenn Greenwald once again refers to paranoia, musing that the NSA will become paranoid in the extreme once they notice what classified data Snowden has set loose to blow their cover. Poitras, Greenwald, MacAskill, and Snowden are anything but paranoid in the extreme. Snowden, most of all, is, rather remarkably, cool, calm, collected, sturdy, thoughtful, and courageous while we watch him contribute to making this documentary. Members of the teams are, after all, working in the face of sure knowledge that they are putting at least their professional lives on the line and opening up the possibility of being harassed stalkees for the rest of their lives. They are hopeful that laws leaning on the side of protecting journalistic good faith and freedom of expression will protect them for at least a limited time. Snowden, himself, is a remarkably generous and caring person, knowing that he will have to come forward without biasing the reporting process. Then Greenwald publishes the second story with Barton Gellman in *The Washington Post*, and the *Guardian* continues its *exposé* of the NSA shortly after. Once again, we watch the group cloistered in the less and less safe Hong Kong hotel room watching Wolf Blitzer on CNN with more breaking news that the documentary group has released. Blitzer tells the world that *The Post* and the *Guardian* have reported on another broad and secret N.S.A. surveillance program: The FBI and the CIA are tapping directly into the central service of nine leading internet companies, including Microsoft, Yahoo!, Google, Facebook, AOL, Skype, YouTube, and Apple. They are currently extracting audio, video, photographs, emails, documents, and connection logs that enable analysts to track a person's movements and contacts over time with no checks or oversights. At the time this scoop of this "super stalk" is released, commentators have begun to suspect a whistle-blowing leaker. Although they still have no idea who it might be, they offer assurances that an investigation as to who is behind it will undoubtedly be launched in no time at all. The more libertarian commentators think the focus will be only on the whistle-blower who leaked and not on whom in the NSA and government at large put these anti-privacy principles into effect. With this discrepancy in predictions, we begin to hear important statements about the morality of the larger privacy–security issue. The group holed up in the hotel hears one side consistent with theirs as an analyst comments that the NSA's unfettered invasion of cyberspace is the biggest intrusion into civil liberties of all time, and look as though they are content that their mission is on its path to accomplishment. They also hear the opposition point of view: security and safety concerns about terrorist attacks are getting short shrift in the name of civil libertarianism.

Meanwhile, many of those who are on to Snowden-as-leaker have begun to make his life difficult and to hint that he is an unwelcome blocker of national security. He learns that his partner, Lindsay Mills, is all right but that his rent checks are not going through. He has been in close contact with her, although she and his family do not yet know where he is and what he is doing, but we sense there will be a break in that secrecy very soon along with more breaking news stories on CNN and the other news networks. Poitras photographs Snowden as he looks out the hotel window. A creepy silence seems to pervade, and he says that the feeling, that I will label " impending stalking" is hard to describe. He says that not knowing what is going to happen the next day is scary but, at the same time, liberating. He refers to an "internal Wikipedia" at GCHQ in Britain where anyone with access to the super high classified levels of intelligence can work on anything they want, making it very hard for him or anyone else to predict what news will break next. We get the closest look possible in this documentary at the defenses and ego strengths that sustain Snowden through his courageous move on behalf of you and me, and trust him when he says he is totally willing to pay the price of risk to himself on behalf of his cause. He engages in a kind of soliloquy directed to the NSA, words that reveal a lot about the character of this most unusual human being: cool, calm, collected, courageous, and justifiably paranoid. He is aware that any day now "they" will make this all about him, at which point

> I'll come out, you know, hey this is a . . . this is not a question of somebody skulking around the shadows. He's a public issue. It's not my issues, you know. These are everybody's issues, and I'm not afraid of you, you know. And you're not going to bully me into signing like you've done with everybody else, and if nobody else is going to do it, I will, and hopefully when I'm gone, whatever you do to me there will be somebody else who will do the same thing. It will be the sort of internet principle of the hydra, you know, you can stalk one person but there's gonna be seven more of us.

Asked if he is getting more nervous, Snowden says,

> No, I think the way I look at stress, particularly because I sort of knew this was coming, because I sort of volunteered to walk into it, I'm already sort of familiar with the idea. I'm not worried about—when something like busts in the door, suddenly I'll get nervous, but I'm usually relaxed, that's the only difference, I think.

Greenwald starts to discuss with Snowden how they will come out with Snowden's identity. The reporter is orchestrating a way to introduce him as a person who has a particular set of political objectives about informing the world about what's taking place at N.S.A—"you're coming out because you want to fucking come out." Snowden repeats that he does not want to skulk around, but also does not want to do the government's job for them. "I think it's powerful to come out and say 'I'm not afraid.'" Glenn Greenwald then speaks up in a way that tells of his personal motivations as a gay man who has come out and is living with a partner in Rio de Janeiro. "You feel the power of your choice . . . you don't have to investigate, here I am." The mutual support and bonding between these two men, one heterosexual, the other homosexual, in an effort to come out as the right antidote to secret stalking, has got to be one of the most potent forces of their particularly effective whistle-blowing. To avoid the shock of potential investigations to come, Greenwald interviews Snowden in anticipation of what might be coming later, from without, at an unknown time. Most of the information they intend to "give" or "leak" exposes that Snowden worked for the CIA and NSA at the highest level of secret privileged access to top classified information and that position afforded him access to the information he is now sharing with the world and, therefore, he should be completely trusted. Psychoanalytically speaking, they are turning potential passive persecution into active effectiveness. This defensive reversal of passive into active is also adaptive in helping both men to master any apprehensiveness they would normally have at being cornered. It is not just the documentary that is brilliantly conceived and executed, but also the conscientious work of the two men who arranged this unbelievably risky, world-shaking outing.

The scene shifts to a busy street in Hong Kong with a colossal sized television screen showing Snowden, as yet unidentified by name, to the world. The issue of extradition from Hong Kong comes up, as he is about to lose his cover. Snowden applies for refugee status through the UN and goes underground until a Wikileaks representative can find him a place of safe asylum. Poitras stays in Hong Kong to complete her filming, but realizes she is being followed, or stalked, and six days later she returns to Berlin. Greenwald returns to Rio and reports to authorities around the world everything he has learned from Snowden about the bulk collection techniques used in the government secret intelligence programs. On June 21, the US government charges Snowden with three felonies, two under the Espionage Act, and asks Hong Kong to extradite him. Two days later, Wikileaks organizes his departure from Hong Kong and provides a representative to escort him to Russia for political asylum, where to this day he is living. Asylum trumps extradition and keeps the debate over NSA spying practices alive.

Poitras continues work on *Citizenfou*r during her exile in Berlin, where her focus is less on the leaks but on world events the initial leaks have stirred up. Among them appears to be a movement afoot to destroy the documentation that Snowden had given the *Guardian* regarding the bulk collection practices of the NSA. A group of lawyers representing Snowden *pro bono in absentia* believe he was charged with three felonies under an error of the Espionage Act, involving the dissemination of national defense information. The law charging Snowden was to be used for spies, not whistle-blowers. The Espionage Act does not discriminate between those leaking information to the press and those selling secrets to foreign enemies for personal profit. The law itself eliminates any kind of defense Snowden might be able to make. The attorneys conclude that the problem is more political than legal, and support his remaining in asylum.

President Obama would have liked a lawful, orderly examination of these laws and not exclusive reliance on the leak the way it happened, so initially, the US government did not cooperate very well in a follow-up of Snowden's revelations. Reactions in Europe were much more supportive. In September 2013, the European Parliament began hearings to investigate NSA surveillance on European Union citizens and companies, and to find ways to prevent government spying. Testifying was Jacob Appelbaum, an encryptions and software developer and journalist, whom we heard earlier in the documentary explaining the meaning and significance of metadata gleaned from linking debit and credit cards with Metrocards or other IDs. Metadata reveals location and purchase contacts, if not more specific content, from intercepted cellphone and internet data of millions of Americans. Appelbaum was one of the few people who gained access to Snowden's top-secret documents that were released during the 2013 global surveillance disclosure. Poitras is clearly sympathetic and remains so throughout the documentary. Another witness, Jeremy Scahill, called for removing the server from identifying the sender or receiver of email messages and questioned the FBI's request to provide information on any client at all without reason to suspect a crime or potential danger to the country. That is, Scahill questioned the rationale for bulk collection. He was not allowed to tell people what was going on in terms of the FBI's presumed invasion of privacy and felt his only ethical choice was to shut down. "It's supposed to be difficult to invade somebody's privacy," but every bit as important as it is to conduct investigations. Therein lies the dilemma that the Snowden affair has brought to our attention. "If we don't have a right to privacy, how do we have a free and open discussion? What good is the right to free speech if it's not protected." Applebaum notes that what we used to call liberty and freedom we now call "privacy." "When we lose privacy, we lose agency because we lose liberty itself." He refers to the myth of the passive surveillance machine, but personally believes that surveillance has to imply control. He says the NSA is actively attacking European and American citizens and anyone that they can. A case in point was investigating Angela Merkel and Hillary Clinton's cellphone records.

In March 2014, Germany began a parliamentary inquiry to investigate NSA spying. William Binney, whom we have already heard from in the opening scene of the documentary, is asked to testify as expert witness. He feels the issues that Snowden has brought to our attention are not limited to America, but apply to all countries. His testimony is interrupted when news breaks that the CIA has a double agent spying against Germany's NSA inquiry. Binney makes it clear that any source that whistle-blows at this point will be under constant surveillance, and if he passed data "I'm sure they'd take him off the street" and concludes that we will have to do as they did in the Nixon years, meet physically on the floor of a parking garage.

I conclude this exposition of *Citizenfour* with reference to the conflict embedded in the message near the ending of documentary: with a call for conversations on the rights and mandates to investigate government agencies that are charged with protecting privacy and liberty of individuals on the one hand, and also on the rights and mandates to secure these same individuals against terrorist targets who wish to do them harm and annihilate them. I hope I have shown how this documentary has added immeasurably to an understanding of the stalking that is inherent in governmental invasions of privacy through bulk collections of metadata and content data of individuals communicating with one another through technologically advanced media communications systems. What we can learn about technologically advanced stalking should also help us understand stalking in all its other forms that are related to the sexual and surveillance issues covered in this book.

The film ends with Snowden in Moscow, joined by his partner, Lindsay Mills, where we see them through an unknown apartment window, cooking together. Poitras, for her provocative final scene, films Glenn Greenwald and Edward Snowden, who have joined each other in some unidentifiable location. They exchange information by writing their thoughts on paper in order to avoid being recorded by any planted audio device, and then shredding their paper correspondence. The last thing we see shredded is a reference to a new whistle-blowing source, as both Greenwald and Snowden pass pieces of paper with obscure notes back and forth to each other, obviously trying to leak something and keep it secret at the same time. The most enigmatic and tantalizing piece of information we read are scribblings of a sequence either of events or of a chain of command involving the new source, ending with the word "POTUS," the acronym for "President of the United States." Obviously, something very important has been shared about a potential bold and risky whistle-blower plan that excites hope and apprehension in both men, while it excites curiosity in us as audience. Is Barack Obama to be a future ally in their cause? Snowden feels that if the newly hinted at plan works, it can raise the situation of whistle-blowing to a whole new level. We all are hopeful that this stalker, hacker, voyeur, spy saga will not end in the shredder but will come out and be righted as it should be.

Privacy vs. *security in high-level government surveillance stalking*

While Edward Snowden has been living out his life courtesy of the asylum offered by the Russian government and Wikileaks, the enigmatic ending of *Citizenfour* has us all guessing what the shredded reference to POTUS might be. In its ceaseless coverage of privacy and security issues in the face of new terrorist threats, particularly those from ISIS, the press began to release a seemingly never-ending series of stories in the months following the Snowden leakage and the release of the film, *Citizenfour.* I have wondered why, after the film won an Oscar at the January 2015 Academy Awards ceremony, it seemed to be playing in fewer, rather than in more, theaters and its publicity definitely diminished. It was impossible to see the film for quite some time after it left the one theater in New York still airing it sometime in February or March, until the DVD was released on August 25, 2015. I began to follow the regular newspaper coverage of surveillance excesses and violations, taking as meticulous notes as I could on a nearly daily basis until the pace of the press outstripped my ability to keep up with coverage for this book. My interests in the relatively simple personal psychological syndromes of erotomania, voyeurism, and surveillance stalking have expanded to fill a bigger niche provided by world-shaking events of enormous psychological consequence regarding the balance of privacy and security on a global scale. Following the ISIS terrorist attacks in Paris and in San Bernardino, California, critiques of the downside of too much surveillance were to be replaced with pleas for more surveillance in the interests of national security. With the primary debates for the 2016 presidential election in full swing, both Democrat and Republican hopefuls addressed the fears and terrors of their constituents by calling now for more, and not less, governmental surveillance. I will try to convey my early attempts to keep up with, and to summarize, my sampling of what might be never-ending current events related to cyberstalking in the remainder of this final chapter of my book. I ask my readers at this point to trust that my coverage of media coverage of world events, mainly those reported in *The New York Times*, will be extremely relevant to the psychology of stalking, particularly to what it feels like to be stalked.

I start here with two everyday examples of media coverage of internet stalking and hacking. Both appeared as articles or Op Ed pieces in *The New York Times* in March 2015. The first deals with the arrest of private investigators who were charged on account of their alleged illegal hacking into the computers and email accounts of individuals who had information that was potentially useful to their clients. I then move on to new laws enacted by the United States Congress in connection with the Patriot Act and other huge scale changes brought about by explosive movements in the technology world that affect everyone living on the planet. Needless to say, these accounts of cyberstalking add heft to the psychoanalytically cohesive account of stalking that I have been working on throughout this book.

On Tuesday March 10, 2015, Jimmy Wales, the founder of Wikipedia, co-authored with Lila Tretikov, the Executive Director of the Wikipedia Foundation, a piece that grabbed my eye: "Stop spying on Wikipedia users" (Wales & Tretikov, 2015). The piece begins:

> Today, we're filing a lawsuit against the National Security Agency to protect the rights of the 500 million people who use Wikipedia every month. We're doing so because a fundamental pillar of democracy is at stake: the free exchange of knowledge and ideas. (p. A21)

A regular Wikipedia user, myself, I was shocked to learn that I was being stalked once again, this time in an additional modality, on the internet. I was just getting accustomed to being harassed by advertisements popping up on my email every time I ordered an item of clothing online, or even clicked on an image of a particular dress or jacket that appealed to me. This monitoring of my fashion preferences was not altogether a bad thing: some computer was being fed, and was feeding back to me, images of things I desired and showed me the way I could obtain them if I had the means to do so. Pop-up images reflected a relatively benign downside in disrupting my concentration on email content. In time, though, however beneficial to my interests these minor privacy invasions might have been, they began to be increasingly bothersome around the time that I had been studying the *Citizenfour* DVD for an entire weekend, and feeling dizzily informed about the danger posed by too broad a scope of mass internet data collection by U.S. government intelligence agencies. My excitement at what I learned from *Citizenfour* about feelings induced by privacy invasions was pretty well matched by my fear of the danger of terrorist attacks. Why, I began to wonder, should anyone get to know my interests, and even private curiosities, by spying on me via the internet? And why should everybody else as well be subjected to the same obvious invasions of privacy as I had been? On the other hand, I would like to continue walking out of my front door and over to my office without being bombed into oblivion. Being cyberstalked seemed a small price to pay.

Wales and Tretikov go on to describe Wikipedia's lawsuit against the NSA in the interest of protecting its users. Wikipedia contended that the NSA's mass surveillance violates the Fourth Amendment, which protects the right to privacy as well as the freedoms of expression and association. Previous lawsuits against the organization, such as that by AT&T subscribers, have made similar claims. This lawsuit sounds, then, like its predecessors, with the exception that it has been filed after Snowden's leak and the release of the documentary, *Citizenfour*. Most people read Wikipedia anonymously, and the individuals who write for its website and are overseen by parent company, Wikimedia, prefer to remain anonymous. Many contributors cover controversial issues that are particularly problematic for those who live in countries with repressive governments. "These volunteers should be able to do their work without having to worry that the United States government is monitoring what they read and write." Whenever someone overseas views or edits a Wikipedia page, it is likely that the NSA can intercept any international text-based traffic related to those reading and writing activities. The NSA can access, via mega and more specific collection, that person's location, identity, political and religious beliefs, sexual orientation, and medical conditions. This case is one of many that indicate how prophetic the film *Enemy of the State*, discussed earlier in this chapter, was of the Snowden affair. The column goes on:

> The notion that the NSA is monitoring Wikipedia's users is not, unfortunately, a stretch of the imagination. One of the documents revealed by the whistle-blower Edward J. Snowden specifically identified Wikipedia as a target for surveillance, alongside several other major websites like CNN.com, Gmail and Facebook. (p. A21)

Wikipedia is presumably asking the court to order and end NSA's "dragnet surveillance of Internet traffic," but not specifically targeted parties suspected of crime or terrorism. The Wales and Tretikov piece concludes:

> Privacy is an essential right. It makes freedom of expression possible, and sustains freedom of inquiry and association. It empowers us to

read, write and communicate in confidence, without fear of persecution. Knowledge flourishes where privacy is protected. (p. A21)

I have just scanned and reported on selected articles in *The New York Times* appearing in the month of March and earlier in 2015. They suggest, as I did in Chapter Eight, that it is beginning to look as though one cannot duck hacking at all. During the month of May, then on through October, and into January of 2016, the topic has been rolling on ceaselessly. In the spring of 2015, we learned that the entire NSA intelligence operation had been hacked, perhaps by a foreign power, China. On April 27 2015, David Sanger and Nicole Perlroth caught our attention with their *New York Times* headline: "White House takes cybersecurity pitch to Silicon Valley" (p. A3). The President, or POTUS, wanted to negotiate with those most involved in matters of encryption to guarantee more privacy without loosening up on security. The article highlighted the idea that President Obama is presently leaning more in the direction of security than in the direction of privacy in what has clearly boiled down to a major concern since the scandals around the NSA started with Snowden's whistleblowing. The article caught my attention for many reasons, including the fact that I had just returned from San Francisco, which seemed very different from the marvelous city it had always been before it became the center of high-tech Silicon Valley. Apparently Apple, Google, and Facebook, the high-tech mainstays of Silicon Valley, have been developing encryption technology communities, which could easily be now more dedicated to privacy and freedom of expression than to security and protection against terrorism, and the President would like this potentially dangerous imbalance to be looked into. Jeb Johnson, the newest president of Homeland Security, along with Ashton B. Carter, Mr. Obama's recently installed Secretary of Defense, in investigating "Post-Snowden cryptography", believe that encryption is making it harder for your government to find criminal activity and potential terrorist activity, albeit more protective of individual civil liberties and a much needed obstacle to privacy invasions. Mr. Obama, as early as February 2015, had expressed sympathy with those who were striving to protect security, while saying at the same time that it had to be balanced against privacy and liberty. Yet, in October, *The New York Times* questioned the safety of encryptions, and reported that the Obama administration, embarrassed by Snowden's revelations of mass surveillance by the National Security Agency and the theft of federal personnel records by foreign hackers, has ordered all publicly accessible websites run by the executive branch to use HTTPS encryption by the end of 2016. I could not help but wonder if this order was the one referenced in *Citizenfour* when Greenwald scribbled the acronym POTUS to Snowden on the paper, subsequently shredded, he passed to him. The order for encryption strikes me as analogous to an order for protection as the only legal safeguard against personal stalking. This very tenuous balance of power swinging volatilely between privacy and security seems to be on everyone's minds. It has been said, for example, that the newest iPhone operating system leaves Apple no way to decode data in cellphones, and friendly cryptographers are saying that the need for encryption is greater than ever, to guarantee some control over the greatest amount of information in history that has ever been collected. The pro-encryption faction worries about restraint of trade if we are going to allot security primacy in the privacy–security conflicts of our day.

As it turns out, encryption is a double-edged sword, depending on who is in charge of potentially indecipherable coding, Silicon Valley or ISIS allies. I jump ahead to December of 2015, following the attack by two home-bred ISIS terrorists on the developmental facility in San Bernardino. Investigators of that mass killing have unearthed that American terrorists who are supported by ISIS have been receiving instructions by encrypted ISIS commands that nobody yet can decipher. As I was writing this section, I was thinking that there would undoubtedly be more reports before my manuscript sees the light of day. Since I was then thinking I would like to see this book published earlier rather than later, I return now to May of 2015, only seven months before the time I was writing this section and perhaps well over a year from when this book is to be published. I hope my reader is following my dip into non-linear time at this juncture.

Just as I was beginning to write this section, on May 5, 2015, a *New York Times* breaking news alert came through on my computer screen with the following announcement. I quote it here in its entirety just to give the flavor of what it felt like to be writing this book in the midst of daily actively breaking news that made it so hard to write because the stories were on the very same topic I was writing about and always a step ahead of me in their processing of information. I began to feel stalked by the influx of news invasions of my privacy as a psychoanalytic writer on the topic of stalking, even as the influx provided me with information that, at the same time, has made my topic as current as any can be. The announcement read:

> The lower house of France's Parliament overwhelmingly approved a sweeping intelligence bill that, if it wins in the upper house, would give the government broad surveillance powers with little judicial oversight. The measure would give the intelligence services the right to gather potentially unlimited electronic data from Internet communications, and to tap cellphones and capture text messages. It would obligate Internet companies to comply with government requests to sift through subscribers' communications.

According to Alissa Rubin (2015), who broke the story, the French Parliament is taking a great stride in the opposite direction from American lawmakers, who, as I have just noted, are considering altering the limits of the broad surveillance powers assumed by the U.S. government after September 11, 2001. The French, in what seems to me at the moment to be an unbalanced reaction, have overwhelmingly approved a bill that could give authorities their most intrusive spying abilities ever with no judicial oversight. This proposed extension of power seems to be a reaction to the terrorist attacks in and around Paris this past January 2015, especially those directed at the offices of the satirical newspaper, *Charlie Hebdo,* and at a kosher grocery. The new surveillance powers lean in completely the opposite direction of the new U.S. negotiations with the Silicon Valley cryptographers, which aim to protect civil liberties by curbing extreme privacy invasions: they would give French intelligence services the right to gather potentially unlimited electronic data. The provisions of the French bill would allow the intelligence services, the equivalent of our NSA, to tap telephones, read emails, and force internet providers to sift through virtually all of their subscribers' communications. Internet companies, civil libertarians, and privacy advocates call the law a creation of a "French Big Brother," referring to the George Orwell novel, *Nineteen Eighty-Four* (1949). The groups that oppose the bill question and highlight the issue of whether the dangers of additional terrorist attacks require these extreme measures of privacy eradication. They have raised the question of who would then be the surveillance stalkers to fear most—the terrorist Islamic State, ISIS, or our own governments in their extreme counterterrorism reaction to the external threats. Each, they believe, have utilized cyberspace to advance their own interests and to destroy the opposition. Of course, this question arose nearly a year before the even more devastating ISIS terrorist attacks on Paris.

At that moment I thought *The New York Times* had wound up its exposition of stalking, hacking, and the NSA, but then the Friday May 8, 2015 edition of *The Times* overwhelmed me with a massive coverage of the topic that I, too, was covering on that day. The front-page lead news story, plus another one in the middle of the International news section, and yet again a major piece on the editorial page, were all devoted to presenting news on the dangers of surveying phone records in bulk. The ever-disturbing security *vs.* privacy conflict had reached global proportions as never before. I could not help but think, as I read my morning *Times* and drank my tea, that I was being news-stalked by stories that scared me. Whatever I read that day seemed to contain strong evidence that I was one of many citizens of the world who had become victims of telephone stalkers and internet hackers who worked at, or for, the highest government levels. I began to think about what it felt like to be stalked and wondered if everyone else was feeling the "justified paranoia" that plagued me that morning and has continued ever since.

I shall summarize here a portion of that day's breaking news stories. The long lead article by Charlie Savage and Jonathan Weisman (2015) began:

> A federal appeals court on Thursday ruled that the once-secret National Security Agency program that is systematically collecting Americans' phone records in bulk is illegal. The decision that comes as a fight in Congress is intensifying whether to end and replace the program or to extend it without changes. (p. A1)

The rest of the long article went into details about how the U.S.A. Patriot Act cannot be legitimately interpreted to allow the bulk collection of domestic calling records. On the very same day, May 8, news broke about the controversy over the electronic surveillance that has been building in Europe, including a push in France to increase domestic spying, an event I have referred to briefly, above, and a decision by Germany to reduce cooperation on surveillance with the United States.

In that very issue, another article (Smale, 2015) expresses the same and apparently growing sentiment that spying in cyberspace has gone too far and, in fact, might never have predicted a terrorist attack, which was its justification for existing in the first place. Her article, entitled, "Germany limits cooperation with U.S. over data gathering" appears to be part of a wake-up-call that not all nations are supportive of the stalking, hacking, bugging, and spying epidemic initiated by the USA against its own citizens and those hailing from other countries. Next, Smale spoke out against Germany's Chancellor Angela Merkel's victimization that had been referenced in *Citizenfour* two years earlier. Clearly, she thought, the hacking into Merkel's email account and sweeping up her cellphone number must have spurred on this growing, destructive, counter-spying initiative that matches the destruction of the very spying it is designed to eliminate. According to Smale, populist German outrage at its government for cooperating with American intelligence has swelled since 2013, when the Snowden documents revealed the extensive sweep of the USA's data collections in Germany and throughout Europe. The German reaction contrasts with France's increase in spying activity after the *Charlie Hebdo* attacks and deepening fears the world over of home-grown terrorists. This French variety of surveillance stalking obviously holds great terrorist potential in itself and, apparently, spawns equally dangerous counter-terrorist movements.

Finally, in that same May 8, 2015 issue, an editorial entitled "Illegal phone-data sweeps" praised the ruling made in New York by a federal three-judge panel the previous day that held that the government's vast, continuing, and, until recently, thanks to Snowden, secret sweep of American phone records is illegal. On this view, Congress could not have intended to approve a program whose true scope almost no one outside the NSA fully comprehended; that is, until Edward Snowden leaked its details and documents to the world. In the nearly two years since these revelations shocked America and started a heated debate on the proper balance between privacy and national security, the NSA, which conducts the data sweeps, has defended its actions. That organization

> contends that Congress knew exactly what it was doing when it authorized the Patriot Act in 2010 and 2011, after the collection program had begun . . . It is particularly galling that the government

> cannot even point to evidence that any terrorist attack has been thwarted by the collection of all this data. (p. A24)

The editorial argues for substantial debate, which, it says, "thanks to Mr. Snowden, is well underway." I should like to add that this necessary debate will go far to place limits on the potentially terroristic aspects of cyberstalking that I am emphasizing throughout this part of the book.

Several days later, on May 12, 2015, *The Times* published an article by Jeremy W. Peters, a political bombshell that surprised many readers in its coverage of Rand Paul, a candidate for the Republican Party primary for the 2016 election for President. Apparently, Paul was not afraid of offending the conservative wing of his party, which would weigh in heavily on the side of greater surveillance and less privacy. Peters also alluded to the voyeurism of surveillance but did not develop the theme as I am encouraging my psychoanalytic and other readers to do on their own with my guidance. In addition, an editorial published in that newspaper on the same day took the position that Rand Paul did Americans a singular service by drawing attention to the fact that their civil liberties remain at stake as Congress drifts toward a renewal of the Patriot Act that is likely to do too little to rein in government surveillance programs. Many regular *Times* readers were surprised that a far-right conservative libertarian wanted to dump the Patriot Act in its entirety, and not just the portions advocating bulk collection of private information. The conservative Paul presented himself as the sole Republican defender of civil liberties against Big Brother's prying eyes. He was said to agree with the major Democratic primary candidate, Hillary Clinton, who took a civil libertarian position by coming out in favor of balancing privacy rights against the NSA's defense of extreme surveillance measures. Paul's stump speech applause line was: "What you do on your phone is none of the government's damn business."

By May 14, two other pieces on cyberstalking appeared. One announced that the U.S. House of Representatives voted to restrict phone sweeps by the NSA. According to the story, the House of Representatives overwhelmingly approved legislation to limit, but not end, the federal government's bulk collection of phone records. The House did this by approving a specific change in the Patriot Act without discarding the Act in its entirety. Only records relevant to an investigation could be collected, improving the equilibrium between protecting both security and privacy. The debate has begun and there is clearly another side, as in right-wing Republican Mitch McConnell proclaiming that the legislation limiting the Patriot Act will neither keep us safe and secure nor protect our privacy and liberties. So, as the surveillance efforts exposed by Edward Snowden go on being questioned and debated, more and more conflict emerges, whether that conflict is between agencies of our federal government, between houses of parliament abroad, or between our government and those of our closest allies, particularly Germany. On that same day, May 14, 2015, *The Times* ran an editorial on "Shortcomings of cybersecurity bills" (p. A26). Its main point is that all of the new proposed cybersecurity legislation could help make American networks somewhat less vulnerable to hackers, but it would do so at a cost to the privacy of individuals. The writer argues for fixing the shortcoming of these bills so that both issues are addressed. That is, the editorial policy of *The New York Times* has been evolving for some time, now, into a plea for some kind of conflict resolution within the legislative bodies that could bring such harmony about.

Of course, while *The New York Times*, along with *The Washington Post* and the *Guardian*, has views compatible with those proposed by Snowden in the documentary, *Citizenfour*, it hardly represents the totality of thinking around the globe. But the gap could be closing. On May 20, yet another article was published in the same New York City newspaper. Scott Shane (2015) commented on Edward Snowden's life in exile in Russia, emphasizing his response to the court ruling two weeks prior that the first NSA program he disclosed, which collects records in bulk of millions of Americans, is now illegal. That was the ruling I have referred to above in which the House of Representatives voted overwhelmingly to transform the program by keeping the bulk phone records out of government hands. President Obama endorsed that change at that time while the Senate was debating it. Snowden has since said that the House vote will affect every other surveillance program in the USA going forward. The vote led to Apple and Google angering the FBI by stepping up encryption on the internet and by scrambling communications on smartphones in order to protect customers from the kind of surveillance Mr. Snowden exposed. I like to imagine that all of these events related to NSA surveillance that occurred in the month of May 2015 were the very ones that Glen

Greenwald and Edward Snowden sensed might occur when they were writing, sharing, and then shredding the communications that marked the ending of *Citizenfour* and that suggested eventual support from "POTUS," the President of the United States. I also like to imagine that my guess will eventually prove to be accurate. At the time of this writing, I am calling attention to these issues because the debate about Snowden's actions is ongoing. Some American officials tell a very different story, many of them expressing fury at what Snowden did, believing that his calls for personal liberty and privacy have been made at the expense of national security and safety. Some partisans would have us believe that Snowden's revelations taught terrorists, including those from ISIS, how to dodge the NSA's eavesdropping and are not relevant to privacy invasions. Those extremists who believed Snowden endangered our security and safety were mainly fueled by a desire to shame the government. So, we see pseudo-psychologizing, and, in connection with the upcoming 2016 election, unabashed politicizing. The jury is still out on which arguments fit the facts best, and how we can enlist encryption techniques to fight terror instead of promoting it.

In that same month of May, a front page of *The New York Times* Arts section carried a serious book review of a novel (Matthews, 2015) that dealt with important aspects of the psychology of any stalkee who became a victim of government surveillance. The article was entitled, "Shadowing a spy turned author" (McGrath, 2015). This review and the pending House vote on the Patriot Act bring me to the final section, "Epilogue" of my book. In my Epilogue, I will try to summarize what it feels like to be a stalkee, with special emphasis on the terrors of having one's privacy invaded. The example that closes Matthews' book is the case of an ex-CIA spy who wrote a thriller about how to duck omnipresent surveillance cameras and planted surveillance operators. We are treated to a tongue-in-cheek rendering of New York City today, designated here as SDRDB, or "The Social Democratic Republic of de Blasio." An ex-CIA stalkee may have to walk for thirteen or more hours to make sure she is not being followed. She stays in heavily trafficked areas and tries to look nonchalant as she passes the surveillance cameras lurking from above at every street corner. Doormen are suspect, as they are also the eyes and ears who see and hear everything. Like any stalkee, ex-operatives spend a lot of time walking around trying to avoid being followed and to escape surveillance. There are cameras everywhere, Mr. Matthews said, that can be live-monitored. How reminiscent of the visuals of the film, *Red Road,* covered in Chapter Six of this book. "You never try to elude or escape from surveillance . . . You want to lull them into thinking that you're not operational on this particular day." For the spy in question, the police communication tower is in plain sight. I am also reminded of the opening scene of *The Conversation,* in which Ann and Mark, the adulterous couple, are in plain sight of the operatives in Harry Caul's surveillance van, and know someone is following them and recording their conversation. To fake nonchalance about being stalked, they take advantage of the crowd, and choose the noisiest spots to continue their "conversation", which is a counter-spy dialogue calculated to throw their surveillance stalkers off guard by creating suspicion that they, the couple, are to be the victims of a killing rather than the perpetrators that they apparently turn out to be.

On May 29, *The New York Times* offered editorial support for the renewal of the Patriot Act, which gives federal authorities vast surveillance powers, but came out against authorization for that part of the program that the government uses to sweep up all Americans' phone records in bulk. That was the previously secret part of the NSA program that whistle-blower Edward Snowden had disclosed: intelligence personnel were gathering up phone records of millions of Americans who were not under investigation on a routine, systematic basis, or targeted for any crime or any other wrongdoing. On June 3, Op Ed contributor Frank Bruni referred to the NSA as America's peeping Tom. On that same day, while writing this material, I was waiting anxiously for news of a resolution. What a relief to know that the Senate passed the amended bill that outlawed bulk collection by the government of every American's telephone records and allocated the collection job to the telephone companies while, at the same time, retaining the necessary security provisions against terrorists. The House has yet to act and will do so sometime in November of 2016. As of the time of writing my initial draft of this chapter, when President Xi Jinping of China was visiting the USA, we were reminded that Chinese officials are believed to be behind many cyber attacks against American companies and government agencies. Governments should be able to intercept communications and investigate crimes and terrorist plots. But they should place sensible limits on surveillance and require their officials to meet a high burden of proof before they are allowed to listen in on phone calls, read emails, and troll through the web browsing histories of individuals; that is, stalking. Balancing both aims, the authority to investigate terrorism threats and spies by regulated surveillance *and* the protection of civil liberties, freedom of expression, and privacy is the goal most of us, I think, hope to see achieved in our lifetimes.

Today, September 15, 2016, is the day I am sending in my first edited proofs of *Stalker, Hacker, Voyeur, Spy* to Karnac Books. Just as I am packing up everything for its journey to London, I found an Op Ed piece in *The New York Times* that is truly irresistable for me to refrain from citing before I let go of this fairly final draft. Kenneth Roth, executive director of Human Rights Watch, and Salil Shetty, secretary general of Amnesty International make a plea to "Pardon Snowden". "He opened our eyes and changed our country. Let him come home" (p. A27). The authors argue for Snowden's release from asylum in Russia to return to the United States. Whistle-blowing to protect human rights

> should not be something that gets you locked up for a lifetime or compels you to live in exile. The President [yes, POTUS] has an opportunity to correct the injustice. It's time to pardon Mr. Snowden and bring him home, not to face the music, but to work for the security and privacy of us all. (p. A27)

EPILOGUE

On learning that one's privacy has been invaded by stalking

What does it feel like to be stalked? What does it feel like to stalk desperately? What does it feel like when your privacy has been invaded by sexual stalking, surveillance stalking, hacking into your internet accounts, or being followed by a private eye when a sexual partner becomes suspicious that you have been unfaithful? What does it feel like to have an order of restraint taken out against you, or to have your living and working space bugged, or when the government spies on you with high-tech surveillance methods? Among those who know of my interest in studying stalking psychoanalytically, many have asked these and similar questions frequently. Theirs are the questions I have sought to address throughout this book, no matter what the stalking situation. Questions such as these raise important issues about both members of the stalking couple, stalker and stalkee. Couples might have been involved in erotomania, unrequited love, and revenge. They might have been involved in a voyeuristic pursuit that brings sexual, aggressive, and sadomasochistic pleasure. They might have been involved in for-profit financial and professional gratifications resulting from private eye eavesdropping. They might be smitten celebrity stalkers, or they may be celebrities who variously delight in their conquests and in their exposure to the media. They might have been involved as perpetrators or victims in well-rationalized bulk collection of private telephone and internet information. In all of these instances, both stalker and stalkee are bound to have strong feelings affecting both their inner private lives and their interactions with one another; that is, both intrapsychically and interpersonally.

Each variety of stalking brings about different kinds of feelings amenable to psychoanalytic psychological study Following the order of their appearance in this book, I succinctly summarize here the main psychoanalytic issues associated with every form of stalking I have included. Vengefulness and the wish to invade the lives of the stalkee and his or her family members are frequent aftermaths in cases in which the rejected erotomanic sexual stalker's love is unrequited. Invasive revenge is illustrated in two clinical vignettes and in the films *Play Misty for Me* and *Fatal Attraction*. Voyeuristic sexual stalkers, such as the protagonists in *Rear Window* and *Peeping Tom*, experience polymorphous perverse pleasure, particularly sadistic, by invading the privacy of their victims. Their victims, in turn, vary in the degree to which their own exhibitionism complements the stalker's yearnings. Surveillance stalkers, as we have noted in *The Conversation*, *The Lives of Others*, *Caché*, and *Red Road*, experience a range of satisfactions and frustrations, including the voyeurism, pleasures, and anxieties that accompany the living out of primal scene fantasies. Professional surveillance operatives, private eyes, eavesdroppers, and other invaders of personal space may revel in self-enhancing justification, and even praise and fame for their actions, which, in other contexts, would be judged amoral and/or punishable. These entrepreneurial stalkers receive kudos for a job well done by being paid, esteemed, and acclaimed. Their victims suffer the fears, tortures, and terrors of being followed by shadowy, sometimes sinister, presences. On occasion, however, even such victimized stalkees might enjoy boosts to their egos when they know they are important enough to have so much invested in their demise or capture. Celebrity stalkers gratify erotomania and the illusion of merger at certain times, and, at others, may thrive on their vicarious acquisition of fame and fortune. Internet and telephone stalkers of the more benign sort, such as those I have presented as case vignettes, satisfy insatiable curiosity about their stalkees along with some degree of satisfaction for disrupting the lives of those once significant others who have rejected them. Cyberstalkers at the highest level of government agencies, as portrayed in *Enemy of the State* and *Citizenfour*, are rewarded particularly well by empowerment. Like Snowden, they might feel stronger even as they risk their jobs when they begin to question and expose the governmental stalking policies that had been their lifeblood.

To broaden our psychoanalytic perspectives on stalking to include the issues of privacy and security in newly familiar cyberspace as well as in the more extensively familiar psyche, it is important to realize that psychoanalysis today does not think of meaningful psychological conflict as located only between the so-called agencies of the mind: the id, the ego, and the superego. Although these traditionally conceived conflicts exist and are ordinarily taken into account in any psychoanalytic explanation or investigation into conflict, they belong only in the intrapsychic realm of mental activity, and to only one sector of that area. Classically, intrapsychic conflicts have been limited to troubling issues of sex and aggression as they are represented in the mind. Now, conflicts involving security and safety *vs.* freedom and self-expression are given as prominent consideration as are conflicts involving sex and aggression. Sex and aggression, on the one hand, and security, safety, and privacy, on the other, while hypothetically separable into different realms, are also intrinsically interrelated. Sexual or aggressive stalking might disrupt a person's security and safety for many reasons; for example, the experience of painful affects emanating from exposure to the unbearable amounts of sadism and destructiveness associated with invasions of privacy that range from the personal to the governmentally supported.

We have all become victims of everyday cyber attacks. Take the simple example of documented logs of one's purchasing preferences in the advertisements that pop up on the right side of our computer screens every time we sign on to our personal email account. Sometimes we develop a psychological blind spot and do not even notice that we are being pursued on our screens with unexpected, unrequested information. It is worrisome to realize that we are not paying much attention to something that has popped up before our very eyes. If we become too conditioned to scotomatizing the unimportant, might we not also start to automatically blot out the important and the urgent? When we finally notice the intrusion on our private and personal screens, and realize we are bothered by the idea that someone knows our preferences and is dogging us, following us, and throwing stuff in our face, we wonder if we have become paranoid in now worrying about an intrusion we did not even notice before. The term, "justified paranoia" has become a frequently used oxymoron to describe a common reaction to a "normalized" universal practice. Thinking we are being followed when we actually are being followed is justified; it is not paranoid. Worrying that a justified concern might be abnormal, if only in its intensity and persistence, does often lead to routine obsessional and, ironically, paranoidal kinds of thinking that have also been referred to as "justified paranoia." We can also develop such obsessional preoccupations about our own fearfulness when some individual or agency invades the privacy of our personal communications in our telephones and computers. As the distributors of *Enemy of the State* published on their DVD cover, "It's not paranoia if they're really after you" (Simpson & Bruckheimer, 2009).

I am clearly not alone in my feelings of unease. On October 15, 2015, *The New York Times* put out a special section entitled "Bits," that dealt exclusively with hacking on a global scale as well as the relation between security and privacy, emphasizing the idea that privacy and security use many of the same technologies. Quentin Hardy, in an article entitled "Machines vs. malice," comments that people worry about companies as well as governments that try to figure out private information. Hardy asks, "Which should scare me more: a big Chinese hacking or companies constantly trying to look at me and figure out my online behavior?" His answer is that when companies harass personality, character, and lifestyle with a barrage of tailored advertisements and "personalizations," that erosion of the private sphere is, over the long run, more insidious than a hack. As Shane (2015) has noted, many people in the USA and beyond share an unnamable sort of abstract anxiety about the menace posed by government snooping, especially when it is fully empowered by technology. The questions I am raising in connection with all the consciousness raising provided by this growing shared fearfulness of being cyberstalked relate to how these national and global conflicts between privacy and secrecy play out within a psychoanalytic frame of reference. In addition to wondering whether governmental conflicts mirror, parallel, or double our individual or inner psychic conflicts, we must also look unflinchingly into the ways these governmental conflicts between privacy and security are impacting on individual psychic wellbeing, and what sorts of inner and outer adjustments we might make to restore equilibrium.

For some, myself included, it is almost impossible to process the fact that the privacy, security, dependability, and safety we once took for granted are eroding insidiously in modern times. "I must be paranoid" has to be replaced with "It is really happening to me." I am not crazy to believe that my records can be swept up at any time. Territory that I once thought was safe is now territory that can be very dangerous. I constantly hear the admonitions, "Don't write anything you don't want everyone to see in an email. Use the telephone instead, but be careful that you are not being bugged."

Just as there is a complementary relation between persecutors and their victims, there is an important relationship between stalker and stalkee, and hacker and hackee. Understanding the stalkee's motives and fantasies is every bit as important as understanding the stalker's or hacker's motivations. One is likely to know more about what it *feels* like to be invaded in stalking and hacking if one is a victim than if one is a perpetrator. It takes some victims of stalking by hacking a long time to truly understand what is involved for them personally to have their privacy invaded. In any kind of bullying, for example, there is an important part played collusively and often unconsciously by those who endure it. Sometimes, unfortunate victims have "set up" the very stalking situation they ache to avoid. Appreciating that victims often provoke others to do to them what they fear most does not imply that we blame the victims of stalking, any more than we blame victims of sexual or terrorist assault. We intend only to identify one or another variety of unconscious collusion between perpetrator and victim. We, as psychoanalysts, certainly would want to understand why some people are more concerned about invasions of their privacy than others. We would also do well to study the range of reactions to having discovered that one is being stalked vengefully for not requiting another's love and for being hacked and discovering it in the process of everyday communications. To be convinced that one is being stalked, hacked, bugged, or spied upon does not need to imply a paranoidal, even a justified paranoidal, reaction. Signals are the whispers that alert us to events that are on the brink of occurring. Raising the questions in this Epilogue, however, is a first and necessary step to the expansion of that knowledge. The psychological realities of stalking and the objective realities of stalking, hacking, bugging, peeping, tapping, eavesdropping, spying—all of the invasions of privacy related to the broader rubric, stalking—have real, objective effect on the workings of the psyche.

One of the reasons I have included films as my data source for a deeply penetrating understanding of stalking, other than that they are abundantly available, is the close connection between fact and fiction, fantasy and reality. Steven Spielberg's first film and directing debut, an original masterpiece on stalking, is *Duel* (1971). It stars Dennis Weaver as a terrified motorist on a remote and lonely road, stalked by a mostly unseen and unknown driver of a mysterious tanker truck. To bring closure to my Epilogue, I turn briefly to yet another film, *In Fear* (Lovering, 2013). Like *Duel*, this film focuses on the terror wreaked when you have no idea who your stalker is and who actually puts your life in danger. In this little known British horror film, director Lovering focuses exclusively on the fears and terrors of a couple that is being stalked by an unknown stalker. His protagonists, Tom (Iain de Caestecker) and Lucy (Alex Englert), are driving from a pub to a nearby hotel where they plan to spend the night before proceeding on to a festival. In this cinematic experiment, designed to scare audiences and actors alike, director Lovering keeps his three-person cast as much in the dark as his film audience about who is stalking them. The verisimilitude of the fear of being stalked is thus maximized in both audience and cast. The couple's stalker, presumably someone they met at the pub, follows them and totally throws them off balance by moving the arrowed "500 meters to the hotel" sign to point in a different direction each time they pass it. The couple ends up driving in a maze as their quiet bewilderment morphs into screaming terror. One can only say that brain washing, mind manipulation, or, better yet, "mind fucking" has conflated with stalking to maximize the experience of terror. That is, director Lovering and the stalking terrorizer are carrying through disorienting psychological manipulations of the minds of the protagonists and audience alike. I have heard of other stalkers who gain access to their stalkee's homes and move things around to psych them out in order to induce a paranormal experience of fear. In *In Fear,* someone or something seems to be stalking the protagonist couple by calling into question the actual way their minds see the world. When they eventually confront head on the most likely source of their terror, Max (Allen Leech) a man from the pub, the terror wreaked upon them by mind manipulation only continues on its irreversible trajectory. Although all, that is, the actors, the characters they portray, and the viewing audience, are harried by an invasive stalking presence, none has any idea why and by whom their fear has been raised to such unbearable levels. Most important, director Lovering has kept all on edge in this unique experimental film about *violence and fear as a state of mind.*

If we had to search for a feeling, from the most basic to the most global, common to all stalkers and all stalkees, I would say the answer lies somewhere on the spectrum of power lost and gained in emotional distance regulation. When you stalk erotomanically to avenge your unrequited love, and when you stalk by high-tech surveillance in cyberspace to terrorize people worldwide, you gain a measure of imagined and real power over your "others", who then become your prey. When you feel that power, you imagine that you are closer to the intimacy you seek than you would if you had not succeeded in invading the privacy of others. If you were to restrain your predatory impulses, you would increase the emotional distance toward the optimal that you are trying to maintain. Stalkees know that somebody so desperately wants them or is watching them because they feel unable to leave them be. No matter how invaded you feel, you also gain a sense of power by simply knowing that they seem to be unable to let you alone. As powerful as stalkers may feel and seem to be to others when they stalk, they are powerless to establish a grain of *valuable* intimacy. "Big Brother" has been watching you from time immemorial. The years 1984–2016 have gained the status of archetype for the years gone by that has alerted us to the surveillance variety of stalking. In all likelihood, all versions of stalking that we can identify and more to come that most of us have not imagined will continue until the end of time as we know it.

I conclude by voicing my hopes that my attempts to cover the breadth and depth of stalking in many, if not most, of its variations, will meaningfully fill a gap in the general and psychoanalytic literature on the topic. It has been a challenge and a major spur to my work that so many people have questioned me about stalking, and, although troubled by their concerns, I have enjoyed hearing the examples that friends, colleagues, and strangers have offered from the minute they have heard of my interest. I hope I have opened up a new area for inquiry and sharing that will appear munificently not too long from now before someone does a Psychoanalytic Electronic Publishing

(PEP CD ROM) search, or a general Google on "Stalking," and that people will follow through to gain some shared understanding if they come across the title, *Stalker, Hacker, Voyeur, Spy*.

REFERENCES

Abbott, G. (Director) (1955). *Damn Yankees*. USA: Warner Brothers.

Ainslee, G. (2006). Stalker and stalked: Be careful what you wish for. Paper presented to Panel on "Stalking," 26th annual meeting, Division of Psychoanalysis (39), American Psychological Association, Philadelphia, April 20.

Allen, W. (Director) (2005). *Matchpoint*. USA: DreamWorks Pictures.

Andrews, M. (2016). Feds' plan to ease privacy rules on addiction treatment spurs debate (March 25, 2016). Available at: www.npr.org/sections/health-shots/2016/03/22/471313442/feds-plan-to-ease-privacy-rules-on-addiction-treatment-spurs-debate

Arnold, A. (Director) (2007). *Red Road*. UK: Verve Pictures.

Basseches, H. I. (2006). Chair and Discussant, Stalker and stalked: obsessed with desire. Panel on "Stalking," 26th annual meeting, Division of Psychoanalysis (39), American Psychological Association, Philadelphia, April 20.

Beebe, B., & Sloate, P. (1982). Assessment and treatment of difficulties in mother–infant attunement in the first three years of life: A case history. *Psychoanalytic Inquiry*, *1*: 601–623.

Bentham, J. (1995). *The Panopticon Writings*. London: Verso.

Binion, R. (1993). *Love Beyond Death: The Anatomy of a Myth in the Arts*. New York: New York University Press.

Bloomfield, O. H. (1987). Human destructiveness: an essay on instinct, fetal existence and infancy. *International Review of Psycho-Analysis, 14*: 21–32.

Brennan, K. (2008). *In His Sights*. New York: HarperCollins.

Brooks, D. (2015). Leaving and cleaving. *New York Times*, March 3, Op Ed Column, p. A29.

Bruni, F. (2015). The education assassins. *New York Times*, May 31, Op Ed Column, p. SR3.

Coppola, F. F. (Director) (1974). *The Conversation*. USA: Paramount Pictures.

Daly, C. D. (1943). The role of menstruation in human phylogenesis and ontogenesis. *International Journal of Psychoanalysis, 24*: 151–170.

Davenport, M. (1936). *Of Lena Geyer*. New York: Grossett and Dunlap.

Dowd, M. (2005). *Are Men Necessary? When Sexes Collide*. New York: G. P. Putnam's Sons.

Dunn, P. (2014). Sexual voyeurism in Hitchcock's *Rear Window*. Paper presented to the Association for Psychoanalytic Medicine, New York, May.

Eastwood, C. (Director) (1971). *Play Misty for Me*. USA: Universal Pictures.

Ebert, R. (1998). Film review, *Enemy of the State*, RogerEbert.com November 20.

Fenichel, O. (1946). *The Psychoanalytic Theory of Neurosis*. London: Routledge and Kegan Paul.

Freud, S. (1905d). *Three Essays on the Theory of Sexuality. S. E., 7*: 123–246. London: Hogarth.

Freud, S. (1915c). Instincts and their vicissitudes. *S. E., 14*: 109–140. London: Hogarth.

Freud, S. (1916d). Some character types met with in psycho-analytic work: criminals from a sense of guilt. *S. E., 15*: 309–333. London: Hogarth.

Freud, S. (1918b). *From the History of an Infantile Neurosis. S. E.*, 17: 1–122. London: Hogarth.

Fried, W. (2016). *Critical Flicker Fusion*. London: Karnac.

Gabbard, K., & Gabbard, G. O. (1993). Phallic women in the contemporary cinema. *American Imago, 50*(4): 421–439.

Gast, L. (Director) (2010). *Smash His Camera*. USA: Magnolia Pictures.

Gediman, H. K. (1985). Imposture, inauthenticity, and feeling fraudulent. *Journal of the American Psychoanalytic Association, 33*: 911–935.

Gediman, H. K. (1992). Resurrection fantasies in art and in the love life of an older man. Paper presented to the New York Freudian Society, New York City, December 3.

Gediman, H. K. (1995). *Fantasies of Love and Death in Life and Art*. New York: New York University Press.

Gediman, H. K. (2005). Premodern, modern, and postmodern perspectives on sex and gender mixes. *Journal of the American Psychoanalytic. Association, 53*: 1059–1078.

Gediman, H. K. (2006). Reflections on stalking obsessions and stalking fantasies. Paper presented to Panel on "Stalking," 26th annual meeting, Division of Psychoanalysis (39), American Psychological Association, Philadelphia, April 20.

Gediman, H. K. (2008). Lonely stalking: A perverse transformation of the search for idealized romantic love. Paper presented to the Fourth Joint International Conference on Psychoanalysis, "Loneliness and Yearnings." University of British Columbia, Vancouver, Canada, July 25–27.

Gediman, H. K. (2009a). Stalking: Case histories and movie portrayals. Paper presented to Discussion Group, "Self Psychology. " Moderators, Curtis Bristol and Sandra Hershberg, American Psychoanalytic Association, National Meeting, New York City, January.

Gediman, H. K. (2009b). Gender differences among sexual stalkers: voyeurism and erotomania in the films *Peeping Tom* and *Fatal Attraction*. Paper presented to IPTAR Conference, "A Dialogue between Psychoanalysis and the Arts." New York City, October 25.

Gediman, H. K. (2016). Erotomania and sociopathy in celebrity stalking. Paper presented to the Virginia Psychoanalytic Association, Richmond, February 19.

Gediman, H. K., & Lieberman, J. S. (1996). *The Many Faces of Deceit*: Northvale, NJ: Jason Aronson.

Goldberg, A. (1995). *The Problem of Perversion*. New Haven, CT: Yale University Press.

Goldstein, M. (2015). Need some espionage done? Hackers are for hire online. *New York Times*, January 16, p. A1.

Gornick, L. (1994). Women treating men. *Journal of the American Academy of Psychoanalysis, 22*: 231–257.

Gottlieb, R. M. (1994). The legend of the European vampire. *Psychoanalytic Study of the Child, 49*: 465–480.

Gottlieb, R. M. (2000). Hannibal. *Journal of The American Psychoanalytic Association, 48:* 1017–1019.

Haneke, M. (Director) (2005). *Caché*. France: Les Films du Losange.

Hardy, Q. (2015). Machines vs. malice. *New York Times*. Thursday, October 15, p. F2.

Harris, A., & Sklar, R. (1998). Wild film theory, wild film analysis. *Psychoanalytic Inquiry, 18*: 222–237.

Hermann, I. H. (1976). Clinging-going-in-search. A contrasting pair of instincts and their relation to sadism and masochism. *Psychoanalytic Quarterly, 45*: 5–36.

Hesse, E., & Main, M. (1999). Second-generation effects of universal trauma in nonmaltreating parents: dissociated, frightened and threatening behavior. *Psychoanalytic Inquiry, 19*: 481–514.

Hesse, E., & Main, M. (2000). Disorganized infant, child, and adolescent attachments. *Journal of the American Psychoanalytic Association, 48*: 1097–1127.

HIPAA Journal (2015). The age of healthcare data breach: 40% of Americans now victims. *HIPAA Journal*, August 29, 2015. Available at: www.hipaajournal.com/the-age-of-the-healthcare-data-breach-40-of-Americans-now-victims-8083/

Hitchcock, A. (Director) (1954). *Rear Window*. USA: Paramount Pictures.

Hitchcock, A. (Director) (1958). *Vertigo*. USA: Paramount Pictures.

Hitchcock, A. (Director) (1960). *Psycho*. USA: Paramount Pictures.

Howe, P. (2005). *Paparazzi and Our Obsession with Celebrity*. New York: Artisan Books.

Jaffe v. Redmond (1996). United States Supreme Court. http://caselaw.findlaw.com/us-supreme-court/518/1.html

Jones, E. (1927). The early development of female sexuality. *International Journal of Psychoanalysis, 8*: 459–472.

Jones, E. (1929). Fear, guilt, and hate. *International Journal of Psychoanalysis, 10*: 383–397.

Kales, E. F. (2003). Body double as politic: Psychosocial myth and cultural binary in "Fatal Attraction." *International Journal of Psychoanalysis, 84*: 1631–1637.

Kamir, O. (2000). *The Maintenance of Cultural Myths: The Case of Stalking*. Ann Arbor, MI: University of Michigan Press.

Kaplan, L. (1991). *Female Perversions*. New York: Doubleday.

Lacan, J. (2006)[1970]. *Ecrits*, B. Fink (Trans.). New York: Norton.

Le Carré, J. (1974). *Tinker, Tailor, Soldier, Spy*. New York: Knopf.

Lieberman, J. S. (2000). *Body Talk: Looking and Being Looked at in Psychotherapy*. Northvale, NJ: Jason Aronson.

Lovering, J. (Director) (2013). *In Fear*. USA: Anchor Bay Entertainment.

Lyne, A. (Director) (1987). *Fatal Attraction*. USA: Paramount Pictures.

Manninem, V. (2000). The face of fear: Castration and perversion. *Scandinavian Psychoanalytic Review, 23*: 103–215.

Maslin, J. (1998). Film review, *Enemy of the State*: The walls have eyes, ears, and cameras. *New York Times*, November 20. Available at: www.nytimes.com/movie/review?res=9404E3DD1530F933A15752C1A96E958260

Matthews, J. (2015). *Palace of Treason*. New York: Scribner's.
McGinley, E., & Sabbadini, A. (2006). *Play Misty for Me* (1971). The perversion of love. *International Journal of Psychoanalysis, 87*: 589–597.
McGrath, C. (2015). Shadowing a spy turned author. *New York Times,* May 27, p. C1.
Miller, L., & Twomey, J. E. (2000). Incoherence incognito. *Contemporary Psychoanalysis, 36*: 427–456.
Morris, W., & Scott, A. O. (2015). The French identity through film. *New York Times,* November 28, p. C1.
Mulvey, L. (1975). Visual pleasure and narrative cinema. *Screen, 16*: 6–18.
Mulvey. L. (1989). *Visual and Other Pleasures*. Bloomington, IN: University of Indiana Press.
Newman, A. (2008). Stalked: A decade on the run. *New York Times,* July 31, p. G1.
Nilsson, B. (2007). *La Nilsson: My Life In Opera*. Boston, MA: Northeastern University Press.
Nin, A. (1954). *A Spy in the House of Love*. New York: Penguin.
Obama, B. (2012). Statement by President Obama. In: *Consumer Data Privacy in a Networked World: a Framework for Protecting Privacy and Promoting Innovation in the Global Digital Economy*. Available at: www.whitehouse.gov/sites/default/files/privacy-final.pdf
Ogden, T. H. (2002). A new reading of the meaning of object-relations theory. *International Journal of Psychoanalysis, 83*: 767–782.
Orwell, G. (1949). *Nineteen Eighty-Four*. London: Secker and Warburg.
Panksepp, J. (1998). *Affective Neuroscience: The Foundations of Human and Animal Emotions*. New York: Oxford University Press.
Patient Privacy Rights (2016). The truth about HIPAA. Available at: https://patientprivacyrights.org/truth-hipaa/
Person, E. (1988). *Dreams of Love and Fateful Encounters: The Power of Romantic Passion*. New York: Norton.
Peters, J. W. (2015). Paul tries to stake territory as lone candidate who'd guard civil liberties. *New York Times,* May 12, p. A15.
Poitras, L. (Director) (2014). *Citizenfour*. USA: Radius-TWC.
Pollit, K. (2004). Webstalker. *The New Yorker*. January 19, p. 38.
Ponemon Institute (2015). Fifth annual benchmark study on privacy and security of health care data. Available at: www.ponemon.org/library/fifth-annual-benchmark-study-on-privacy-security-of-healthcare-data.
Powell, M. (Director) (1961). *Peeping Tom*. USA: Universal Pictures.
Powell, M., & Pressburger, M. (Directors) (1951). *Tales of Hoffman*. UK: British Lion Films.

Risen, J. (2006). *State of War: The Secret History of the C.I.A. and the Bush Administration*. New York: Free Press.

Riviere, J. (1929). Womanliness as masquerade. *International Journal of Psychoanalysis, 10*: 11–33.

Roth, K., & Shetty, S. (2016). Pardon Snowden. *New York Times*, September 15, p. A27.

Rubin, A. J. (2015). Lawmakers in France move to vastly expand surveillance. *New York Times*, May 6, p. A1.

Sabbadini, A. (2000). Watching voyeurs: Michael Powell's *Peeping Tom* (1960). *International Journal of Psychoanalysis, 81*: 809–813.

Sabbadini, A. (2014). *Moving Images: Psychoanalytic Reflections on Film*. London: Routledge.

Sanger, D. E., & Perlroth, N. (2015). White House takes cybersecurity pitch to Silicon Valley. *New York Times*, April 27, p. A3.

Savage, C., & Weisman, J. (2015). N.S.A. collection of bulk call data is ruled illegal. *New York Times*, Friday May 8, p. A1.

Scott, A. O. (2007). Film review of *Red Road*. *New York Times*, April 13. Available at: http://query.nytimes.com/gst/fullpage.html?res=9D03E0DE133FF930A25757C0A9619C8B63.

Scott, A. O. (2014). Intent on defying an all-seeing eye. Film review of *Citizenfour*, a documentary about Edward J. Snowden. *New York Times*, October 24, p. C1.

Scott, K. L. (2007). The star and the stalker. *Opera News, 74*: 24–31.

Scott, T. (Director) (1998). *Enemy of the State*. DVD issued 2009, Jerry Bruckheimer, producer.

Shane, S. (2015). Snowden sees some victories from a distance. *New York Times*, Wednesday May 20, p. A1.

Shelby, R. D. (1997). The self and orientation: the case of Mr. G. In: A. Goldberg (Ed.), *Conversations in Self Psychology* (pp. 181–202) (*Progress in Self Psychology, Volume 13*). Hillsdale, NJ: Analytic Press.

Simpson, D., & Bruckheimer, J. (Producers) (2009). *Enemy of the State*. USA: Touchstone Pictures.

Sklarew, B., & Akhtar, S. (2015). Psychoanalysis and film: *Peeping Tom*. Discussion Group. American Psychoanalytic Association National Meeting, New York City, January.

Smale, A. (2015). Germany limits cooperation with U.S. over data gathering. *New York Times*, Friday, May 8, p. A8.

Solomon, B. C. (1997). Discussion of Shelby's "The self and orientation: the case of Mr. G." In: A. Goldberg (Ed.), *Conversations in Self Psychology* (pp. 203–212) (*Progress in Self Psychology, Volume 13*). Hillsdale, NJ: Analytic Press.

Spielberg, S. (Director) (1971). *Duel*. USA: Universal Pictures.

Spitz, E. H. (1989). *Art and Psyche*. New Haven, CT: Yale University Press.

Thompson, E. (1927). *An Indian Day*. London: Alfred A. Knopf.

Thomson, D. (2007). *Red Road*: It's 2007, and big sister is watching. Film review. *The Washington Post*, May 25. Available at: www.washingtonpost.com/wp-dyn/content/article/2007/05/24/AR2007052402495.html

Travers, P. (1998). *Enemy of the State*. Film review. *Rolling Stone*, December 10. Available at: www.rollingstone.com/movies/reviews/enemy-of-the-state-19981120.

Vidor, C. (Director) (1946). *Gilda*. USA: Columbia Tristar.

Von Donnersmarck, F. H. (Director) (2007). *The Lives of Others*. UK: Lionsgate.

Von Sternberg, J. (Director) (1930). *The Blue Angel*. Germany: UFA.

Wales, J., & Tretikov, L. (2015). Stop spying on Wikipedia users. *New York Times*, Tuesday, March 10, p. A21.

Warren, S., & Brandeis, L. (1890). The right to privacy. *Harvard Law Review*, *IV*(5). Available at: http://groups.csail.mit.edu/mac/classes/6.805/articles/privacy/Privacy_brand_warr2.html

Zellner, H. (2000). Review of Panksepp's *Affective Neuroscience: The Foundations of Human and Animal Emotions*. *Neuropsychoanalysis*, *2*: 272–276.

Zusman, W. (1998). *The Conversation*: Psychic reality, neutrality, and reaction formation. *Psychoanalytic Inquiry*, *18*: 251–256.

INDEX